# 3D GAME PROGRAMMING FOR TEENS

ERIC D. GREBLER

**THOMSON**

COURSE TECHNOLOGY™

Professional ■ Technical ■ Reference

ISBN: 1-59200-900-X
Library of Congress Catalog Card Number: 2005929776
Printed in the United States of America
06 07 08 09 10 PH 10 9 8 7 6 5 4 3 2 1

**Publisher and General Manager, Thomson Course Technology PTR:**
Stacy L. Hiquet

**Associate Director of Marketing:**
Sarah O'Donnell

**Manager of Editorial Services:**
Heather Talbot

**Marketing Manager:**
Heather Hurley

**Senior Acquisitions Editor:**
Emi Smith

**Project Editor:**
Dan Foster, Scribe Tribe

**Technical Reviewer:**
David Rivers

**PTR Editorial Services Coordinator:**
Elizabeth Furbish

**Interior Layout Tech:**
Interactive Composition Corp.

**Cover Designer:**
Mike Tanamachi

**CD-ROM Producer:**
Brandon Penticuff

**Indexer:**
Larry Sweazy

**Proofreader:**
Sandy Doell

**THOMSON**
──────★──────
**COURSE TECHNOLOGY** ™

Professional ■ Technical ■ Reference

Thomson Course Technology PTR,
a division of Thomson Course Tecnology
25 Thomson Place
Boston, MA 02210
www.courseptr.com

# Acknowledgments

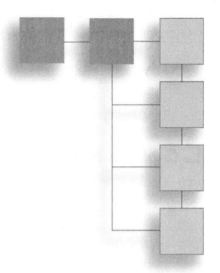

Putting together a book like this is truly a team effort, and thanks must first be extended to all the fine people at Thomson Course Technology. In particular, I'd like to point out the efforts of Dan Foster, David Rivers, Emi Smith, and Stacy Hiquet for bringing this project to life.

Thanks also to David Brinnen, Adam Kruvand, and Ralph Baer for their generous donation of some of the files and photos used in the book.

Thanks to my wife, my son, and the rest of my family for their constant source of inspiration and love.

## About the Author

**Eric Grebler** is an IT professional, author, and certified trainer who has demystified the world of computers for thousands of people. Eric has written books on a wide range of technical topics including desktop publishing, audio sequencing, graphics, and operating systems.

# CONTENTS

# INTRODUCTION

Congratulations on taking your first step to becoming a 3D game programmer by buying this book! If you are looking at this introduction online or are flipping through the pages while standing in a bookstore... What are you waiting for? It's time for the adventure to begin.

Unfortunately, I don't have a crystal ball or great psychic ability, so I can't say for certain exactly who you are, but I think I have a few good guesses. You might be a teenager who is interested in getting started in 3D game programming, and you're looking for a great resource to get started. If so, you've come to the right place. Or, you might be the parent of a teenager or young adult who is looking for a good resource for their child to start 3D game programming. Again, if so, you've come to the right place. My last guess is that you may not be a teenager or the parent of a teenager at all, but you may just be someone who is interested in getting into 3D game programming, and you're looking for a great resource for beginners that isn't intimidating and won't get you lost in a wilderness of heavy technical jargon and difficult math computations. Don't let the title of this book restrict you from diving right in; this book is designed specifically for *anyone* who is interested in starting the journey to 3D game programming.

Here's what I'm assuming: You love games, but you have little or no programming experience. The good news is that you don't need any experience. You just need the will to learn and some time. The only tool that you need to use this book properly is a computer with a CD drive. I'll provide you with everything else. Our journey will involve the use of three different programs: one for programming (Blitz3D), one for graphic design (CorelDRAW), and one for 3D modeling (Autodesk 3ds Max), all of which are included on the accompanying CD or can be downloaded free of charge from the Internet.

## How to Use This Book

This book is divided into three informal sections. Chapters 1 through 4 are theory-based chapters that give you a brief introduction to gaming, its history, the skills necessary to become a programmer, the game process, and the types of tools available. Chapters 5 through 16 are the real meat of the book, where you'll dive right into actual programming. Each chapter deals with specific types of tasks and the code necessary to accomplish those tasks. While you'll create mini-programs in almost every chapter, you'll put everything together into a final game in Chapter 17.

How you choose to use this book is entirely up to you. Some people will read it from beginning to end, starting with the theory and then moving on to the programming and then the final game.

If you want to roll up your sleeves and start right away, you may want to gloss over the theory section and then come back to it after you've gotten into the programming. Whatever method you choose, I strongly suggest that you go through Chapters 5 through 16 in order, since the concepts and ideas build from one chapter to the next. Once you complete the book, you may want to jump back and forth through different chapters to refresh yourself on certain topics.

If you want to tell your friends that you bought a book and can program games right away, you might even want to start at Chapter 17, create the final game, and then start back at the beginning of the book to see exactly how you accomplished what you did.

## The Learning Process

In much of this book you'll learn by dissecting. That is, I'll present you with some code that performs a specific task, and then we'll look at the code line-by-line to see exactly what has been accomplished.

By no means does this book cover every aspect and scenario that you'll encounter while programming 3D games, but its goal is to give you the solid groundwork and practical experience for understanding and creating games.

Because games can be comprised of thousands of lines of code, there will be instances in this book for which you'll need to add lines to an existing piece of code. In most of these instances, the new code that you need to add will be shown in **bold**. This will help you easily see where to place the new lines in relation to the existing code.

## Files Used with This Book

In addition to the applications that you'll need when programming, the accompanying CD contains files that you'll use with different parts of the book. Rather than spending time copying code line-by-line from the book, in many instances I'll ask you to start a project by opening a file that you'll find on the accompanying CD.

So what are you waiting for? Let the journey begin.

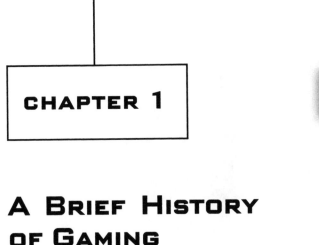

# CHAPTER 1

# A BRIEF HISTORY OF GAMING

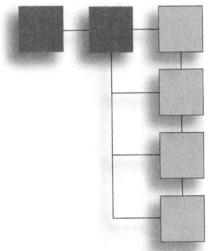

When I was a kid, my father regularly took my brothers and me to the Museum of Science and Technology in Ottawa, Ontario. The highlight of these trips was going through what they called the "Crazy Kitchen." The "Crazy Kitchen" was a replica of an ordinary kitchen with the exception that everything was slanted (including the floor), which made walking through it quite a challenge. In 1983 the appeal of the "Crazy Kitchen" took a back seat to a new exhibit that they had created at the museum—an exhibit that would change the lives and inspire hundreds, if not thousands, of budding young gamers. As we walked into the new exhibit, we were greeted by a large flashing sign that read "Computer Electronics." As we made our way past oversized plastic displays of the inside of a computer, we came to an area that contained five or six "stations." These stations were made up of a seat, a keyboard, and a monitor, and there was one station that always had a big crowd gathered around it. It was at that station that I first laid my eyes on a computer video game. You may have heard of the game that I saw that day; it was called Breakout, a very basic computer game. The game was made up of a white rectangle that bounced back and forth as it tried to break through a wall of other white rectangles.

Although Breakout wasn't the first computer game created, it was the one that inspired me to get into gaming. My father built our first few computers, and we were hooked on programming games. Back then there was a magazine called *Compute* that contained pages and pages of programming code that you could type to create your games. We used a programming language called Atari Basic to

**Figure 1.1**
An image of Pong, one of the first commercial video games.

create our games, which were simple by today's standards, but still gave us hours of entertainment.

To say that video games have come a long way since the days of Breakout would be a complete understatement. From simple white rectangles to Pong (see Figure 1.1) to 3D worlds, life-like sports games, and underwater adventure worlds, the world of video games has been growing at an exponential rate. You might ask the question, "Why is it important to know about the history of video games?"

The truth is, you could skip this chapter completely and still learn about how to program 3D games. In fact, you could skip the first part of this book and still learn how to program a 3D game. But you have to remember that programming is only one element of creating 3D games, and by studying the history of gaming you can:

- **Create better games.** Understanding how historic games have worked, what their appeal was, and why some worked while others flopped will help you in the process of creating your own games.

- **Get game ideas.** Retro games are the perfect source for inspiration when thinking of games to create.

- **Become an expert.** Imagine a NASCAR driver who only knows how to step on the gas pedal. He doesn't know how to brake, steer, or pass other cars; he only knows how to accelerate. He wouldn't last very long, would he? To become an expert in the field of gaming, you really have to know about all aspects of gaming, including its history.

- **Impress employers at interviews.** You might have aspirations of working for one of the big gaming companies one day. Maybe Microsoft, Sony, Nintendo, or Lucas Arts will interview you and ask what you know about their games or the history of their company. Nothing is more impressive than being able to show that your knowledge is well rounded.

- **Beat mega winner Ken Jennings at Jeopardy!** You never know when your knowledge of gaming will come in handy. Whether it's impressing your friends, teachers, or game show hosts, a little extra knowledge can always come in handy.

So let's get started on our journey through time. I promise that it will be a lot more exciting and interesting than any history lesson you've learned in school.

## A Quick Timeline

A lot has happened in gaming over the past 30 years, and to cover it all would take another entire book. Here I'll share a look at some of the most important moments in gaming and when they occurred.

### 1958—The First Video Game Invented

In 1958, a man by the name of Will Higinbotham, a physicist who worked for the Brookhaven National Laboratory, invented a video game called "Tennis for Two," which was an electronic version of Ping Pong. The game was created on an oscilloscope (see Figure 1.2), which is a device with an electronic screen that measures a trace of voltage or wave shape.

### 1961—Spacewar

Spacewar was created by Steve Russell and a team of several others at MIT (Massachusetts Institute of Technology). Spacewar (see Figure 1.3) was a multiple player game in which two ships moved around firing missiles at one

**Figure 1.2**
Arguably the first video game, Tennis for Two was played on an oscilloscope.

another. The two ships, one called "wedge" and the other called "needle," fought on a backdrop of stars. The game was played on a computer called a "PDP-1," which was about 6 feet tall and 3 feet wide.

## 1967—Television Video Games Created

Until this point in time, video games were created to run on computers, which in those days could be the size of an entire room. In 1967, a man named Ralph Baer created the "Brown Box," which was a game device that you could connect to a regular television set in order to play video games. This device was licensed to a company called Magnavox which released it as the "Odyssey" in 1972.

## 1971—The First Video Arcade Game

An arcade game is a machine that is usually operated by a coin. You place a coin into the slot and you are able to play the game. In 1971, Nolan Bushnell and Ted

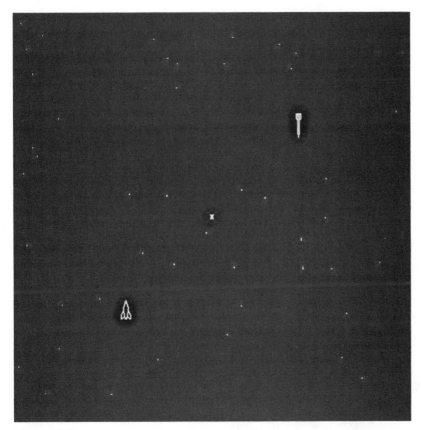

**Figure 1.3**
Spacewar was the first multiplayer video game—quite a bit different from the games we're used to now.

Dabney created the first video arcade game. The game was called "Computer Space" (see Figure 1.4) and involved controlling a spaceship that shoots at flying saucers. Ted Dabney and Nolan Bushnell later went on to create the famous video game company Atari.

## 1972—Magnavox Odyssey Brings Games Home

In 1972 the Magnavox Odyssey, based on Ralph Baer's invention, was released to the general public. The Odyssey ran on batteries and had no color and no sound. The Odyssey (see Figure 1.5) played several games including volleyball, hockey, tennis, football, and more. There were color plastic overlays depicting the background of the games that you would tape to your television screen. The Odyssey also had game cartridges, and it offered a rifle and several other accessories.

**Figure 1.4**
A promotional ad for Computer Space, the first video arcade game. Today these units are considered a collector's item and sell for over $2,000.

**Figure 1.5**
The Odyssey was the first commercially available home video game unit.

**Figure 1.6**
People lined up around the block of Sears stores during Christmas 1975 to get their Pong game systems.

## 1975—Atari Releases Pong

Although Pong had been available as an arcade version for several years, it was released as a home arcade version in 1975. Pong (see Figure 1.6) was an electronic version of table tennis where players would move their paddles to hit a ball (a white rectangle) back and forth. It was sold by Sears and was hugely successful. At first the Pong systems only played Pong, but later Atari added several other games. You could either play against the computer or two players could play against each other.

## 1977—Atari 2600

The Atari 2600 (see Figure 1.7) was a home video game system that put Atari on the map as a serious gaming system. It came with two joysticks and paddle controllers. There was a library of nine games at first, each of which came on a separate cartridge which you would insert into the unit in order to play. The Atari 2600 was hugely successful, and in 1979 they sold a million units. The Atari 2600 became even more popular after Space Invaders was licensed by the company in 1980—they earned 2 billion dollars in profits that year.

## 1978—Space Invaders

Space Invaders (see Figure 1.8) is considered to be one of the most influential video games of all time. It was designed by a man named Toshihiro Nishikado

**Figure 1.7**
The Atari 2600 was a staple in many homes of young gamers in 1980.

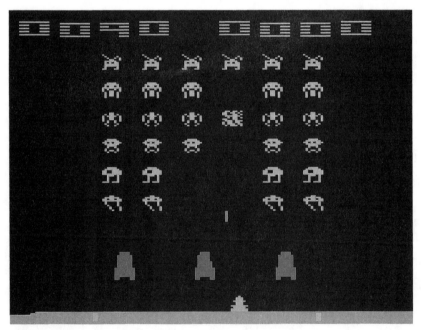

**Figure 1.8**
Space Invaders took the world by storm and instantly hooked millions of people on video games.

and was produced by a company called Taito which licensed it to Midway Games. In the game, the player controlled a gun that could move back and forth across the bottom of the screen and would shoot at aliens while they approached at an increasingly rapid rate. The game was so popular that it caused a coin shortage in Japan and the government was forced to produce more coins.

## 1979—High Score

In 1979, Atari released Asteroids, an arcade game in which you control a ship that needs to avoid and destroy asteroids that are hurling about the screen (see Figure 1.9). The game was immensely popular and had a new feature that had never been seen before: it allowed players to enter their three-letter initials on the screen after they obtained a high score. The name would remain on the screen so that others could view the high score list.

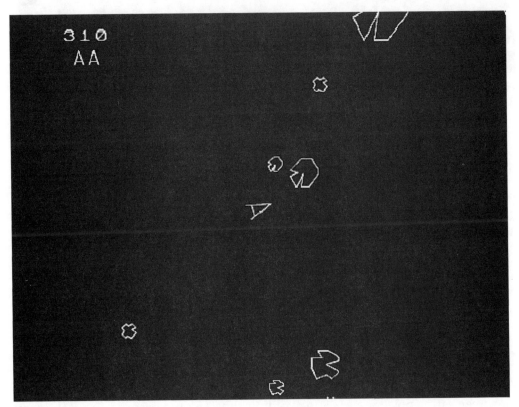

**Figure 1.9**
Notice the score and the name "AA" in the top left corner of the Asteroids game screen.

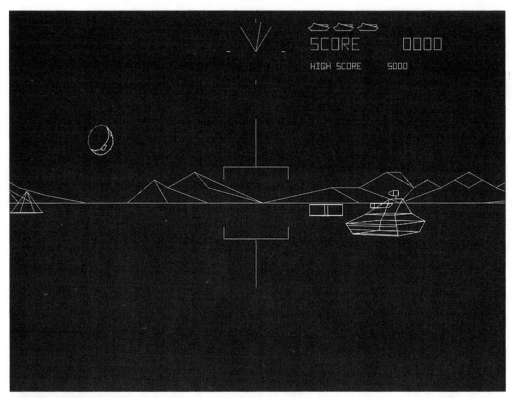

**Figure 1.10**
Battlezone was the first real commercially successful 3D game.

## 1980—The First 3D Game

Atari created Battlezone in 1980 (see Figure 1.10). It was the first real 3D video game. There had been other 3D games in the past, but this was the first to use real 3D objects like mountains, a moon in the sky, and various obstacles. Battlezone was an army-style game in which you controlled a tank that shot at enemy tanks. You played the game by looking through a pair of goggles which provided the perspective as if you were actually in the tank. The U.S. government was so impressed by Battlezone that it adapted it for military training.

## 1980—Pac-Man

Who would have ever thought that a pizza-shaped character running around the screen eating power pellets and avoiding ghosts would become one of the most popular games of all time? That's exactly what happened in 1980 when Midway

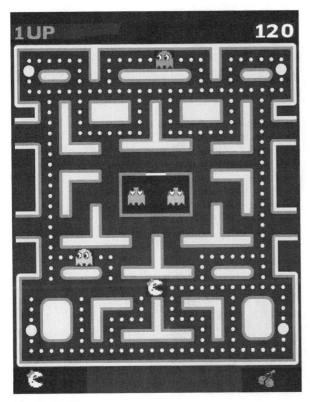

**Figure 1.11**
Ms. Pac-Man was one of the popular spin-offs of the Pac-Man series of games.

Games distributed Pac-Man, which was created by a company called Namco. Pac-Man was quite different from most of the existing games at the time. Rather than shooting at something, it was more like an exciting combination of a puzzle and adventure game. Pac-Man was the first video game brand to become popular outside of the video game itself. T-shirts, hats, dolls, board games, mugs, and many other products (see Figure 1.11) displayed the Pac-Man characters.

## 1981—Hello Mario

In 1981, a game called Donkey Kong was released by Nintendo and was a hit from the start. The game seemed to be modeled somewhat after the movie King Kong. The villain was a giant gorilla that held captive a beautiful prisoner. The gorilla held the woman in a cage at the top of the screen and hurled down barrels. The hero, Mario, had to jump over as he climbed ladders trying to reach the top (see Figure 1.12). This was the first time we met Mario—a character who later became

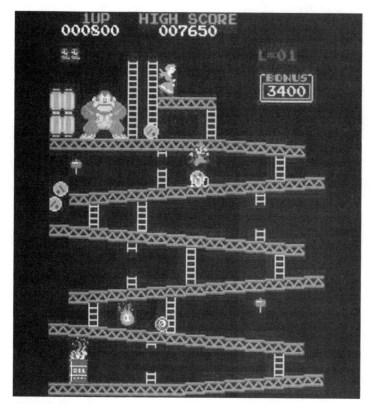

**Figure 1.12**
Mario was first seen here in the hit game Donkey Kong.

very popular in other games released by Nintendo including Mario Bros and
Super Mario Bros.

## 1983—Video Game Crash

From the mid '70s to early '80s, the video game market was growing at an
outstanding rate. This all changed in 1983, the year of the "video game crash."
During this year many video game companies went out of business or got out of
video games entirely. There were a variety of reasons that the gaming market
crashed, including the introduction of inexpensive home computers, a lack of
good games being released, and a weak economy.

## 1983—Dragon's Lair

Dragon's Lair (see Figure 1.13) was the world's first fully animated video game
that worked on a laser. While other games were starting to get old, boring, and

**Figure 1.13**
Dragon's Lair cost a dollar to play when all other games were 25 cents.

outdated, Dragon's Lair injected some much-needed life into the video gaming industry. Players controlled the main character, Dirk the Daring, and as they moved the joystick, the animation on screen would play a scene based on the movements. I remember playing this game at the local arcade when I was a kid, and the one thing that stuck in my mind was that you needed four quarters to play, while every other game was just one quarter. I guess you get what you pay for; Dragon's Lair was the most popular game in the arcade!

## 1985—NES and Super Mario Bros

The NES (Nintendo Entertainment System) has been credited with turning the gaming industry around after the video game crash of 1983. It was released in October of 1985 and was an instant success. The NES was an 8-bit gaming console that included two games: Super Mario Bros and Duck Hunt. Super Mario Bros was the first video game in which the action scrolled sideways rather than up and down. It once again starred the popular Mario character and also brought along his brother Luigi as the second player. The game is one of the most popular of all time, with over 50 million copies sold. In 1991, Nintendo followed the success of the NES by releasing the Super NES, a 16-bit video gaming console.

## 1985—Tetris

Alexey Pajinov created Tetris, a puzzle game in which the player had to fit together blocks as they fell from the top of the screen. Although Tetris was originally created for the PC, it really owes its popularity to the Nintendo Game Boy. When you purchased a Game Boy, the Tetris game cartridge was included, so Tetris reached millions of gamers. To this day, Tetris remains extremely popular and is just as addictive as it was when first created over 20 years ago.

## 1989—Game Boy

With the popularity of the NES, Nintendo wanted to create a unit that was portable but still gave the gamer the NES experience. The Game Boy was released in 1989 and was a small, hand-held video gaming device with an LCD screen. Although its design and capabilities have changed over the years, the Game Boy line still remains very popular among young gamers. Other Game Boy incarnations include Game Boy Color, Advance, Advance SP, Micro, and Nintendo DS (see Figure 1.14).

**Figure 1.14**
One version of the popular Game Boy portable gaming system.

## 1993—Atari Jaguar

Although it wasn't commercially successful, the Atari Jaguar was the first gaming console with a 64-bit processor. It was a more powerful system than any on the market at the time, but Atari just didn't have the marketing power to make the console a success, and there simply weren't enough games being developed for it.

## 1993—Doom

If you are in to 3D gaming at all, you've probably heard of Doom, which was the pioneer of "first-person shooter" games. Doom, created by id Software, was made available as shareware (free limited version download) and was used by over 10 million people in its first two years. Doom's popularity has spawned a variety of follow-up games and even a movie.

## 1995—PlayStation

The PlayStation was a CD-ROM–based gaming console released by Sony in 1995. It was a 32-bit console with a quality of graphics that had not been seen before. The main appeal of the games on the PlayStation was that they were in 3D. The PlayStation was actually born out of a relationship gone bad with Nintendo. Sony was developing a CD-ROM system for the SNES CD-ROM, but when the relationship went sour, Sony decided that they would develop it on their own, and thus the PlayStation was born. Sony has come out with a variety of successors to the original PlayStation, including PSOne, PlayStation 2, and PSP (PlayStation Portable), followed by the release of PlayStation 3 in 2006.

## 1996—Nintendo 64

As its name suggests, Nintendo 64 was a 64-bit game console. While similar consoles of the time were using CD-ROMS, the N64 (as it was commonly known) still used ROM cartridges. The release of the N64 also saw the first 3D version of a Mario Bros game in Super Mario 64.

## 2000—PlayStation 2

Over four times more powerful than the original PlayStation, the PlayStation 2 was the next giant step in the evolution of gaming. People lined up around the block and went on huge waiting lists to get their hands on this latest gaming phenomenon. Besides its impressive performance, the PlayStation 2 had another

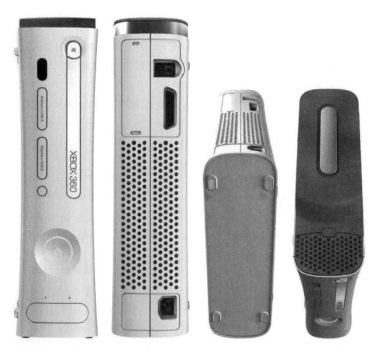

**Figure 1.15**
The Xbox 360 is the latest in powerful 3D gaming.

great feature—it was backward compatible, meaning PlayStation and PSOne games could be played on it. To date, almost 100 million units have sold.

## 2001—Xbox

In 2001, Microsoft announced to the world that is was stepping into the world of gaming consoles with the creation of the Xbox. The Xbox was a 64-bit gaming system that was built more like a PC than a traditional gaming console. It had a built-in hard drive, a DVD-ROM drive that you could use as a regular DVD player, and Internet capabilities. In 2005, Microsoft released the Xbox 360—a much more powerful version than the original Xbox (see Figure 1.15).

So that's your journey down memory lane. It by no means covers all that has happened over the last 30 years of gaming, but you should now have a good idea of the highlights. Now it's your turn to make gaming history. Read on . . .

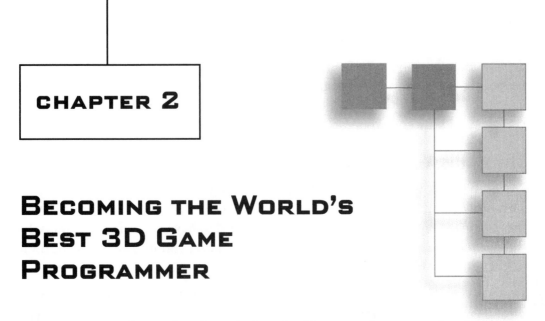

# CHAPTER 2

# BECOMING THE WORLD'S BEST 3D GAME PROGRAMMER

As you stare out the 12-foot bay window, looking over the mountain-view resort lake, watching as speckles of sunlight dance off the water ripples, you look down at your watch. It's 3:25 in the afternoon, quitting time, and you consider playing a few rounds before heading home to your palatial mansion.

The corner office that they gave you two years ago looks more like a high-tech war room than a corporate boardroom. Six 42-inch plasma screens glisten on the far wall, each connected to a different gaming system or high-powered gaming machine. The two oversized leather recliners that face the screens engulf you as you climb inside and prepare to blast through enemy invaders in your latest creation.

Just as you prepare to fire up your favorite system, you hear a few raps on your solid oak office door. The president of the company darts in, his eyes wide, his smile gleaming from ear to ear. "We got the call!" he bellows out. He assumes that you know what call he's talking about, and you do. The National Gaming Institute (NGI) convened a special meeting two months after the release of Aki—Alien Destroyer, the hit 3D game you programmed that has broken all sales records and has made you a programming superstar. Your boss continues, "The NGI has voted to put you into the Video Gaming Hall of Fame as the Best Programmer Ever!" You lean back in your recliner, and a warm smile comes across your face as you start to plan your acceptance speech. Only one thought seems to come to your head: "Thank goodness I read *3D Programming for Teens* all those years ago."

So how exactly do you go from being interested in 3D game programming to becoming the world's best programmer? That's exactly what I'll discuss in this chapter. I'll go over the key skills you must have to become an amazing game creator, and how and where to get those skills.

## The Skills You Need

Down the road, you may have the goal of creating and designing games on your own or working as part of a team at a gaming company. Regardless of what you decide, to become a game developer you will need to have a certain set of skills. In this section I'll discuss the key skills you should have, and in the next section I'll talk about how to acquire those skills.

Don't worry if you don't have certain skills or are not strong in one particular area; there are plenty of jobs and opportunities for people with specific skills. For example, let's say you are a great graphic designer but your programming skills are so-so. Not to worry, the gaming industry needs plenty of great graphic designers.

The best way to see what skills you need is to take a look at what employers look for when they are hiring employees. The following is an actual job posting for a game programmer that does a great job of summing up most of the important skills you'll need:

*Our company is looking for an experienced game designer with focus on game-mechanics and implementation. It is also a big plus if you have other complementary artistic skills. You will work closely with a team of designers, programmers, and artists to bring life and fun into next-generation console games. This job is available immediately and is full-time on location.*

*Qualifications:*

> *Excellent written and verbal English skills*
>
> *Strong problem solving skills*
>
> *Strong team skills and the ability to take initiative*
>
> *Excellent social skills*
>
> *Basic understanding of programming (actual programming skills is a great plus)*
>
> *At least two years of game industry experience*
>
> *A passion to develop innovative game-play*

## Programming Skills

It may seem quite obvious, but to be a good game developer you need to be able to program. In the following chapters you'll learn all about the different programming languages that are available for you to learn. You certainly don't have to know how to program in every language; it's more important to know the thinking behind the programming process. Once you've learned one programming language, you'll find that learning others is much easier. A lot of the commands are similar and many of the things you learn about one programming language are transferable to another.

## Graphic Design Skills

I consider myself a graphic designer, but there's something you should know about me—I can't draw. You don't necessarily need to be a great artist or be gifted with raw talent in order to be a graphic designer. I'll give you a terrific example. I couldn't draw a perfect circle if my life depended on it, but with the tools available I don't need to. There are a ton of graphics programs out there that can create a perfect circle for me. In the next chapter I'll cover the different graphic design programs that are available to you, but just as with programming, the skills and concepts are more important than the actual tools you use. For example, if you know how to create a circle in a program like CorelDRAW, you'll easily figure out how to create a circle in Adobe Illustrator. Graphic design plays a huge role in the development of a video game. You could have the greatest story in the world, but if it can't be told graphically, your game will not be a success. Figure 2.1 is an example of some realistic 3D artwork.

## Team Skills

You may have dreams of sitting in front of your computer, designing and creating the perfect 3D game by yourself and selling millions of copies. The reality is that most games that have any commercial success were created by a team of individuals. There is so much that goes into a 3D video game that many different individuals with different expertise are required. An average commercial 3D game requires programmers (many of whom will have their own specific expertise), a 3D animator, a 3D modeler, a texture artist, graphic designers, marketing and sales people, and potentially many others. The team sizes can range from just a few people to several hundred. Being able to work with others is fundamental to becoming a good game developer. When working with a team you need to have tough skin. Not all your ideas will be accepted, you won't

**Figure 2.1**
The goal of the graphic designer is to create realistic, believable graphics that bring the game story to life.

necessarily like all of the people on your team, and you may not get all the credit you deserve. But the advantages of working with a team far outweigh the drawbacks. A team atmosphere can generate productivity, increase motivation, and ultimately create a better game. I'm sure you've heard of the saying "Two heads are better than one," and that certainly applies to creating a game. Working well with others goes a long way to helping you go far in gaming.

## Math

That's right, I said *math!* I hate to say it, but math is essential to the world of programming. As you get deeper and deeper into programming you'll find that math plays an increasingly important role. The good news is that you can get started in 3D programming without knowing all that much about math. When you get to the programming section of this book, the math concepts will be clearly explained in an easy-to-follow format. Beyond this book, as you advance into 3D game programming, you'll have to pick up additional math skills including trigonometry, physics, and 3D math concepts. The more you know about math, the easier it will be to overcome obstacles and find solutions to problems that you come across.

## Patience

Have you ever heard any of these sayings: "Rome wasn't built in a day," "Good things come to those who wait," "Patience is a virtue"? All of these apply to the world of game development. Building your skills as a game developer takes time and patience. It will take a long time before you are able to create the types of 3D games that you find on the shelves of your favorite electronics store. Becoming a game developer is a journey—one that may have a few bumps in the road. The programming section of this book will allow you to see results instantly and give you a great start in programming, but once you are off on your own and continue to build your skills, you may—no, you *will*—experience some problems. The biggest frustration you'll find are bugs. Bugs are problems with the program code you have created that prevent your game from running properly. The key to overcoming these problems is patience. Know that every new programmer has experienced these same problems and that a solution is out there.

## Communication Skills

You probably wouldn't think that communication skills would be all that important in becoming a game developer, and you'd be right if you thought that all there was to being a game developer was programming on your own. As I said earlier, creating a great game involves working with others. In order to work with others, you need to be able to communicate, both verbally and in writing. For example, let's say that you had a great vision for how a character in your game should look. You've got a picture in your mind down to every detail, facial texture, type of clothing, eye color, facial expressions, etc. If you are unable to convey your vision either verbally or in writing to your graphic designer, the character won't turn out as you had envisioned.

## Grace Under Pressure

This skill is particularly important if you are working in a gaming company. Most gaming companies have release cycles. This means that in order to remain competitive, they have to make sure that their games are completed and available to the public by a certain date. As release dates get closer and closer, there is always a lot of pressure on the game developers to meet deadlines. Being able to handle stress and pressure is of utmost importance to game developers, and not only to those who work in big gaming companies. Even if you are just playing around with 3D programming on your own, it is easy to get frustrated and stressed out when your game isn't working properly or you get stuck.

## Attention to Detail

Not everyone is detail oriented, which is one of the essential skills to have when programming. If you gloss over something, it's easy to make a mistake, or leave something out of your coding that will prevent your program from working properly. Paying attention to details will also help you when trying to debug or solve problems in your programs. Some people naturally look closely at the details, while others, like me, really have to work at it. The good thing is that this is a skill that is easily learned; you can actually force yourself to become detail oriented.

## Creativity

It's easy to say that in order to be a game developer you need to have creativity, but what exactly is creativity? Isn't it something that you either have or you don't have? The truth is that everyone has creativity in their own way. Creativity can be applied in so many different areas to game development from the story to the design, to problem solving, to marketing and selling. The key is to try and find in what area you are most creative and apply that creativity to the gaming process. If you lack creativity in a specific area, don't worry; you can always borrow the creativity of others. By incorporating other people into your gaming process, you can make up for areas where your skills are lacking.

## How to Get the Skills

The good news about developing games is that there are so many different job options available to you that you don't need to have all of the skills in all areas. For example, a programmer doesn't need all of the skills that a graphic designer needs, and a 3D modeler doesn't need the same skills as a beta tester. In the preceding section, I covered the different types of skills that you need. But how do you get them? Truth be told, for some of the skills you are either born with them or you aren't. For others, you can learn and increase your proficiency by doing the following.

## Play Games

Here is some really good news. One of the best ways to become a really good game developer is to play games! Just like a professional football player will watch hours and hours of game tape to perfect his performance, playing games will actually help you become a better game programmer. As you play games, you'll learn to understand what makes some games more appealing than others. You'll also learn about the different components of a game that you might want to include in your program. As you play, think about what you like or don't like about the game—is it the action, the story, the special effects, the atmosphere, the controls, the characters, or something else? Try to play a variety of games on different platforms (PC, PlayStation, Xbox, etc.). Don't just play first-person shooters, or puzzle or simulation games; play all different types of games, both old and new. This will help to provide you with the inspiration needed to create your own 3D game.

## Practice, Practice, Practice

Just like with piano lessons, practice makes perfect. The best way to get really good at something, including 3D game programming, is to practice. This book provides you with the perfect opportunity to practice. In the programming section you'll find quite a bit of gaming code that will help you get started. Experiment with the code provided, try changing it slightly, and explore on your own how changing the code affects the program. Try dreaming up your own games and bringing them to life by programming them from examples in this book. The more you practice, the better you will become.

## Read

This book is meant to be a steppingstone on your journey into programming. It will provide you with the basic tools and concepts you need to get going, but by no means is it a be all and end all. There are hundreds of different books on the market that cover all aspects of gaming, from programming to math to game design to you name it. No one person is an expert in every area of gaming, and as you get deeper into 3D game development you'll find that you'll be drawn to a particular area and may want to become an expert in that area. Whether it's game design, online gaming, C++ programming, or any other topic, you'll find many books that will help quench your thirst for game knowledge.

## Get Out There

One of the best ways to gain the skills necessary to become a game developer is to get involved with the gaming community. You'll find that you'll learn much by staying in tune with the community. New technology, trends, and hot games are always topics of discussion in these communities, and you can stay on top of the latest news, techniques, job openings, and events by getting plugged in. Following are a variety of different ways that you can get involved with the gaming community.

### Online Forums

The fastest and easiest way to see what's going on is to go online and get involved with online gaming forums. There are hundreds of different forums, each focused on a particular aspect of gaming. What you'll see on each forum will vary, but in general they provide discussion groups, answers to frequently asked questions, tutorials, manuals, event listings, job postings, and product reviews. The best way to find a forum is to simply conduct a search on the Internet. For example, if you wanted to find 3D game forums, simply type that in on your search and you'll find plenty.

### Trade Shows

Trade shows are a great opportunity to not only see what's new and hot in gaming but also to meet face to face with the key players in the industry. At a trade show you will typically see a cross section of the entire industry, including both big and small gaming companies, software vendors, graphic design companies, and much more. It's a terrific opportunity to network and check out possible future employers. I'm assuming that you don't have the budget to travel all around the country to attend different trade shows, so your best bet is to check your local computer papers for upcoming shows and events. The Internet is also a terrific resource when looking for shows. Keep in mind, however, that many trade shows are open only to people already in the gaming industry, and typically you have to be over 18 to get in. Some of the most popular annual trade shows are E3 (Electronic Entertainment Expo) and DigitalLife.

### User Groups

A user group is a group of individuals who live in a particular area who share common interests in a particular technology. Typically, they meet once a month to share ideas, help one another, and listen to presentations on a variety of topics. Being a member of a user group has its advantages. Along with being able to network with people with common interests, many companies offer discounts and special promotions to members of user groups. Finding a user group in your area is simply a matter of conducting a search on the Internet. In the search field, type in the type of user group you are looking for (for example, "C++ user group" or "Xbox user group") and you'll find a user group that you may want to join. Another option is joining an online user group. If you go to http://groups.yahoo.com you'll be able to conduct a search for different online user groups that you can join (there's even a 3D Game Programming group on the site.)

### Magazines

Magazines are another terrific resource for gaining the skills you need to become a game developer. If it weren't for magazines, I probably would never have gotten my start in programming. When I was young, I subscribed to a magazine called *Compute* that gave me line-by-line codes that I could enter to program video games. There are dozens of different computer, gaming, and programming magazines available. The main advantage of magazines is that they keep you up to date with the latest news, information, and trends. Some magazines that may be of interest to you include:

- *Computer Games*
- *Computer Gaming World*
- *GamePro*
- *PC Gamer*

In addition to actual print magazines, there are dozens of online gaming and programming magazines that can provide you with a lot of valuable information.

## Find a Mentor

A mentor is a person who has achieved the position that you would like to achieve and who can provide you with advice, help, and motivation as you attempt to reach your goals. For example, if your goal was to become a programmer at Nintendo, you would try to find someone who is currently a programmer at Nintendo to become your mentor. How do you get someone to be your mentor? Just ask. You'd be surprised at how willing people are to help others who simply ask for help. If you can get someone to agree to meet with you online once a month so that you can ask them questions about how they got to where they are, and what advice they have to give, you'll find that having a mentor can be extremely valuable. Where do you start? If you don't happen to know anybody, start with a company's general e-mail address, and send a message telling them that you are a young programmer looking for a mentor and ask if they could recommend someone. It's as easy as that. Don't get discouraged if some people or companies aren't willing to mentor you. Just keep trying others until you find a mentor who's willing to work with you.

## Take a Course

Everybody learns in different ways. Some people like to read and practice, others prefer to learn in a classroom environment. There are hundreds of different courses available at community centers, colleges, and private schools. However, I would suggest that you do not take a course right away. First get your feet wet by going through this book and several others to get an idea of what direction you'd like to take with your game programming. Once you determine the area or areas you'd like to specialize in (e.g., C++, DirectX, JavaScript, etc.), you'll find plenty of courses, either in a classroom setting or online.

## Have Other Interests

It may sound silly, but another very important factor for becoming a successful game developer is to have other interests. It's very easy to get too wrapped up in a game you are creating, spending hours in front of the computer spinning your wheels and getting frustrated. Life is about balance, so as exciting and rewarding as creating games can be, it's important to have outside interests. I know of many programmers who experienced burnout because they worked too hard and didn't have enough balance in their lives. Don't make the same mistakes they made. Take plenty of breaks, read books, go outside, play sports, and, most of all, make sure you are having fun!

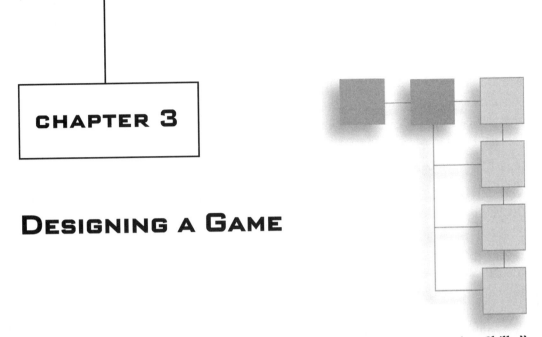

# CHAPTER 3

## Designing a Game

I used to teach a class called "Speak at Your Peak—Effective Presentation Skills," and one of the key fundamentals I would impart to the class was to remember the seven P's: **P**rior, **P**roper **P**reparation **P**revents **P**oor **P**erformance by the **P**resenter. The basic point is that planning in advance makes all the difference in the world. When building a house, a contractor doesn't just buy some wood and start hammering away; he follows a detailed plan that has been outlined by an architect. The same holds true in programming. If you just sat down in front of the computer and started trying to program a game without a proper plan, you would get frustrated very quickly and things wouldn't turn out as you would have hoped. I'll be completely honest with you: creating a game is a lot of hard work. It takes hours and hours of work and a lot of energy, but in the end it is very rewarding. In this chapter I will discuss the proper way to create a plan for your video game. The methods that I will be discussing are the ones used by most of the largest and most popular gaming companies. As a beginner to programming, you don't necessarily have to follow each of these steps in detail to create your first few programs, but it's a good idea to get a solid grasp on the process so that when you're ready to create your first commercially viable game, you'll understand what is involved.

## The Big Idea

It all starts with an idea. Perhaps you got an idea for the perfect program the first time you laid eyes on a video game. Or maybe you woke up in the middle of the night with a dream about a game that will put you into the gaming hall of fame.

Maybe you and your friends brainstormed and came up with a terrific idea. Or perhaps you don't have an idea at all. Where do ideas for video games come from? Read on. . . .

## An Old Video Game

One terrific source of inspiration for a video game is old video games. In the 30 years of video games, thousands of different programs have been created. Perhaps you'd like to take a classic game and create a 3D version of it. If you're creating video games for practice or just for you and your friends to play, you can use just about any idea. If you are developing a game that you would one day like to sell, one important thing to remember is that you should look to old video games for inspiration, but never blatantly copy them. Most games have a copyright, which means that it is illegal to copy the idea and put it into your own game. You have to make a significant change to the program to be able to call it your own. A good idea is to take the things that you like best from other games and combine them into your own unique idea. Pac-Man (see Figure 3.1) is one of many old games that you can use as inspiration.

## A Book

Another great place to get ideas for video games is books. You can take just about any story and turn it into a video game idea. Everything from nursery rhymes to comic books to novels can be used as inspiration for a video game. Just imagine the three little pigs fighting off the big bad wolf in a space adventure. As with all ideas that you get from other sources, make sure that you change the idea enough or give it a twist so that you won't get into any copyright trouble.

## A Sport

There have been hundreds of different video games created for just about every sport on earth, but that doesn't mean that you can't create your own unique sporting video game. The key is to have a twist or make your game different from what is already available. Try and think creatively or "outside the box" when thinking of how to make a cool sporting video game. One idea is to simply change the type of players. How about a game of ice hockey where cats take on dogs? Or perhaps a baseball game where aliens take on humans? Another way to add a twist to a sporting video game is to change the location. Have a football

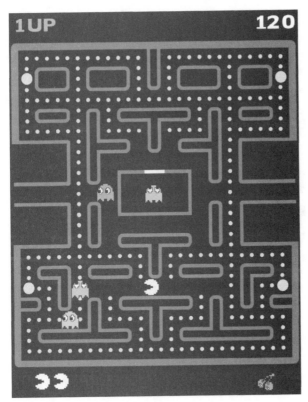

**Figure 3.1**
An old video game, like Pac-Man, can provide great inspiration for a new one.

game (see Figure 3.2) take place on the moon with zero gravity or create a golf match underground. Finally, you can also invent your own sports from games that you've made up. When my older brother and I were young, we'd hollow out boxes and have races rolling down our backyard hill. I could easily create a video game using those box races as my idea. The key is to stretch your imagination to create something that would be fun and interesting and appealing to gamers.

## A Board Game

There's no better way to bring a board game to life than by making a 3D video game version of it. There are thousands of board games that you can use for video game ideas. As I already mentioned, you don't want to make a copy of an existing board game (see Figure 3.3); you want to take an idea from a board game and make it your own by changing the characters, events, and surrounding, and giving it a twist. You can also create your version of popular games that have

**Figure 3.2**
Many video games are based on a sport or combination of different sports.

**Figure 3.3**
You can bring a board game to life by making it into a 3D game.

no copyright such as chess, backgammon, tic-tac-toe, S.O.S., or checkers. It's important that you make your game appealing so that people will want to play it.

## An Event in Your Life

Our lives are stories that are played out on a daily basis, and they are the perfect inspiration for video games. Every day something happens to you or you see something that could be the idea behind a video game. Did a car splash a puddle on you on your way to work? You could make a video game where the player tries to avoid being splashed. Were you put in detention for behaving badly in school? You could make a game where the player tries to escape detention. Did your parents make you shovel the driveway to earn your allowance? You could make a game where the player has to shovel driveways and avoid obstacles to earn his allowance. The point that I am trying to make is that if you don't have an idea for a video game, you're not looking around. There are dozens of things that happen to us on a daily basis that can be used as the inspiration for the next great video game.

## A News Event

Every night on the news there are good stories, bad stories, silly stories, and sad stories that all can be used as inspiration for a video game. The other day there was a story about a lady who locked her dog in the car by accident while the car was running. She had to convince the dog to try and unlock the door by putting his paw on the button. Eventually he did press the button and unlocked the doors. It's a bit of a silly story, but still one that can be used as a video game idea where the player would be the dog trying to press the right button to unlock a door. Whether it's a silly local story or an important national event, the news can be a great source for video game ideas.

## A Sitcom, Drama, Game Show, or Movie

The next time your mother asks why you are watching so much television, you can tell her that you are doing research for your future career as a game developer. Just by flicking the channels on your television, you can get hundreds of ideas for video games. There are many video games on the market that have been inspired from game shows or scenes from television or movies. Some examples of these include Star Wars Battlefront, The Simpsons Road Rage, Shrek Superslam, James Bond 007, and Jeopardy, and there are dozens of others.

## Planning Your Game

So now that you've got a great idea for a video game, the real work begins: the planning stage. In this stage you have to map out and plan the different aspects of your game. In other words, you'll be creating the road map that the programmer will follow when developing the code for the game. (In most cases, the programmer will be you, especially when you first start making games.)

## Type of Game

The type of game you choose will determine the amount of programming work necessary. For example, creating a full football game simulation will be more difficult to program than a tic-tac-toe simulation. The idea for your game may have already determined what type it will be; otherwise, you will need to choose the type. Following is a list of the most common game types.

- **First-Person Shooter.** These are very popular in the world of 3D gamers. Examples of popular first-person shooters include Doom (see Figure 3.4), Halo, and Half-Life. In a first-person shooter, the player sees the world as if

**Figure 3.4**
Doom was a pioneer in 3D first-person shooter games.

he were actually in the video game. Typically, the only thing players will see of themselves is their hands holding a particular weapon as they fight through different scenes.

■ **Racing**. This type of game is pretty much self-explanatory. Players race against one another or the computer in order to get to the finish line first. The type of characters, vehicles, obstacles, and environments that can be used in a racing type game are endless.

■ **Platform**. A platform game is a type of video game where the player typically has to move up or sideways from platform to platform, fighting off enemies and collecting items in order to complete a level. Some of the most popular historic platform games include Super Mario Bros, Sonic the Hedgehog, and Donkey Kong (see Figure 3.5).

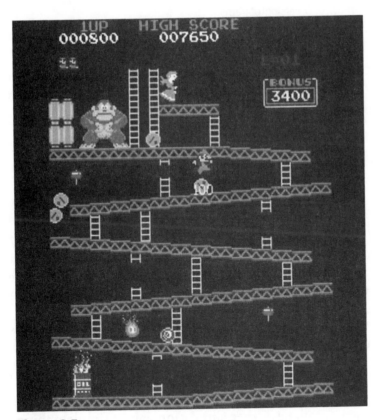

**Figure 3.5**
Donkey Kong was one of the first platform games.

**Figure 3.6**
Consider making your own 3D version of Tetris.

- **Puzzle**. Perhaps the most famous puzzle game of all time is Tetris (see Figure 3.6), a game where you need to fit together blocks as they fall from the top of the screen.

- **Fighting**. In a fighting game, the player must defeat one opponent before moving on to the next scene or opponent. Many strategy and role-playing games incorporate fighting as part of their scenes.

- **Role-Playing**. This type of game encompasses many different categories of games. In almost every type of game, there is some sort of role-playing. In a role-playing game, the character takes on a role and goes through an adventure. Typically, the character walks through worlds, taking on different challenges in order to arrive at a certain location or achieve a certain goal.

- **Sports**. This type of game is pretty much self-explanatory; the game is a video version of the real sport.

- **Simulation**. Simulation games simulate some type of real-life action. For example, a flight simulation video game gives the player the experience that he is really flying an airplane. Other simulation games simulate things like operating tanks, cars, and trains. There is also a subset of games within this type that include simulating not so "real-life" situations like creating and managing an airport, a train station, a planet, or a family. Examples of these include The Sims and Railroad Tycoon.

## The Story Line

The things that happen in your game, the characters, and the environment all make up the story line. As a game developer, you need to create the story of your video game by writing it down long before you start programming.

### Plot

Just like in a novel, the plot of a game is a description of the events that happen. It's important that you write out the plot of a game as it will be part of the road map that you'll follow when programming your video game. The plot will include the events in the game, the goal of the game, the number of levels in the game, and more. If you think about it, even the plot of a simple game like Space Invaders has many aspects to it. Following are the events of Space Invaders in bullet form.

- The player controls a space ship that moves back and forth horizontally along the bottom of the screen.

- The player's ship fires a single missile whenever the space bar is pressed.

- Alien ships appear in several rows, each row containing a different type of alien ship.

- The alien ships move left and right horizontally across the screen.

- Whenever the group of alien ships moves all the way to the left or right side of the screen, they fall one level closer to the player's ship.

- Whenever the group of alien ships moves all the way to the left or right side of the screen, their speed increases.

- Whenever an alien ship is hit by the player's bullet, the alien ship is destroyed.

- The alien ships randomly fire missiles down at the player's ship.

- The player's ship is protected by four oval-like objects that act as shields.

- When an alien missile hits the shield, part of the shield is destroyed.

- The player gets 10 points for every alien ship that he destroys.

- When all of the alien ships are destroyed, the player moves on to the next level.

- The aliens move faster on each progressive level.

- If the player's ship is hit by an alien missile, the ship is destroyed.

- The player has a total of three ships to begin with.

- Each time the player advances to a new level, he receives a new ship.

As you can see, even though Space Invaders is a relatively simple game, the plot is quite involved. In commercial games like Doom or Halo, it takes a special team of writers months to develop the plot of a game, including the details of player movements, scenes, fights etc.

### Characters

Typically, one of the main appeals of video games are the characters that are played within them. Whether a character is good or evil, if a character appeals to gamers, they'll be more interested in playing the game. Characters like Pac-Man, Mario, and Donkey Kong were so popular that they have become part of our pop culture. When developing the characters for your game, you have to answer some of the following questions:

How many characters will you have?

How tall will a character be?

What will the characters wear?

Will they be fast or slow?

Will the characters be male, female, or have no sex?

Does the character talk?

Will the character hold any weapons?

How does the character walk/move?

What are the expressions on the character's face?

How will the character interact with other characters?

What will make your characters appealing?

How will the characters react to and interact with their environment?

### The Environment

When creating a 3D game, you are given the responsibility of playing God. You have the ability to create any kind of world that you like. You can choose the appearance and details of the sky, the ground, the trees, the rivers, the roads, and the animals, and you can choose whether it's day or night, overcast or sunny, and so on.

In the programming section of this book, you will create environments for your world by using a feature called *texture mapping*. Think of texture mapping as a piece of wrapping paper that you would wrap around a gift. If you wrapped a ball with wrapping paper that had a pattern of grass, the ball would appear as if it were covered in grass. That's exactly how you create your environments in 3D games. You wrap a texture, which is usually a picture that repeats itself, over different objects.

The type of world you create will depend on the plot of your game. If it's a deep, dark, mysterious plot, the world you create should reflect that by having dim lighting—perhaps with some fog and set at night. On the other hand, if you have a lighter plot, bright lighting, high detail, and happy characters would be most appropriate. The bottom line is that your game is a package made up of many elements, and those elements (including the plot, the environment, the sounds, and the characters) should all complement one another.

## Storyboarding

Once you have written down your ideas for a story line, it is time to create a storyboard. A *storyboard* (see Figure 3.7) is a visual representation of the characters and action in your game. Think of a storyboard as the comic strip version of your video game. In a storyboard, you draw a rough sketch of how each scene in your video game is to be played out. In most cases, a storyboard is a black-and-white rough drawing with some text that describes the action.

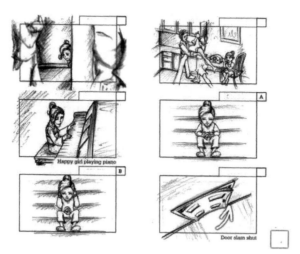

**Figure 3.7**
A storyboard will bring your game to life before you've done any programming.

Because each scene of a video game can have so many different outcomes, depending on the magnitude and complexity of your video game, a storyboard can be extremely long. Although it might take a while to create, a storyboard is very important, especially in the process of creating a commercial video game for which there are dozens of people working on the same project. The storyboard shows the programmers, artists, and designers what the game should look like once complete.

## Controls

In addition to what happens during your game, you'll have to consider how it happens. By that I mean you'll have to decide how objects are controlled. Will the characters in your game move on their own? Will they be controlled by keyboard, mouse (see Figure 3.8), joystick, or some other means?

Another very important consideration in 3D game programming is the movement and positioning of the camera. The camera acts as the player's eyes in the video game. In some games you can control the camera by being able to "look around," while in others the camera cannot be controlled and will only follow the play as determined by the programmers. You'll need to determine in advance how and if you want the camera controlled and where you would like to position the camera. For example, if you were creating a flight simulator game, you

**Figure 3.8**
How will the player control the game?

would have to decide where you want the perspective of the player to be. Will the player's view be from inside the cockpit? From outside the plane? From the side of the plane? Or will the player have the option of changing the camera view?

## Sounds and Music

Have you seen any of the *Star Wars* movies? Imagine watching some of those movies with the sound turned off. Not only would it be hard to figure out what is going on because you wouldn't hear the dialog, you'd also be missing one other very big component—emotion. Just as in movies, the music in video games can add to the story line by creating a sense of fear, tension, excitement, joy, trauma, or other emotion. When designing your game, you'll have to decide where and when you will want audio to play.

There are a variety of questions you can ask yourself when deciding how and where music and sounds will be played.

Will there be music playing in the background during the entire game?

Will there be different music for different scenes/levels/worlds?

What sounds will be made when a weapon is fired?

What sounds will play when players collide?

Will there be music for the Welcome screen?

What sounds will play when a player is destroyed?

Make sure that the choices you make complement the game play and don't overshadow or distract from the game.

## Creating a Design Document

If you are just creating a game on your own or with your friends, you don't really need a design document, but it's important to know what one is in case you ever plan on working in a 3D gaming company. A *design document* puts together all of the components you've written down for your game into one document that will be used as the complete plan for building the game. Design documents are also created in gaming companies to help sell the idea of the game to the people who make the final decisions. Depending on the size of the game, a design document can sometimes be up to several hundred pages.

Now that you have a clear, written concept of the game that you are creating, it is time to start programming it. That brings up a dilemma. You have dozens of options that you can choose from for programming and designing your game. There are different languages and software packages for each aspect of a game. In the next chapter I'll discuss the most popular choices available.

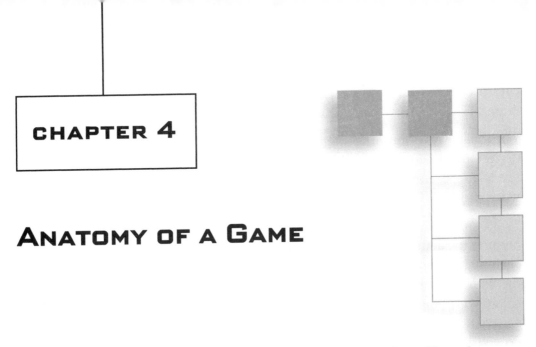

# CHAPTER 4

# ANATOMY OF A GAME

Unfortunately, at some point or other in our lives, most of us will need to go to the hospital for an x-ray. The doctor examines this information to determine what's wrong with us on the inside. Think of this chapter as an x-ray of 3D games. You'll see how and why a 3D game works and what combination of programs it takes to put everything together.

All 3D games are created in some type of programming language. Whether we create the code ourselves or we work with objects for which the code is generated automatically, the underlying fact is that all games require some type of computer language behind them. In this chapter I'll discuss the different programming options available for 3D gamers. Programming languages are just one of the parts that make up a 3D game; you'll also typically need a graphics program and 3D modeling program, depending on how elaborate your game will be. I'll discuss some of the options that are available to you. Finally, I'll cover the flow of a game, and how the code creates what you see on the screen.

## Programming Languages

There are dozens of different options when it comes to choosing a programming language for your game. A programming language communicates with your computer, telling it how and where to display objects on the screen and how to react to inputs from the player. Each language has its own unique way of communicating with the computer. This method of communication is called the *syntax*, and whenever you use a language you'll have to learn its syntax.

With many programming languages, you enter the code directly into any kind of text document following a specific format. After your code is created, it needs to be compiled. Compiling a program means taking all of the code that you entered and turning it into a file that can be executed to run your game.

Because the action happens so fast in a 3D game and the graphics are constantly changing, the language that you create your game in needs to be able to interpret the code quickly. There really is no magic language that you should use to create your games. The reality is that if you are serious about becoming a 3D game programmer, you'll probably end up learning several languages. So which do you pick? It really depends on a variety of different factors, some of which include:

- Your experience, if any, with the programming language

- The type of game you are creating

- The cost of the language

- The platform you want your game to be able to run on (Windows, Linux, Nintendo, Macintosh etc.)

- The ease of use of the language

- The portability of the language

In the following sections, I'll cover some of the most popular options available to you.

## C++

C++ is the choice of many 3D game programmers and is probably one of the most popular languages. With C++, you enter code, much like any other computer language, in a text document. There are a lot of reasons why C++ is a great choice for creating 3D games. First of all, because it is such a popular language, there is a lot of support, information, manuals, and other resources available for the language should you get stuck at any point in your programming—and trust me, you *will* get stuck at some point; every programmer does! Aside from having help readily available, the games you create using C++ can be compiled for use on virtually every platform. In other words, the games you create using C++ can be used on just about every type of computer or gaming machine.

The main disadvantage of C++ and the reason we won't use it for the programming in this book is that it is difficult for beginners to learn and use. Not only do you have to learn C++, but you also need to understand the various libraries that can be used in the creation of your game. It's much better to start off with an easier language, understand the concepts of programming, and then slowly graduate to using C++.

## Java

The main advantage of programming in Java is that after you've created a program, it is compiled and then runs on something called the JVM, or Java Virtual Machine. The JVM can be run on almost every type of computer platform, so you don't have to modify your code to get it to work on different machines. It's like owning your own pair of skis instead of having to rent them at each different ski resort. Think of each different ski resort as a different platform (Xbox, Windows, Linux etc.). If you brought your own skis to each resort, you could just go on the hill and start skiing, but if you rented, you'd have to take the time to learn to use different skis (modify the code) at each resort you visited. Java also makes it easier to create programs intended to run on the Web. Java code is similar to C, so again there is a bit of a learning curve for the new user. Microsoft has a similar programming language to Java called C#.

## Visual Basic

Visual Basic, created by Microsoft, is a flavor of an older programming language simply called Basic. Visual Basic is very popular with programmers who create business applications but is also starting to gain some ground as a language that can be used by 3D game programmers. Visual Basic is called "visual" because you can actually create the visual components of your programming by placing or dragging them on the screen, while the code is created for you. To properly create 3D games, you'll also need to use DirectX. Unlike many other programming languages, you must purchase Visual Basic from Microsoft in order to use it legally.

**Note**
_____

**DirectX**

> As a 3D game programmer, you should have at least a basic understanding of DirectX. In this book you won't actually be using DirectX, but if you progress in your endeavors as a 3D game programmer, eventually you'll learn to work with DirectX. DirectX is a group of different technologies that gives 3D game programmers a set of application programming interfaces, which are referred to as API's. API's let a game grab and use different resources on your computer, including things like joysticks, music, graphics memory management, graphics rendering and the control of the keyboard and mouse. As I said, this topic is a little more advanced, but for now it's just good to know what it is.

## Blitz3D

Blitz3D is one of dozens of different programming languages that take an existing language—in this case Basic—and make it not only easier to use, but also make it so that it is specifically designed to handle 3D functions. I've selected Blitz3D for use in this book for several reasons. The first is that it is relatively easy to use and learn compared with some of the other options that are available. Blitz3D is also free to use from a learning perspective. The only thing that you can't do with the free version of Blitz3D is compile your game into an executable file once you're done. For the purpose of learning Blitz3D, this doesn't make a difference since you can still preview and test your games. You just can't make them into executable files. Another advantage of using Blitz3D is that if you decide that you'd like to purchase the full version, it is only $100, which is relatively inexpensive when compared to some other languages. While there aren't a lot of printed resources available to help you if you get stuck, there is a large user community that is always willing to share answers. Blitz3D has a simple user interface, as seen in Figure 4.1.

## 3D Modeling Software

One of the most appealing parts of 3D games are the graphics. Most are so lifelike that they bring the action in your games to life. Programs like Blitz3D allow you to create some basic shapes that you can use in your games, but if you really want your games to stand out, you need to use a 3D modeling package that will allow you to create the backgrounds, characters, and objects that you are used to seeing in a 3D game. As with programming languages, there many different options available to you. Here are a few considerations that you should keep in mind

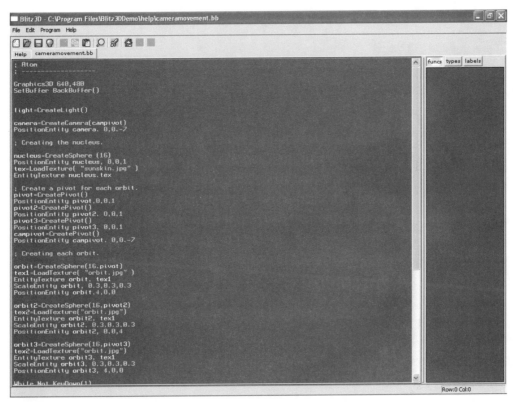

**Figure 4.1**
Blitz3D has a simple user interface that makes entering code relatively easy.

when deciding on a modeling package:

- Cost—Some 3D modeling packages can be very expensive.

- Ease of use—Many of the programs are very complicated with hundreds of different options.

- Compatibility—You need to make sure that the models you create in your software package are supported by your programming language.

There are dozens of different 3D modeling packages available, but from a gaming industry standpoint there are two standards: Maya and 3ds Max.

## Maya

From video games to television to movies, you've probably seen 3D models that were created in Maya. This is the premier 3D modeling tool of the entertainment community. Maya has thousands of different tools and effects that you can apply

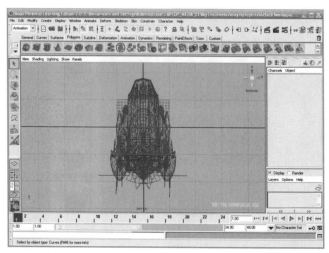

**Figure 4.2**
Maya is one of the most powerful 3D modeling programs on the market.

to your animations. It is extremely powerful, which means, unfortunately, that it can be difficult to learn and master. Figure 4.2 shows a screenshot of this powerful application.

## 3ds Max

3ds Max is the most popular 3D animation and modeling software package in the world. Like Maya, it offers hundreds of possible tools and configurations. It too is used in many video games and broadcast productions. Later in the book, you'll use 3ds Max to create some 3D models that you will incorporate into your games. Blitz3D allows you to easily incorporate 3ds files into your games. Figure 4.3 shows you the user interface of 3ds Max.

## Graphics Programs

Just as you need 3D modeling software to create characters and objects for your games, you'll need other graphics programs to enhance the look of your games. Using these graphics programs, you'll create Welcome screens, Pause screens, textures for objects, and height maps (all of which I will discuss later in the book.) Once again, as with the modeling software, you've got dozens of choices available to you. You certainly don't have to use either of the two packages listed here, but they are by far the most powerful and universally accepted in the industry.

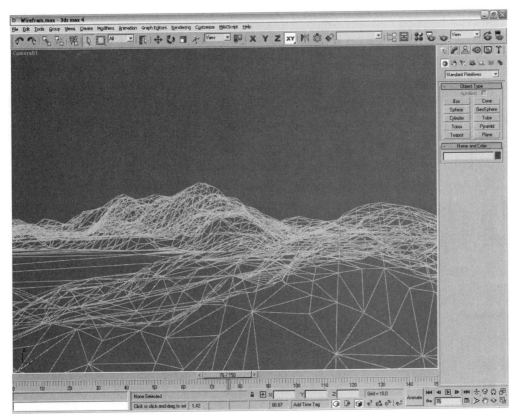

**Figure 4.3**
3ds Max is the program you'll use in this book to create 3D models.

## Adobe Photoshop and Illustrator

Adobe Photoshop is considered the leader in image editing and is used by thousands of people. Adobe Photoshop and Illustrator are packed with dozens of tools to help you create all sorts of images, textures, and drawings that can be used in your games. From both Photoshop and Illustrator, you can export your files to a variety of formats that are supported by Blitz 3D. There are also hundreds of resources available to help you learn and master this software.

If you are new to graphic design, Photoshop and Illustrator can be quite intimidating, especially if you've never used the software before. It'll take a bit of time and practice before you feel comfortable using all of the features. If you want a good head start into Photoshop, I suggest reading *Photoshop CS Fast & Easy* by Eric Grebler, published by Course Technology, ISBN 1-59200-345-1. (I know, it's

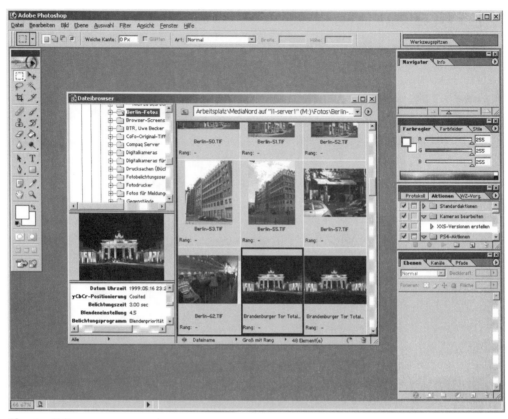

**Figure 4.4**
Adobe Photoshop is the industry-leading image editing software.

a shameless plug!) Figure 4.4 shows a screen capture of Adobe Photoshop and Figure 4.5 shows images created in Illustrator.

The main difference between the two programs is that Photoshop deals primarily with bitmap or raster graphics while Illustrator deals primarily with vector graphics. Without going through a long, drawn out explanation, in a nutshell, bitmaps are images made from tiny little squares called pixels. Bitmaps are what we call resolution dependent, basically meaning if you expand a bitmap larger that it was originally created, you'll see the little squares that make up its content. Vectors are lines and fills that have their basis in a mathematical formula so they can be expanded or reduced without noticing a difference in their quality. Both types of images have their advantages and disadvantages, but regardless of which you choose, the images will have to be converted to a file format that Blitz3D understands.

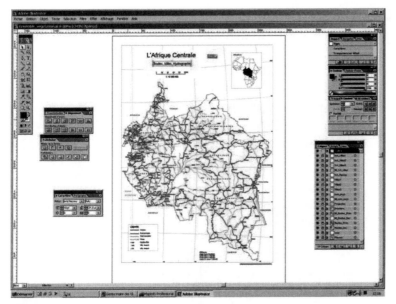

**Figure 4.5**
Adobe Illustrator allows you to create, manipulate, and export vector images.

## CorelDRAW Graphics Suite

Although not as popular as Adobe's graphics options, CorelDRAW is the most powerful and easy-to-use graphics suite on the market. Not only can it do all of the things that can be done in Photoshop, it has tools that are easy to manipulate, it has more capabilities, and it costs a fraction of the price of Illustrator and Photoshop. Later in the book, I will take you through several different projects using both CorelDRAW and Corel Photo-Paint that will ultimately end up in the games you create. Figure 4.6 shows an image of the CorelDRAW user interface.

## Audio Programs

In addition to what you see on the screen, the sounds that emanate from your game can add a dynamic effect. There are hundreds of thousands of different sound effects that you can purchase or download over the Internet to enhance your game. You also, of course, have the option of creating original audio from scratch by recording it directly to your computer. Whether you want to add dialog or create your own sound effects, there are hundreds of different digital audio packages out there. Some of these packages are designed for high-end

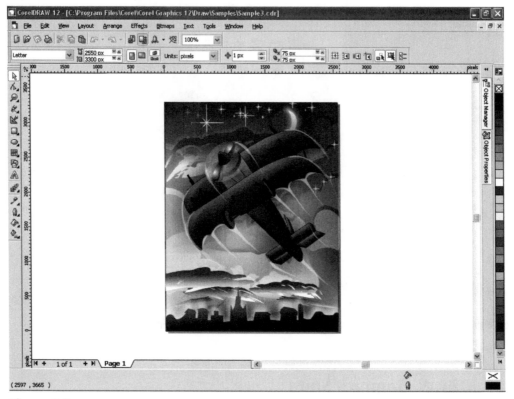

**Figure 4.6**
CorelDRAW is the program you'll use to create textures, Welcome screens, and Pause screens.

studio recordings, so be aware that they can get expensive. Other packages, which simply allow you to record from your computer and do minor editing are available for little or no cost. Some of these packages include:

- Adobe Audition

- Home Studio

- GarageBand

- Digital Performer

- Cubase

In addition to the commercial packages listed above, you can test out a variety of packages by going to www.download.com and searching for "audio recording" to find a list of software packages available for free download. If you are just looking to create some quick audio recording and doing no editing, you can use the free Sound Recorder program that comes with Windows. It can be accessed in most versions of Windows by clicking Start > Run to bring up the Run dialog box. Then type **sndrec32** and click OK.

## Code Flow

In the next chapter we'll actually begin exploring the Blitz3D programming environment, but regardless of what language you use, the code you enter will be translated into a game following a specific flow. When you read a document in English, you start from the top and move to the bottom. That's exactly how the computer will read and execute the code you enter for your computer game with one major difference.

At some point, a section of the code will start to repeat itself and loop over and over. This part of the code is called the *main loop,* or the *game loop.* Think of your video game as a cartoon animation. To create the illusion of movement, an animation contains different frames that appear on the screen, one at a time, and typically very quickly so that you can't tell one frame from another. If an object changes locations from one frame to the next, it will appear to be moving when the animation is played, as in Figure 4.7.

That is exactly how things work in the 3D games that you'll be creating. The game loop contains the code that actually plays the frames over and over. Think of the game loop as the projector that is running the animation. Once the game loop is ended, the game will end. The code outside the game loop is mostly used to set up the scenes or create objects, as seen in Figure 4.8. If this sounds a little confusing, don't worry, things will become much clearer as you start to create your own programs in the following chapters.

**Figure 4.7**
A 3D game works much the same as an animation: objects change size, shape, or location from frame to frame.

Game Code

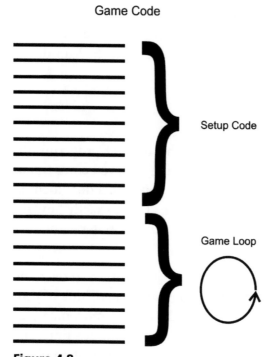

**Figure 4.8**
The game loop is typically near the end of the program code and repeats over and over until the game is stopped.

The thing to take away from this section is that the flow, or the order in which you enter code in the program, is important because the code you enter first will be carried out first unless you specify otherwise. That's why it's important to enter the code in the order you see it in this book; otherwise, you may run into some problems and the games you create may not work properly.

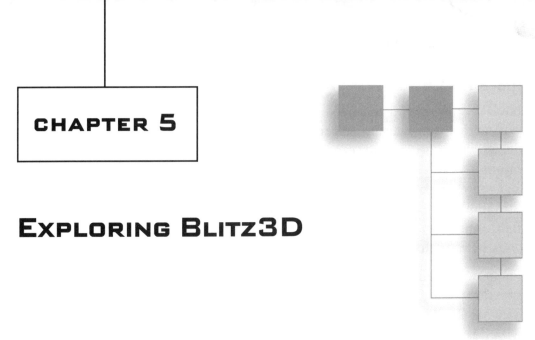

# CHAPTER 5

# EXPLORING BLITZ3D

Most of the programming you will do in this book will be done using the compiler called Blitz3D. Blitz 3D is based on the programming language called BASIC and is an excellent program to work with when first starting 3D game programming. The code you write for your programs themselves is just text, so you could actually use any word processor or text editor to create your code and then simply copy and paste it into Blitz3D when it comes time for compiling. There are several reasons why you'd want to use Blitz3D when entering your code. First, it will automatically recognize code and format it so that it "looks" okay. For example, if you were to enter the code for creating a sphere, which is `createsphere`, Blitz3D would format it properly as `CreateSphere`. This may sound like a small thing, but when sharing your code with others, it's nice to have a level of consistency. Another good reason for using Blitz3D to enter your program is that it color codes the commands you enter. This makes it easy to distinguish between different parts of your code, especially when debugging your program. This chapter will explore the user interface of Blitz3D and cover some of the basics of entering code and programming. I'm a strong believer in learning by doing, so this chapter will just be a brief introduction to the Blitz3D interface; the real learning will happen in the following chapters where you'll begin entering actual code that will be the foundation of your games.

## Installing Blitz3D

Blitz3D is the compiler you'll be using to create your games. To be truthful, the version that you are using isn't really a compiler, it is just an interpreter because it doesn't let you create an executable from your programs. What does all that mean? You will be using the free version of Blitz3D. It allows you to enter code and run your games. What it does not allow you to do is "compile" your game or turn it into an executable file that can be shared with others. If you want to have this feature, you'll need to purchase the full version of Blitz3D from the Web site www.blitzbasic.com.

For now, install the free version that will allow you to create and run your programs. Start by locating the file called Blitz3DDemo183.exe on the accompanying CD. Double-click on the file and the installation wizard will begin. The wizard is really quite simple to use; you just have to click the Next button several times until you get to the final screen where you can click the Install button (see Figure 5.1). Blitz3D will now be installed on your computer and you can begin programming.

**Note**

**Downloading Blitz3D**

If for some reason you don't have the CD that came with this book, you can download the program from www.blitzbasic.com.

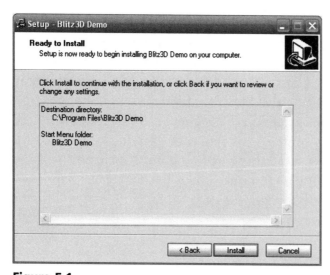

**Figure 5.1**
After clicking the Next button several times, you will arrive at the final screen of the wizard where you can click the Install button to install the program on your hard drive.

## Launching Blitz3D

The program itself can be launched from the Start menu in Windows. Once open, Blitz3D defaults to the Help window. To exit the Help window you need to either open an existing file or create a new one.

1. Click Start > All Programs (or just Programs depending on your version of Windows). You'll now see a list of different installed programs, and with any luck, you should see the Blitz3D Demo icon.

2. Click on the Blitz3D Demo icon and then click Blitz3D to launch the program. A dialog box will appear in which you'll need to click the Okee Dokee! button. The program should launch and you should see the Help screen as in Figure 5.2.

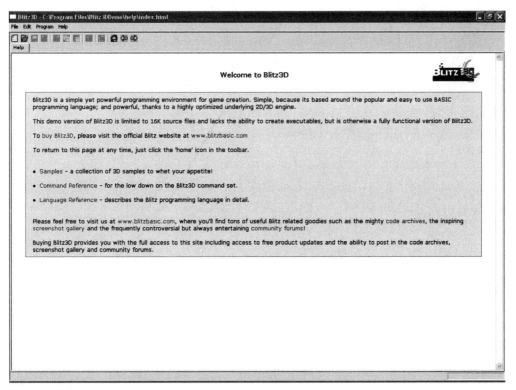

**Figure 5.2**
When you launch Blitz3D, the Help screen opens by default.

3. Click the New button to open a new tab in which you can enter code for your game (see Figure 5.3).

**Figure 5.3**
Press the New button to start programming.

## Getting to Know the User Interface

The User Interface, or UI, is a fancy name for what you see on the screen when the program is open. The UI for Blitz3D is actually quite simple, and the components are easy to understand and use.

### The Menu Bar

Like most programs, Blitz3D has a menu bar across the top of the screen (see Figure 5.4). To access the menu bar, you click on the desired option that will bring open the menu and then click on the desired command. Most of the options in the menu bar are also available as buttons in the toolbar.

**Figure 5.4**
The menu bar in Blitz3D is similar to that of many programs.

### The Toolbar

There are only a dozen buttons on the toolbar, and each is relatively straight-forward. Here's a look at each individual button and its function.

■ **New.** Pressing this button will create a new blank document (see Figure 5.5).

**Figure 5.5**
The New button will create a new blank document.

- **Open**. When you press this button (see Figure 5.6), the Open dialog box will appear, from which you can navigate your computer's hard drive and select a file to open.

**Figure 5.6**
The Open button brings open a dialog box from which you can select a file to open.

- **Save**. Pressing this button (see Figure 5.7) will save your current document. If you haven't already saved your document, the Save As dialog box will open where you can give your document a name and then save it.

**Figure 5.7**
The Save button is used to save your programs.

**Note**
_____

**Saving**

Blitz3D has a nasty habit of saving changes to a program even if you haven't pressed the Save button. This could potentially be a problem, especially if you've made changes to an existing file that you don't want to keep. For this reason, I would suggest always saving your files with a new name after they have been opened. That way the original file won't be affected. A good habit to get into is to save your files and add the date so you can keep track of the most current version and always have a backup. Let's say, for example, that you start entering code for a program you call "game." The first time you save the program, name it "game." The next time you save your program, use the Save As feature (you can access Save As from the File menu) and give your program a new name like "game_1" or "game_Jan_15." On subsequent saves, you can give your game new names like "game_2," "game_3," and so on. Doing this will ensure that you always have a backup and you can return to a previous point in your programming should you make any changes that have been inadvertently saved.

_____

- **Close**. Pressing the Close button (see Figure 5.8) will close the current document.

**Figure 5.8**
The Close button closes the currently open program.

- **Cut.** You can select code by clicking and dragging across it. Once selected, it will appear highlighted. When you press the Cut button (see Figure 5.9), the text will be removed and placed on the computer's virtual clipboard. Once it has been cut, it can be pasted elsewhere.

**Figure 5.9**
The Cut button will remove the current selection to the clipboard.

- **Copy.** When you have text selected, you can copy it to the virtual clipboard by pressing this button (see Figure 5.10). It can now be pasted elsewhere.

**Figure 5.10**
The Copy button copies the current selection to the clipboard.

- **Paste.** When you press this button (see Figure 5.11), the contents of the clipboard that you have cut or copied earlier will be pasted at the point where the cursor is.

**Figure 5.11**
The Paste button pastes the contents of the clipboard.

- **Find.** Programs can contain hundreds to thousands of lines of code and finding a certain portion of code that you are seeking can be like finding a needle in a haystack. When you press the Find button (see Figure 5.12), a

**Figure 5.12**
The Find button opens the Find dialog box.

dialog box will appear from which from you can enter text. After you enter the text and press the Find button in the dialog box, Blitz3D will look for the code you have entered.

- **Run.** Pressing this button (see Figure 5.13) will launch the program that is currently open.

**Figure 5.13**
The Run button will launch your game.

- **Home.** Pressing this button (see Figure 5.14) will open the main Help page. From here you can explore help options, samples, and command and language references.

**Figure 5.14**
The Home button opens the Help page.

- **Back/Forward.** Once you are on the Help page, you can navigate back and forth through individual Help pages using the Back and Forward buttons (see Figure 5.15).

**Figure 5.15**
The Back and Forward buttons can be used to navigate through the Help pages.

## Switching Programs

Blitz3D allows you to have many different programs open at any given time. To help you navigate through those open programs, there is a bar directly under the toolbar that will allow you to move through your different files. By clicking on the tab that contains the program name, you can make that the active document (see Figure 5.16). When you have many programs open at once, not all tabs will

**Figure 5.16**
Click on any of the tabs to switch to a particular open program.

be visible, but you can use the arrow keys to navigate through the different programs.

## The Side Panel

On the right-hand side of your screen, you should notice a panel that has three buttons at the top named funcs, types, and labels (see Figure 5.17). By clicking these, you can view the functions, types, and labels in your program. I'll discuss all of these later in the book.

**Figure 5.17**
This panel summarizes the functions, types, and labels you have in your programs.

## Entering Code and Comments

How do you enter code in Blitz3D? Just type away (see Figure 5.18). The actual code you enter will be explored throughout this book, starting in the next chapter. At first glance, the code that you enter might not make any sense at all. Every computer language has its own way of "talking" to the compiler and its own way of working. Let's look at an example. Let's say you wanted the computer to create a sphere. Unfortunately, you can't just type "computer, create a sphere for me, please." Instead, here is the actual code you would enter:

```
mysphere=CreateSphere ()
```

In Blitz3D you need to name the object you create. This name is called an *identifier*. In this example, I've named the sphere "mysphere." Because the code won't necessarily make sense to you or anyone with whom you are sharing your code, it's a good idea to enter comments. *Comments* are a way of using plain English to describe the code in your program. You should enter comments before

**Figure 5.18**
Entering programming code is as simple as typing away.

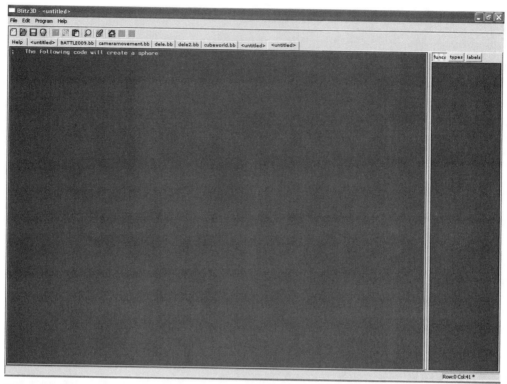

**Figure 5.19**
Creating a comment is as simple as placing a semicolon before your comment.

every section of code you enter. That way, it will be easy to find sections of code and understand what you've done long after you've created it. Entering comments is as simple as using a semicolon. Whenever you enter a semicolon, Blitz3D will ignore everything on that line (see Figure 5.19). For example, if you wanted to enter the comment "The following code will create a sphere," you would enter it as follows:

```
; The following code will create a sphere
```

Notice that all I did was put a semicolon in front of the comment I wanted to add and Blitz will understand that it is a comment. You'll know that you have correctly entered a comment because it will appear in yellow.

Speaking of colors, you'll notice that as you enter code it will appear in different colors. This is one huge advantage that using Blitz 3D has over just entering your code in a word processor. You can find parts of code quickly by looking for a specific color, or you can detect if you've entered code incorrectly if it doesn't turn the color you expected. Go ahead and enter the following code:

```
;Here is some sample code:
Global enemy = 7
Include ''aliens.bb''
```

This code probably makes no sense to you at all right now, and that's okay. I just want you to notice how the code you entered is in different colors. The comments are in yellow, the identifiers are in white, the numerical values are in light blue and the files that are referenced are in green. This color coding comes in handy when you are looking for particular pieces of code.

So that's the user interface in a nutshell. Not too scary, right? In the next chapter you'll dive in and actually start entering code to create some simple objects.

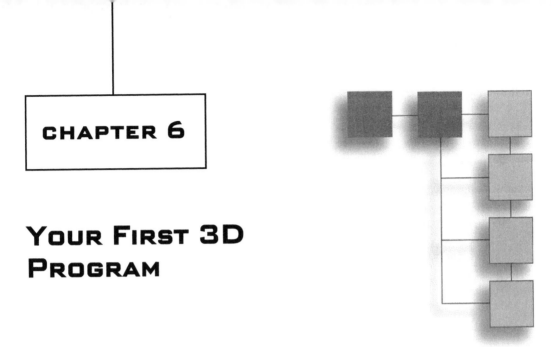

# CHAPTER 6

# YOUR FIRST 3D PROGRAM

Have you ever used one of those paint-by-numbers kits? In the kits, you are given a pre-drawn image that has numbers throughout and several paint colors. You would then paint the appropriate colors in the specified regions. When you were done, you were left with a masterpiece that you had "created" yourself. This chapter is going to be our own version of paint-by-numbers. You are going to copy the code within this chapter to create your first masterpiece. Of course, just copying won't make you a master programmer; the key is to understand what you are typing. After you've copied the content and run the program, I will dissect some of the key areas of the code to give you a broad understanding of how to create games in Blitz3D.

I can make you this guarantee while you are copying the code in this chapter: Unless you have a lot of experience in programming, much of the code you are copying will not make any sense to you. It may seem confusing and perhaps even a little overwhelming. But please don't get discouraged. All of the elements within the program that you are typing will be covered in great detail throughout the book. After you have gone through a few chapters, you'll realize what a simple program this is, and it will all make sense.

## The Jumping Cone Program

So let's get started. Go ahead and open Blitz3D and enter the following code. When you are finished, click the Save button on the toolbar and save your program by giving it a name and clicking the Save button in the dialog box.

```
; Jumping Cone
;_____

camdistance=10
Graphics3D 640,480
SetBuffer BackBuffer()

; Creating the types
type_player=1
type_ground=2

; Create camera
camera=CreateCamera()
RotateEntity camera, 45,0,0

; Creating a light
light=CreateLight()

; Creating a plane and texture
grid_tex=CreateTexture( 32,32,8 )
ScaleTexture grid_tex,10,10
SetBuffer TextureBuffer( grid_tex )
Color 0,0,64:Rect 0,0,32,32
Color 0,0,255:Rect 0,0,32,32,False
SetBuffer BackBuffer()
grid_plane=CreatePlane()
EntityTexture grid_plane,grid_tex
EntityBlend grid_plane,1
EntityAlpha grid_plane,.6
EntityFX grid_plane,1
EntityType grid_plane, type_ground

; Creating a mirror
CreateMirror()

; Creating a cone
cone=CreateCone(64)
EntityType cone,type_player
PositionEntity cone, 0,1,5
ScaleEntity cone ,0.4,0.4,0.4
EntityRadius cone, 0.5
```

```
Texture=CreateTexture(16,16): SetBuffer TextureBuffer(texture)
ClsColor 256,6,56
Cls
Color 12,126,256
Rect 0,0,8,8,1
Rect 8,8,8,8,1
ScaleTexture Texture,.2,.2
EntityTexture cone,texture

; The following code makes the program run

While Not KeyDown( 1 )
y#=0

If KeyDown( 208 )=True Then velocity#=velocity#-0.001
If KeyDown( 200 )=True Then velocity#=velocity#+0.001
If KeyDown ( 31 ) Then velocity#=0
If KeyDown ( 31 ) Then xvelocity#=0
If KeyDown( 203 )=True Then xvelocity#=xvelocity#-0.001
If KeyDown( 205 )=True Then xvelocity#=xvelocity#+0.001
If KeyDown( 57 )=True Then y#=y#+0.5

MoveEntity cone,xvelocity#,y#,velocity#
TranslateEntity cone, 0,-0.1,0
PositionEntity camera,EntityX(cone),0,EntityZ(cone)
MoveEntity camera,0,0,-5
Collisions type_player,type_ground,2,2
Collisions type_ground,type_player,2,2

UpdateWorld

RenderWorld
Flip

Wend

End
```

Now that you have the program entered and saved, go ahead and run it by clicking the Run button on the toolbar. Press the arrow keys to move and accelerate in a particular direction and press the space bar to make the cone jump. Once you are finished checking out your first program, press the Esc key or click the x in the top right corner of the window. The program should look the same as Figure 6.1.

**Figure 6.1**
The code you've entered should produce this cone that you can control.

## Dissecting the Code

As I mentioned at the beginning of this chapter, copying code won't make you a master programmer, but it can help you learn a little about the code that you are creating. Take a closer look at the sections of code for an overview of what you have done.

```
; Jumping Cone
;_____
```

In the last chapter I covered comments, and here we created a comment by adding semicolons at the beginning of the line. We then put in the title of our program, and, to make it stand out, we created a comment on the next line comprised of dashes.

```
camdistance=10
Graphics3D 640,480
SetBuffer BackBuffer()
```

This section of code does a few different things. We created a variable (I'll talk about variables later in the book) called camdistance and gave it a value. The next

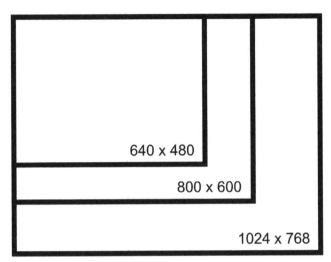

640 x 480

800 x 600

1024 x 768

**Figure 6.2**
Different resolutions produce different screen sizes.

two lines deal with the graphics of our program. They set the size of the screen and tell the program how the graphics should be drawn.

The line `Graphics3D 640,480` sets the resolution (screen size) for our game. In this example, we have set the screen resolution at 640 × 480 pixels. The resolution that you should set for your game will depend on the size of the monitor that the game is to be played on. Obviously, you can't know the size of the monitors of everyone who might play your game, but typically, a game that is 640 × 480 will fit on almost every monitor. Other common resolutions are 800 × 600 and 1024 × 768 (see Figure 6.2). Go back into the code of the program you created, change the resolution, and then run the program to see the difference.

```
; Creating the types
type_player=1
type_ground=2
```

Notice that the beginning of this section of code has a comment that reads "Creating the types." *Types* are a way to group different objects together and will be covered in great detail in Chapter 13, "Collisions."

```
; Create camera
camera=CreateCamera()
RotateEntity camera, 45,0,0
```

Every program you create in Blitz3D needs a camera, since the camera acts as your eyes. In other words, everything you see on screen is being seen through the camera. The camera can be moved and repositioned so that it can follow action onscreen. Chapter 11, "Lights and Cameras," will cover cameras in greater detail.

```
; Creating a light
light=CreateLight()
```

Imagine walking into your room in the middle of the night without turning on the lights. You wouldn't see much, would you? Just like with your room, you need to turn on the lights in Blitz3D in order to see any of the action. There are a variety of types of lights you can create, and they will also be covered in greater detail in the Chapter 11.

```
; Creating a plane and texture
grid_tex=CreateTexture( 32,32,8 )
ScaleTexture grid_tex,10,10
SetBuffer TextureBuffer( grid_tex )
Color 0,0,64:Rect 0,0,32,32
Color 0,0,255:Rect 0,0,32,32,False
SetBuffer BackBuffer()
grid_plane=CreatePlane()
EntityTexture grid_plane,grid_tex
EntityBlend grid_plane,1
EntityAlpha grid_plane,.6
EntityFX grid_plane,1
EntityType grid_plane, type_ground
```

This code may look very jumbled and confusing, but when it is broken down further in upcoming chapters, you'll see that it's not really confusing at all. This code actually creates the ground or the playing surface for our program, and it creates the pattern that you see on the ground.

```
; Creating a mirror
CreateMirror()
```

When you ran the program you may have noticed that the cone was reflected in the ground (see Figure 6.3). The reason this occurs is because we created a mirror in the code above.

```
; Creating a cone
cone=CreateCone(64)
EntityType cone,type_player
PositionEntity cone, 0,1,5
```

**Figure 6.3**
Notice how the cone is reflected in the ground. This was created using the `CreateMirror()` command.

```
ScaleEntity cone ,0.4,0.4,0.4
EntityRadius cone, 0.5
Texture=CreateTexture(16,16): SetBuffer TextureBuffer(texture)
ClsColor 256,6,56
Cls
Color 12,126,256
Rect 0,0,8,8,1
Rect 8,8,8,8,1
ScaleTexture Texture,.2,.2
EntityTexture cone,texture
```

The code above is used to create the cone. In the next chapter I'll cover in detail how to create various types of basic shapes. Not only do we create the cone in this section, we also create, color, and apply the checkerboard pattern you see on the cone.

```
; This following code makes our program run
While Not KeyDown( 1 )
```

```
y#=0

If KeyDown( 208 )=True Then velocity#=velocity#-0.001
If KeyDown( 200 )=True Then velocity#=velocity#+0.001
If KeyDown ( 31 ) Then velocity#=0
If KeyDown ( 31 ) Then xvelocity#=0
If KeyDown( 203 )=True Then xvelocity#=xvelocity#-0.001
If KeyDown( 205 )=True Then xvelocity#=xvelocity#+0.001
If KeyDown( 57 )=True Then y#=y#+0.5

MoveEntity cone,xvelocity#,y#,velocity#
TranslateEntity cone, 0,-0.1,0
PositionEntity camera,EntityX(cone),0,EntityZ(cone)
MoveEntity camera,0,0,-5
Collisions type_player,type_ground,2,2
Collisions type_ground,type_player,2,2

UpdateWorld

RenderWorld
Flip

Wend

End
```

Wow, there's a lot of stuff happening in the previous code. This is the section of code that makes our program run and controls the movement of the cone. This section is usually called the *game loop*. It also sets up some rules that ensure that our cone won't fall through the ground.

Take a look at some of the code in this loop to see what it all means.

```
While Not KeyDown( 1 )
```

This is a very common While statement that you will see in almost every program. I'll talk much more about While statements in Chapter 16, "Programming Fundamentals." This entire line can be translated as follows: "As long as the Esc key is not pressed, do the following things." KeyDown in Blitz3D means a key is pressed on the keyboard. The number in the brackets (1) represents the Esc key. Why does the number 1 mean the Esc key? Every key on the keyboard is represented by a different number, and throughout programming in Blitz3D, you'll use KeyDown to signify what should happen when a certain key is pressed. In the appendix you'll see a keyboard map and the numbers associated with each key.

## Note

### KeyDown versus KeyHit

There are actually two ways to signify a key being pressed on the keyboard in Blitz3D: KeyDown and KeyHit. The difference is a subtle one, yet it is important to know. KeyDown detects whether a key is being held down whereas KeyHit just registers that the key has been pressed. Let's say that you created a game where a bullet would be fired when the space bar is pressed. If you used KeyDown (57) as the code (57 is the number associated with the space bar, as seen in the Appendix), the bullets would continue to fire while the space bar is held down. If you used KeyHit (57), only one bullet would fire until the space bar was released then pressed again. There are other codes such as MouseDown and JoyDown that will signify the pressing of a mouse button or joystick button.

y#=0

This part of the code introduces a variable. Here we are saying that the variable we created called y is equal to 0 at the start of the program. Because it is a variable, this value can change as the program runs. You'll learn more about variables in Chapter 16, "Programming Fundamentals."

```
If KeyDown( 208 )=True Then velocity#=velocity#-0.001
If KeyDown( 200 )=True Then velocity#=velocity#+0.001
If KeyDown ( 31 ) Then velocity#=0
If KeyDown ( 31 ) Then xvelocity#=0
If KeyDown( 203 )=True Then xvelocity#=xvelocity#-0.001
If KeyDown( 205 )=True Then xvelocity#=xvelocity#+0.001
If KeyDown( 57 )=True Then y#=y#+0.5

MoveEntity cone,xvelocity#,y#,velocity#
TranslateEntity cone, 0,-0.1,0
PositionEntity camera,EntityX(cone),0,EntityZ(cone)
MoveEntity camera,0,0,-5
```

This section of code deals with the movement of the cone in our program. Notice that there are a lot of KeyDown statements. In this program, there are several arrow keys and other keys that control the movement of our cone. This section defines each key and what it does. I'll discuss this type of code in detail in Chapter 10, "Controlling Objects."

```
Collisions type_player,type_ground,2,2
Collisions type_ground,type_player,2,2
UpdateWorld
```

This body of code deals with how different objects in your program react to one another. Object reactions are called *collisions* in Blitz3D and will be covered in Chapter 13, "Collisions." The UpdateWorld command checks to see if collisions have occurred.

```
RenderWorld
Flip
Wend
End
```

These lines of code are common at the end of most programs. RenderWorld is the magic abracadabra statement that actually creates everything you see on screen. Flip is a statement that deals with the drawing of the images. Flip takes images that have been drawn on the Backbuffer and brings them to the Frontbuffer (the screen). Every While statement has to be finished with a Wend statement. Since we started a While statement, we need to end it with a Wend. Finally, End terminates the program.

Well, there you have it—your first 3D program. Notice that I said *program* and not *game*. A game typically has a goal or purpose, while this program just has a moving and jumping cone. That being said, all of the elements of this program can be used when creating a game. In the following chapters, I'll cover in detail each of the elements created in this program, and you'll learn how to incorporate them into a game.

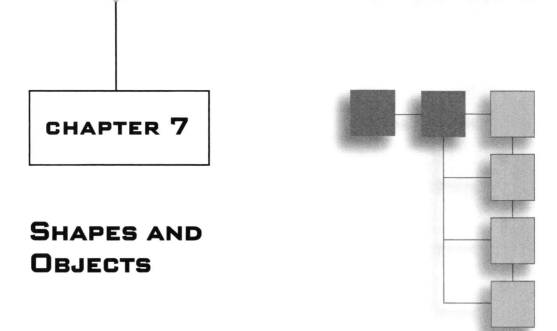

# CHAPTER 7

# SHAPES AND OBJECTS

This chapter explores everything related to creating basic shapes. In addition to learning how to create shapes, you'll discover how to dress them up by adding colors, patterns, and textures. The compiler you're using, Blitz3D, allows you to create several basic 3D shapes including spheres, cubes, cylinders, and cones. Of course, creating a shape is only the first step in the equation. After your shape is created, you'll learn how to position it, resize it, and change its shape.

Although the use of basic shapes is necessary in almost every 3D game, you may want to create something a little more sophisticated. There are dozens of programs on the market that allow you to create 3D objects. Later in the book, you'll explore some of the options you have when it comes to creating 3D objects, but for now, let's get to creating basic shapes.

## Understanding the 3D World

Before we begin, it's important that you understand the concept of a 3D world. Start by looking at your monitor. Your monitor screen is actually two-dimensional; you can't reach in and grab an object on your computer's screen. So 3D games aren't really 3D, they just pretend to be 3D by using a variety of lighting and positioning techniques. Take a look at Figure 7.1. Just like the monitor on your computer, the pages of this book are in two dimensions, but we can create the illusion of three dimensions by cleverly using lighting and positioning. Both objects are simple circles, but the one on the right looks three-dimensional because of the lighting applied to it.

**Figure 7.1**
These two circles started off the same but now look distinctly different. The circle on the left looks two-dimensional but the one on the right looks three-dimensional because of the lighting applied to it.

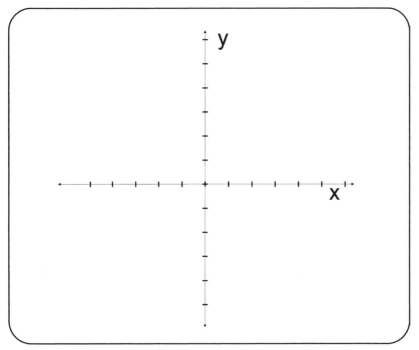

**Figure 7.2**
The x axis runs left to right across your screen and the y axis goes up and down.

A 2D world is made of up two axes: an x axis, which represents the horizontal part of your game, and a y axis, which represents the vertical part of your game. Think of the x and y axes as two rulers going across your monitor—one (the x axis) goes left and right, and the other (the y axis) goes up and down (see Figure 7.2).

Objects that you create in a two-dimensional game are positioned along the x and y axes. Their positions on the screen are called coordinates. Take a look at

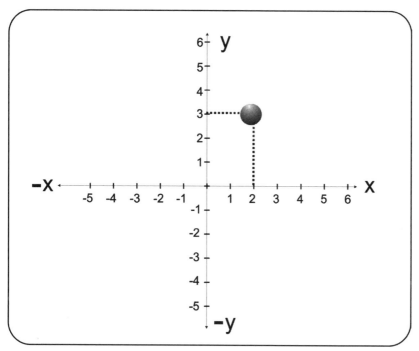

**Figure 7.3**
This object has the coordinate (2,3) because it is two units to the right of the center point and 3 units up.

Figure 7.3, which has an object in the top right corner. The coordinates for this object would be (2,3). The first number represents the object's position on the x axis—in this case, two units to the right. The second number, 3, represents the object's position on the y axis—in this case, three units up.

On the x axis, positive numbers represent objects that are to the right of the center point, and objects to the left are represented by negative numbers. On the y axis, positive numbers represent objects that are above the center point, and negative numbers are those objects below the center point. Take a look at Figure 7.4, which shows several objects in different positions with their coordinates in brackets.

To create the illusion of near or far in a 3D world, the size of the object will change. Take a look at Figure 7.5, which has two objects: one that seems close and one that is far away. We can tell that they are near or far because one is bigger than the other. In a 3D world, there is one more axis, the z axis, which represents objects that are near or far on the screen. On the z axis you can control how near or far an object is.

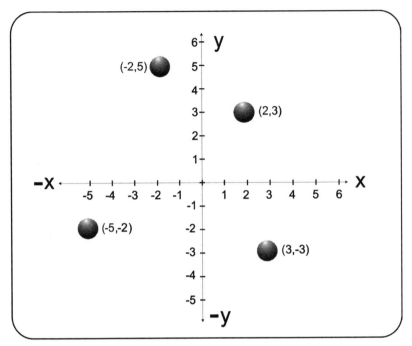

**Figure 7.4**
Each object is positioned at different coordinates.

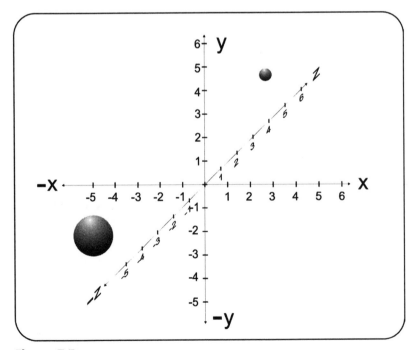

**Figure 7.5**
The z axis controls how near or far an object is.

The position of an object in a 3D program is represented by three coordinates: an x axis, a y axis and a z axis number. Positive numbers on the z axis represent how far away the object is. For example, if the z axis number is 2, the object will be relatively close to the center point while a z axis value of 100 would mean that it is far away. A negative number will mean that the object will be on the close side of the center point, while a positive number represents a position on the far side of the center point. An example of coordinates of an object in a 3D world would be (−3,−,4,−4), which means the object would be at position −3 on the x axis, −4 on the y axis, and −4 on the z axis, as seen in Figure 7.6.

**Note**

**Near or Far?**

Keep in mind that terms like near, far, up, down, and left and right are all relative terms in Blitz3D because your "eyes" are the camera. Although the camera starts at position 0, 0, 0, it can be moved to any position in the 3D universe.

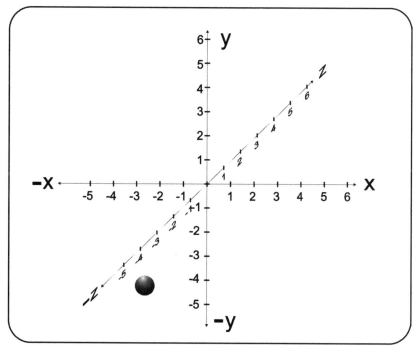

**Figure 7.6**
This object is positioned at location (-3,-4,-4).

## Creating Basic Shapes

When creating a basic shape, you need to tell Blitz3D two things: what type of shape you would like to create and where you would like to position it.

### Creating a Cone

Let's start by entering the code for creating a cone and then going through each line to see what we have accomplished.

```
; Creating a Basic Cone
; ------------------

Graphics3D 640,480
SetBuffer BackBuffer()

; Create camera
camera=CreateCamera()

; Creating a light
light=CreateLight()

; This is the code for creating the cone
cone=CreateCone()
PositionEntity cone,0,0,5

; This following code makes our program run
While Not KeyDown( 1 )

RenderWorld
Flip

Wend

End
```

After you've entered the code, press the Run button to see the masterpiece you have created. With any luck, what you see on your screen should look exactly like what you see in Figure 7.7. After you're done admiring your beautiful work, press the Esc key to close the window and return to our programming session.

Now let's take a closer look at the code itself to see what we've done. In the previous chapter, we touched briefly on some of the code that was necessary to

**Figure 7.7**
With just a few lines of code you should have this wonderful cone.

start our program, see our screen, and make things run, so here we will only concentrate on the specific code we used to create our cone:

```
; This is the code for creating the cone
cone=CreateCone()
PositionEntity cone,0,0,5
```

The first part of the code is cone=. This is what we are calling our cone. If you were to create a game with several cones, you'd want to create a separate name for each cone—for example, cone1=, bigcone=, smallcone=, and smallshape=. The point I'm trying to get across is that this first part of the code is simply a name you are giving your shape. You can call it anything; it doesn't even have to have the word "cone" in the name. You'll see this in practice in our next exercise.

The next part of the code is the CreateCone() command. This command tells Blitz3D to create a cone and give it the name you specified.

The next line of the code indicates where you would like to put your cone on the screen. As you learned earlier, your 3D world is broken up into x, y and z values.

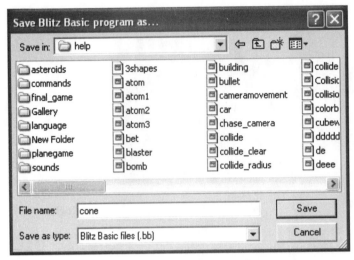

**Figure 7.8**
Make sure to save your files often and with new names for backup.

Using the `PositionEntity` command, you tell Blitz3D where to position a specific object in the 3D world. In the command we used, `PositionEntity cone,0,0,5`, we told Blitz3D to position the object called cone to the values on the screen where x=0, y=0 and z=5.

Now that you've created a cone, save your "game" so that you can always return back to this point. Click File > Save As to bring open a dialog box (see Figure 7.8) where you can select a directory in which to save your program. Call the program "cone" and then press the Save button.

## Creating Multiple Cones

Now that you've created one cone, I'm going to show you how you can create others and position them in different locations on your screen. I'll also demonstrate that you can give your cones any names you'd like. Start off by deleting the cone you created earlier by erasing this code in your program:

```
; This is the code for creating the cone
cone=CreateCone()
PositionEntity cone,0,0,5
```

Now replace that code with the following, and run it once you are finished. You should end up with the same display of cones as seen in Figure 7.9.

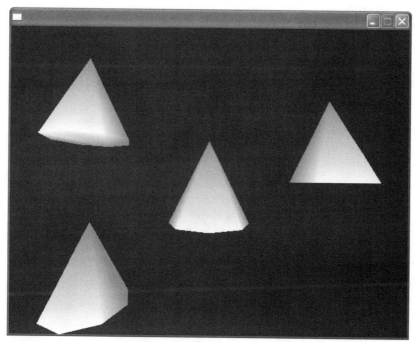

**Figure 7.9**
The objects appear skewed, but they are not.

```
; This is the code we'll use to create four cones in different locations on our
screen.
coneleft=CreateCone()
PositionEntity coneleft,-3,2,5
apple=CreateCone()
PositionEntity apple,3,1,5
cone=CreateCone()
PositionEntity cone,-3,-2,5
coneyisland=CreateCone()
PositionEntity coneyisland,0,0,5
```

Notice that some of the cones have names that have nothing to do with cones at all. Remember that they are just names, and you can call them whatever you'd like, as long as it makes sense to you and others with whom you might be sharing the program code.

**Note**

**Identifiers**

The names that you give to your objects are called identifiers.

You have noticed that some of the cones you created in the last step (see Figure 7.9) appear to be skewed. It's not that the shapes of the cones are altered, it's just that you've moved them around in your 3D world while your source of light and your camera have remained in the same spot. I'll cover cameras and lighting a little later on in the book.

**Note**

**Copy and Paste**

The copy and paste commands can be your best friends as a programmer. You can save yourself a lot of time and effort by copying code. Once you have copied the existing code, you can paste it and then make any desired changes. To select an area of code to copy, simply position your mouse pointer at the point where you'd like the selection to begin and then click and drag to the end of the selection. The selected code will appear highlighted. To paste your selection, press Ctrl+V.

## Creating Cubes, Cylinders, and Spheres

There are several other shapes that you can create using Blitz3D, all of which are created in the exact same manner as you created the cone earlier. The only difference is that the create command you use will be different for each shape.

- `CreateSphere()` – This will create a sphere.

- `CreateCube()` – This will create a cube.

- `CreateCylinder()` – This will create a cylinder.

Don't forget that, when using any of these commands, you'll need to specify a name for the shape you are creating as well as a location. Here is an example of how you would create a cube within a program.

```
; This is the code for creating a cube

cube=CreateCube()
PositionEntity cube,0,0,5
```

**Note**

**Now You Try**

Take a look at Figure 7.10. Try to replicate what you see here on your own. Once you are done, compare your code to the actual code used to create it.

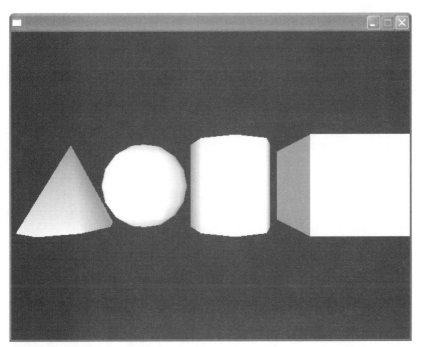

**Figure 7.10**
Try to replicate these shapes.

```
; Creating Basic Shapes
; --------------------

Graphics3D 640,480
SetBuffer BackBuffer()

; Create camera
camera=CreateCamera()

; Creating a light
light=CreateLight()

; This is the code we'll use to create four cones in different locations on our
screen.
cone=CreateCone()
PositionEntity cone,-3.5,0,5

cube=CreateCube()
PositionEntity cube,3,0,5
```

```
sphere=CreateSphere()
PositionEntity sphere,-1.6,0,5

cylinder=CreateCylinder()
PositionEntity cylinder,0.5,0,5

; This following code makes our program run
While Not KeyDown( 1 )

RenderWorld
Flip

Wend

End
```

## Segments

When you create spheres, cones, and cylinders, you can specify the number of segments that each is made of. A segment controls the number of polygons that are used to make up your shapes. This will control how "smooth" the shape will appear on screen.

You may have noticed that the command you used for creating your shape was also followed by a series of parentheses. Typically, those parentheses can contain a definition of the number of segments, and they can define a parent. Don't worry about parents right now, but I will discuss segments. You can specify the number of segments in the brackets. For example, in this instance, the cone would be made of 25 segments:

```
cone=CreateCone(25)
```

Take a look at Figure 7.11, which compares a sphere with 8 segments versus a sphere with 32 segments.

### Note
___

**Default Segments**

If you don't specify the number of segments, the number of segments will be 8 by default.

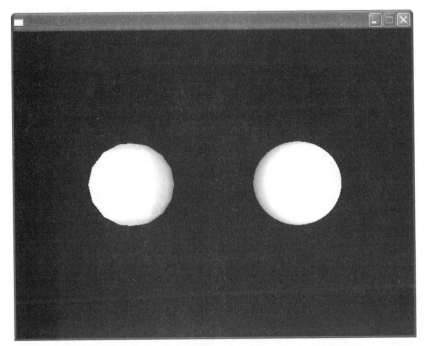

**Figure 7.11**
The sphere with 32 segments on the right appears much smoother.

## Resizing and Reshaping Objects

In most cases, the size of the shape that you have created will need to be adjusted to fit the purpose you had in mind. You can resize or even reshape an object by using the ScaleEntity command. The difference between resizing and reshaping an object is just a matter of what numbers you enter for the x, y, and z values.

## Resizing or Scaling

To resize a shape, you use the ScaleEntity command and use the same number for the x, y, and z values. For this exercise, we are going to use the "cone" file that you saved earlier, so go ahead and open it. If, for some reason, you didn't save the file or you skipped the earlier section on creating a cone, you can find the file on the accompanying CD.

Let's say we want to double the size of the cone we created. To do this we'd add the ScaleEntity command as follows:

```
; This is the code for creating the cone
cone=CreateCone()
```

```
PositionEntity cone,0,0,5
ScaleEntity cone, 2,2,2
```

Notice that the only line we added to double the size of our cone was the Scale-Entity cone, 2,2,2 command. ScaleEntity tells Blitz3D that there is an object whose size we want to change, cone tells Blitz3D the name of the object we'd like to resize, and the 2,2,2 informs Blitz3D that we want the size to double on the x, y, and z axes.

What if we wanted to reduce the size of the cone instead of increasing it? In that case we would enter an integer for the x, y, and z values. For example, if you wanted to scale the cone in half (see Figure 7.12), you would use the following code:

```
cone=CreateCone()
PositionEntity cone,0,0,5
ScaleEntity cone, 0.5,0.5,0.5
```

**Figure 7.12**
The sphere on the right has been enlarged by twice its size using the ScaleEntity command with the values 2,2,2.

Here's a quick reference for some size changes:

- 1/10 the size = 0.1

- 1/4 the size = 0.25

- 1/2 the size = 0.5

- Double the size = 2

- Triple the size = 3

- Ten times the size = 10

**Note**

**ScaleEntity for All!**

The ScaleEntity command can be used on more than just basic shapes that you create. Other objects that you create or import can be scaled using this command.

## Reshaping

Reshaping an object works in much the same ways as scaling or resizing in that it uses the ScaleEntity command. The difference this time is that if you want to stretch or squish an object, the number that you enter for the x, y, and z values will be different. Let's go back and open the saved version of the "cone" file we created earlier to illustrate how we reshape our object. With this code we will stretch the cone along the y axis.

```
cone=CreateCone()
PositionEntity cone,0,0,5
ScaleEntity cone, 1,2,1
```

We entered the numbers 1,2,1 which mean we are going to scale the x axis by multiplying it by 1 (which will result in no change, because any number multiplied by 1 remains the same), multiplying the y axis by 2, which will double the size of the shape along the y axis, and multiplying the z axis by 1. The result is that we end up with a cone that has been stretched along the y axis as seen in Figure 7.13.

**Note**

**Now You Try**

Take a look at Figure 7.14, which is an image of a cylinder that has been stretched along one axis and reduced along another. Try to recreate this effect and then compare it to the actual code below.

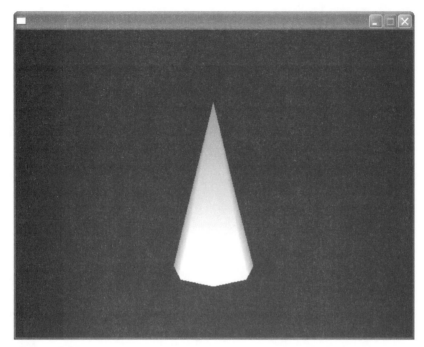

**Figure 7.13**
We stretched this cone by using ScaleEntity cone, 1,2,1.

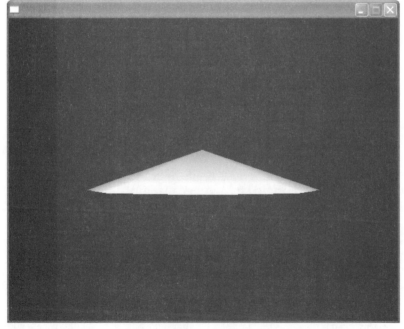

**Figure 7.14**
Try to recreate this stretched cylinder.

```
; Creating a Reshaped Cone
; ---------------------

Graphics3D 640,480
SetBuffer BackBuffer()

; Create camera
camera=CreateCamera()

; Creating a light
light=CreateLight()

; This is the code for creating the altered cone
cone=CreateCone()
PositionEntity cone,0,0,5
ScaleEntity cone, 3,0.5,1

; This following code makes our program run
While Not KeyDown( 1 )

RenderWorld
Flip

Wend

End
```

## Flipping an Object

The process of flipping an object works the exact same way as resizing or scaling, with the exception that you use negative numbers as your x, y, or z values. In fact you can resize, reshape, and flip your objects all at the same time. Just decide along which axis you'd like to reshape and resize your object, and then change the value to a negative number to flip the object. Here's an example of the code you would use to flip your cone along the z axis (see Figure 7.15).

```
cone=CreateCone()
PositionEntity cone,0,0,5
ScaleEntity cone, 1,1,-1
```

## Coloring

So far you've created simple shapes that have been white but appear slightly shaded because of the light source. You'll now learn how to apply a color to your shapes. Once again, start by opening the file "cone" that we created earlier. The

**Figure 7.15**
We flipped this cone on the z axis by using the command ScaleEntity cone, 1,1,-1.

EntityColor command allows you to apply color to an object. Here we will give our cone a color:

```
; This is the code for creating and coloring the cone
cone=CreateCone()
PositionEntity cone,0,0,5
EntityColor cone, 125,201,190
```

After you enter the code EntityColor, you enter the name of the entity you want to color—in this case, it is called cone. You'll then notice three numbers—in this case 125,201,190—which represent the red, green, and blue values. In this case, the 125 would be the red value, 201 would be the green value, and 190 would be the blue value. The colors on your computer monitor are created by mixing different values of red, green, and blue. By entering the three values for red, green and blue (commonly referred to as RGB), you are telling what mix of colors you want to use to color your shape.

Now the million dollar question: How do you know what combination of red, green, and blue make up a specific color? In others words, if you entered 12, 123,

204, what color would you get? Or if you wanted to color an object purple, what numbers would you enter? Well, almost every major graphics program provides a method for you to enter an RGB value to see the resulting color or select a color and get the RGB values.

Corel Photo-Paint, which is included on the accompanying CD, provides an excellent way to get RGB values. After you launch Photo-Paint, follow these instructions to get your RGB values:

1. Press Ctrl+F2 on the keyboard. The Color docker (see Figure 7.16), will open on the right side of the screen, and by default it will be set to RGB mode. You now have several options. You can enter specific values for R, G, and B and see the result of the values in a preview box. You can also click and drag the sliders to manipulate the RGB values.

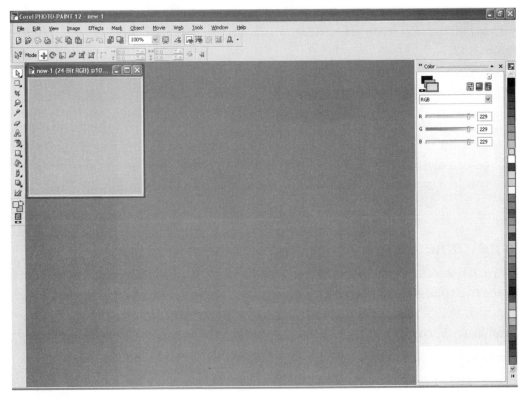

**Figure 7.16**
Pressing Ctrl+F2 will open the Color docker.

**Figure 7.17**
You can select colors from a palette.

2. If you prefer to select a color and then see what the RGB value is, you can click on the Show Color Palettes button, which will show you a square of color palettes. You can scroll through the colors, click on the swatch that you like, and the RGB values will be displayed as seen in Figure 7.17.

## Wireframe

Every 3D object in your game is made up of triangles and polygons. If you want to see the triangle makeup of any object, you can go into wireframe mode (see Figure 7.18). This is best illustrated by creating a sphere and converting it to wireframe. The command you use for wireframe is simply WireFrame. Here is the code for creating a sphere and then converting it to wireframe:

```
; This is the code for creating a sphere and making it wireframe
sphere=CreateSphere()
WireFrame sphere
```

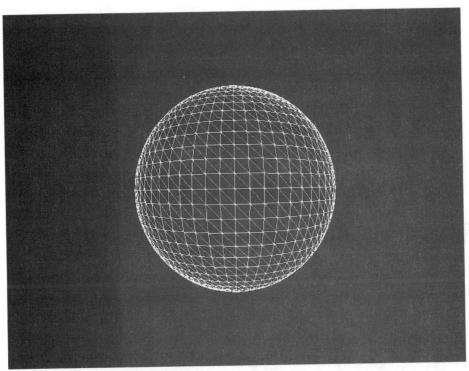

**Figure 7.18**
You can see the polygon makeup of your objects by using the `WireFrame` command.

## Transparency

If you're a fan of the television series *Star Trek* (and if you're reading this book, you probably are), you're probably familiar with the term "cloaking." When a Klingon ship wanted to make itself invisible, it would cloak itself so that it couldn't be detected. We can "cloak" objects that we have created in Blitz3D by using the `Alpha` command. The `Alpha` command allows you to set a level of transparency for an object. Typically, you would set a number for the Alpha between 0 and 1. For example, if you entered an Alpha level of 0.5, the object would be 50% see-through. If you entered a value of 0, the object would be invisible, and if you entered a value of 1, the object would be seen in its entirety. Figure 7.19 shows an example of different alpha values applied to a sphere. Here is the code for creating a cube and then making it 50% transparent.

```
sphere=CreateSphere()
EntityAlpha sphere, 0.5
```

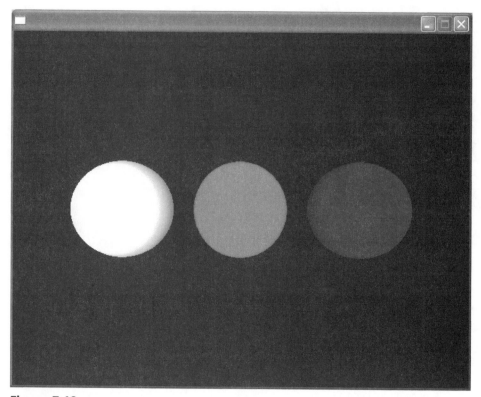

**Figure 7.19**
The sphere on the far left has an `EntityAlpha` of 1, the one in the middle has a value of 0.5, and the one on the right has a value of 0.2.

## Textures and Texture Mapping

This is where things really get interesting. Texture mapping is the key to amazing graphics in 3D games. A very common analogy used for texture mapping is the wrapping of birthday presents. When you wrap the sheet around the gift, the paper takes on the form of the gift. That's pretty much how texture mapping works. You take a flat image, pattern, or text (the wrapping paper) and wrap it around a shape or object you have created or imported.

## Applying Image Textures

To get a "realistic" look for your objects, the best approach is to wrap an image around your shapes. To do this, you must create a texture and then tell Blitz3D what object you would like to wrap that texture around. In the following example, we will create a sphere and then wrap an image around it.

## Note

**Texture Location**

It is very important to note that the file that contains your texture must be saved in the same location as your program file or you must specify the folder where it is located. After you have entered the following code, save it to a location and then copy the texture file to the same location as the program file.

```
; Creating a Sphere with Texture
; ----------------------

Graphics3D 640,480
SetBuffer BackBuffer()

; Create camera
camera=CreateCamera()

; Creating a light
light=CreateLight()

; This is the code for creating our sphere
sphere=CreateSphere(32)
PositionEntity sphere,0,0,5
ScaleEntity sphere, 2,2,2

; Creating the texture
tex=LoadTexture( "texture.bmp" )
EntityTexture sphere, tex

; This following code makes our program run
While Not KeyDown( 1 )

RenderWorld
Flip

Wend

End
```

Run the program and you should see the same textured sphere shown in Figure 7.20.

**Figure 7.20**
You should see this textured sphere when you apply the code.

Let's take a closer look at the code that loaded and applied the texture:

```
; Creating the texture
tex=LoadTexture( "texture.bmp" )
EntityTexture sphere, tex
```

The first part tex= is just a name. You can name your texture anything, but in this case we called it tex. LoadTexture is the actual command that tells Blitz3D to load a specific texture. Within the brackets, you tell Blitz3D which file to load. In this case, the file is called texture.bmp.

Note that the file that you choose to load must be in the same folder that your program is saved in. In this example, texture.bmp would have to be in the same folder that your saved program is in, unless you specify another folder.

The next line, EntityTexture followed by sphere, tex, tells Blitz3D to put the texture, in this case called tex, onto the shape called sphere.

**Note**

**Create Your Own Textures**

Since textures play such an important role in 3D programming, I've devoted a full chapter to them. In the next chapter, you'll use Corel Photo-Paint and CorelDRAW to create a multitude of different textures that you can apply to objects and use for terrains and skies. You'll also explore the creation of other types of graphics for your games, including sprites, Welcome screens, and others.

## Scaling Textures

After you've applied your texture, you may find that it is either too big or too small for the object you are wrapping it around. You can use the ScaleTexture command to increase or decrease the scale of the texture.

Here is the line we would add to our code to scale the texture:

```
; Creating the texture
tex=LoadTexture( "texture.bmp" )
ScaleTexture tex, 2,2
EntityTexture sphere,tex
```

After the ScaleTexture command, you tell Blitz3D which texture you want to scale—in this case it is the one called tex. You then specify how much you would like to scale the object. Because the image you used as your texture was two-dimensional, you only have to enter a number for the amount you want to scale the x and y axes. Any numbers you enter above 1 will increase the size of the texture, and any integer between 0 and 1 will decrease the size of the texture. For example, if you entered 0.5,0.5 for the scale, the texture would be reduced by half.

## Creating Text Textures

You don't necessarily have to have an image to create a texture. Blitz3D gives you the ability to create a texture from text. In other words, you can create some text and then wrap it around an object.

In this example (shown in Figure 7.21), we'll create a sphere and then use some text as a texture that we will wrap around the object.

```
; Creating a Sphere with Text Texture
; ------------------------------------

Graphics3D 640,480
SetBuffer BackBuffer()
```

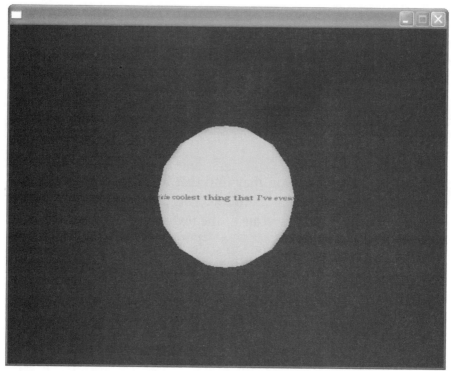

**Figure 7.21**
When you run the program you should see this sphere with the text wrapped around it.

```
; Create camera
camera=CreateCamera()

; Creating a light
light=CreateLight()

; This is the code for creating our sphere
sphere=CreateSphere()
PositionEntity sphere,0,0,5
ScaleEntity sphere, 1.5,1.5,1.5

; Create texture of size 300x300
tex=CreateTexture( 300,300 )

; Set buffer - texture buffer with green background
SetBuffer TextureBuffer( tex )
ClsColor 120,205,12
Cls
```

```
; Draw text on texture
font=LoadFont( "times",15 )
SetFont font
Color 0,0,255
Text 120,250, "Wow this is the coolest thing that I've ever seen!"

; Texture cube with texture
EntityTexture sphere,tex

; This following code makes our program run
While Not KeyDown( 1 )

RenderWorld
Flip

Wend

End
```

Let's take a closer look at the key areas of code used to create and apply this text texture:

```
; This is the code for creating our sphere
sphere=CreateSphere()
PositionEntity sphere,0,0,5
ScaleEntity sphere, 1.5,1.5,1.5
```

I started off by slightly enlarging the size of the sphere so that we could see more of the text.

```
; Creating a texture that is size 300x300
tex=CreateTexture( 300,300 )
```

Here we created a texture using the CreateTexture command. The name of this texture is tex and it's size is 300 by 300 pixels. Next we'll look at the TextureBuffer command we applied:

```
; Set buffer - texture buffer with green background
SetBuffer TextureBuffer( tex )
ClsColor 120,205,12
Cls
```

Here we are going to set the drawing buffer for our texture and choose a color. SetBuffer TextureBuffer( tex ) sets the buffer for the texture called tex. We then set an RGB color for the background of the texture, in this case 120.205,12, which is a greenish color. This is surrounded by ClsColor and Cls, which are used to set the drawing buffer color. After this we coded our text:

```
; Draw text on texture
font=LoadFont( "times",15 )
SetFont font
Color 0,0,255
Text 120,250, "Wow this is the coolest thing that I've ever seen!"
```

This first thing we did was create a name for the font we are going to use—in this case we simply called it font. We then used the LoadFont command to select the font face and size. In this case, we chose the font face "times" and the size was 15. Next, the SetFont command initializes the font we created called font. The Color 0,0,255 sets the RGB color values for the font that we are creating. In the final line, we specify the x and y coordinates for the text (in this case 120,250 and type in the actual text that we would like to appear. Finally we applied the texture to the sphere:

```
; Texture cube with texture
EntityTexture sphere,tex
```

## Object Order

When you have more than one object on the screen, there is a chance that they can overlap each other and you won't be able to see one or the other. Sometimes you'll actually want an object to be hidden by others, and you can create this effect by controlling the order of an object. Let's create a program that contains two spheres that overlap and then change their order using the EntityOrder command.

First, try on your own to create two overlapping spheres, each with different colors (see Figure 7.22), and then compare it to the following code:

```
; Overlapping Spheres
; ————————————

Graphics3D 640,480
SetBuffer BackBuffer()
camera=CreateCamera()
light=CreateLight()
sphere1=CreateSphere()

PositionEntity sphere1,-1,0,5
EntityColor sphere1, 102,23,231
```

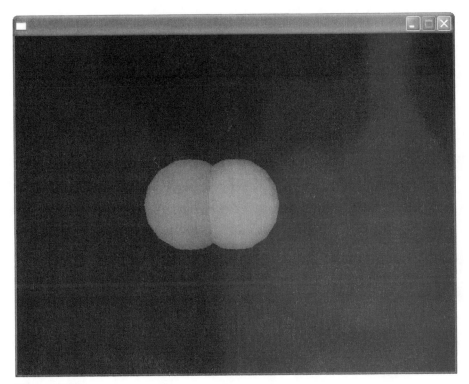

**Figure 7.22**
When two objects overlap they'll blend into one another unless you adjust their order.

```
sphere2=CreateSphere()
PositionEntity sphere2,0,0,5
EntityColor sphere2, 21,78,199
While Not KeyDown( 1 )

RenderWorld
Flip

Wend

End
```

Now when you run the program, you'll see that the two shapes blend together at the point where they overlap. Rather than having the objects blend together, you can have one overlap the other by changing the order in which they are drawn using the EntityOrder command. With the EntityOrder command you can either enter a number below or above 0 to change the order of an object. For example, let's say we had an object called sphere. If we entered the code

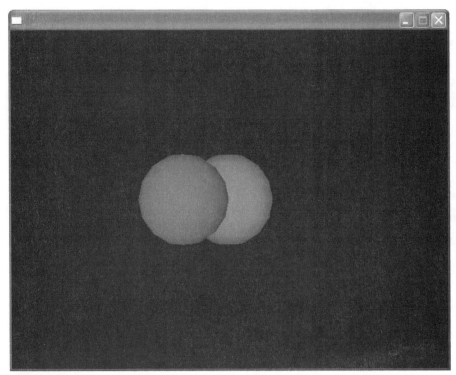

**Figure 7.23**
When you adjust the order of objects, one will appear in front of or behind the others.

EntityOrder sphere, -1, the sphere will be drawn behind other objects; if the code was EntityOrder sphere, 1, the sphere would be drawn in front of the other objects. Let's try this in our code. Add the last line from this section of code:

```
sphere1=CreateSphere()
PositionEntity sphere1,-1,0,5
EntityColor sphere1, 102,23,231
EntityOrder sphere1, -1
```

Now run the program and see how it looks. Then go back and change the −1 to a 1 and run the program again to see how it affects how the spheres seem to overlap (see Figure 7.23).

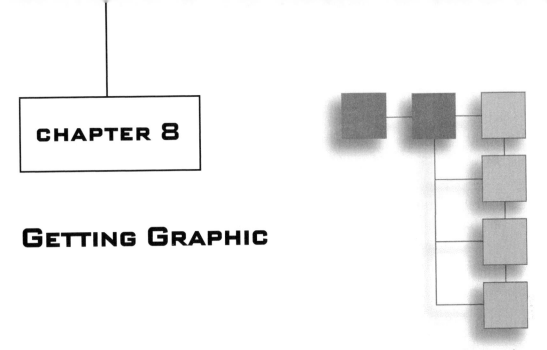

# CHAPTER 8

# GETTING GRAPHIC

It's time to take a break from programming for a minute. I know what you're thinking to yourself: We only started really programming for one chapter and already we are taking a break? Well, because graphics play such an important part in the world of 3D gaming, I thought it might be wise to spend some time showing you how to create some graphics that you'll include in your games. You will need these graphics as you get deeper into the book. Besides, as you'll soon see, creating graphics can be a lot of fun.

There are two categories of graphics that I will cover in this chapter. This first is *heightmaps*. A heightmap defines the landscape of your terrain. In other words, it informs the program where any bumps, mountains, and valleys should occur. The next category of images that you'll create are *textures*. Textures can include the cover to any type of surface including terrains, the sky, walls, and other objects. From grass to mud to ice to brick, you'll create several different types of terrains in this chapter.

All of the graphics that you create in this chapter will be made using either Corel Photo-Paint or CorelDRAW. Both of these programs are found on the accompanying CD and are arguably the most powerful graphics applications on the market. As with most of the technology you are learning in this book, the specific tools you use aren't all that important—it's the process of creating and the thinking behind it that is most important. For that reason, you can use almost any graphics applications to create the same effects we will accomplish here, including Adobe Photoshop and Illustrator, PaintShop Pro, CorelPainter, and many others.

## Heightmaps

A heightmap is an image that defines the landscape of your game. Keep in mind that your game doesn't necessarily need a heightmap, but they are perfect for driving, racing, and role-playing games.

Heightmap images are made in Grayscale mode, which means that there is no color in them, but just 256 shades of gray. You can create mountains and valleys and plains in a heightmap through the use of different shades. Anything that is fully white represents the highest peak while anything that is completely black represents the lowest point (see Figure 8.1).

Now on to the fun part. We are going to create some heightmaps in Photo-Paint. There are hundreds of thousands of possible combinations we can use to create a heightmap, but here I will discuss three different methods. Once you have reviewed these methods, try creating some heightmaps on your own.

## Creating Heightmaps with Textured Fills

Corel Photo-Paint comes with a library of textures that are perfect for creating heightmaps. With a few click of the mouse button your have your perfect heightmap in no time. Start off by launching Photo-Paint. A Welcome screen will appear.

1. Click the New icon (see Figure 8.2). If the Welcome screen doesn't appear, or if you are already in Photo-Paint, just click File > New. A new document

**Figure 8.1**
The image on the left is the heightmap that was used to create the image on the right. As you can see, the areas that were white represent the high points and the areas that were black represent the low areas.

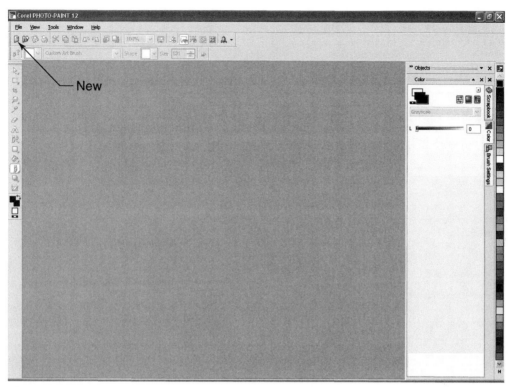

**Figure 8.2**
Start with a new file by clicking the New icon.

dialog box will now appear where you can set the parameters for your heightmap.

2. Take a look at Figure 8.3 and make sure that your settings are the same. In a nutshell, you want the Color mode to be 8-bit Grayscale, the width and height to be 256 pixels, and the resolution to be 72 dpi. You'll probably have to change the units of measurement to pixels to be able to enter these numbers. Click OK once you have all the settings entered.

3. Press the Ctrl key and the Backspace key at the same time. This will bring open the Fill dialog box.

4. At the bottom of the dialog box you will see a row of buttons with little pictures on them. Click the button on the far right called Texture Fill.

5. Now click the Edit button. This will bring open a dialog box where you can choose a texture for your heightmap (see Figure 8.4).

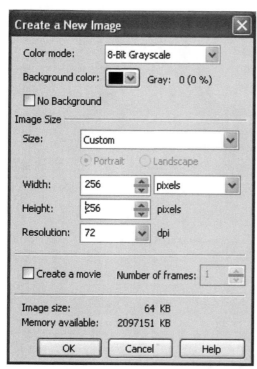

**Figure 8.3**
Enter your image settings for color, size, and resolution.

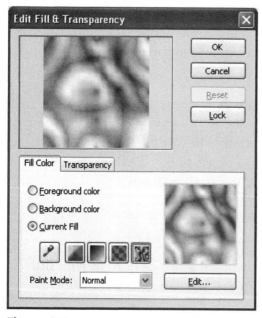

**Figure 8.4**
Choose a texture for your heightmap.

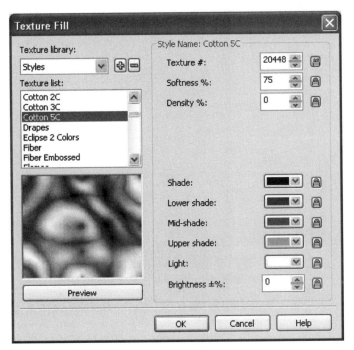

**Figure 8.5**
You can create millions of different combinations by clicking the Preview button.

6. Scroll through the different textures and click on a texture name to see a preview of it. The textures are grouped into seven different categories. You can change categories by clicking on the Texture Library drop-down arrow. There are dozens of different textures to choose from with literally millions of combinations. That's right, I said millions! Every time you click on the Preview button in this dialog box, the pattern will be changed slightly so you can choose from an infinite number of different combinations (see Figure 8.5).

7. Once you find a pattern that you like, you can click the OK button to return to the last dialog box. You'll have to click OK again to be returned to Photo-Paint where you will now see your heightmap. As you make your decision on a heightmap, keep in mind again that the darker an area is, the flatter it will be, while the lighter an area is, the more it will be raised.

8. Now that your heightmap is created, it is a good idea to save it. Generally speaking, you should save it as a .bmp file. In Photo-Paint, click File > Save As . . . to bring open a dialog box (see Figure 8.6) where you can save your file. Click the Save As Type drop-down arrow and scroll until you can select Windows BMP – Windows Bitmap. Now give your file a name: call this

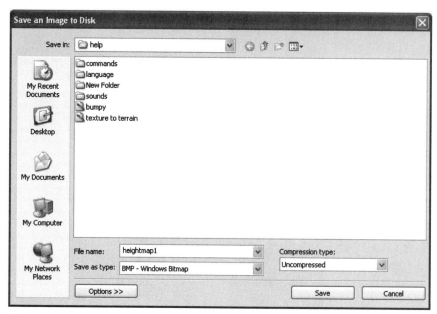

**Figure 8.6**
Save the heightmap as a .bmp file.

heightmap1.bmp, and then click the Save button. That's it. You've created your first heightmap.

## Creating Heightmaps with a Brush

Another way that you can create a heightmap in Photo-Paint, or just about any other graphics application, is to simply paint one. Just remember as you paint that the darker the shade of gray, the flatter the surface will be and vice versa. Start by launching Photo-Paint.

1. Click the New icon. If the Welcome screen doesn't appear, or if you are already in Photo-Paint, just click File > New. A new document dialog box will now appear where you can set the parameters for your heightmap.

2. Take a look at Figure 8.7 and make sure that your settings are the same. In a nutshell, you want the Color mode to be 8-bit Grayscale, the width and height to be 256 pixels, and the resolution to be 72 dpi. You'll probably have to change the units of measurement to pixels to be able to enter these numbers. Click OK once you have all the settings entered.

3. Click on the Paint tool button in the toolbox as seen in Figure 8.8.

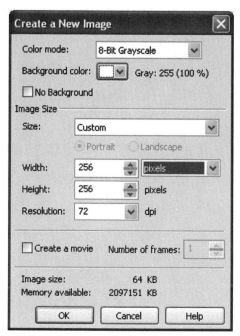

**Figure 8.7**
Enter your image settings for the color, size, and resolution.

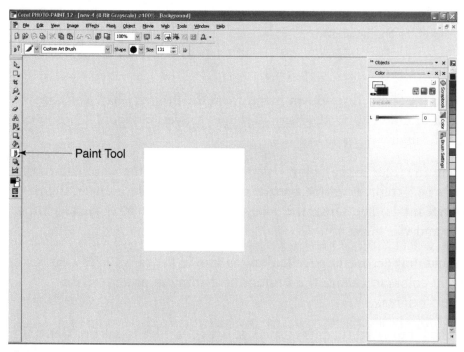

**Figure 8.8**
Select the Paint tool button in the toolbox.

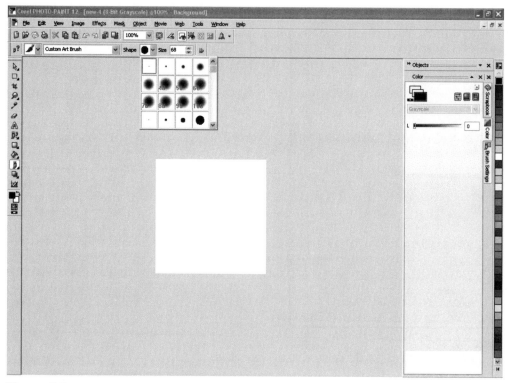

**Figure 8.9**
Choose from any of the brushes displayed.

4. Click on the Shape drop-down menu from the Property bar. You'll now see a list of different brush sizes and shapes as seen in Figure 8.9. You can choose from any of these brushes.

5. Click on any color in the Colors palette. Keep in mind that your color won't actually be a color, it will be a shade of gray because we are working in Grayscale mode. The darker the color you choose, the flatter the heightmap will be and vice versa.

6. Click and drag across the page to draw as seen in Figure 8.10. You can select different colors to change the amount of shading in order to create different heights.

7. Now that your heightmap is created, it is a good idea to save it. Generally speaking, you should save it as a .bmp file. In Photo-Paint, click File > Save As . . . to bring open a dialog box where you can save your file. Click the Save

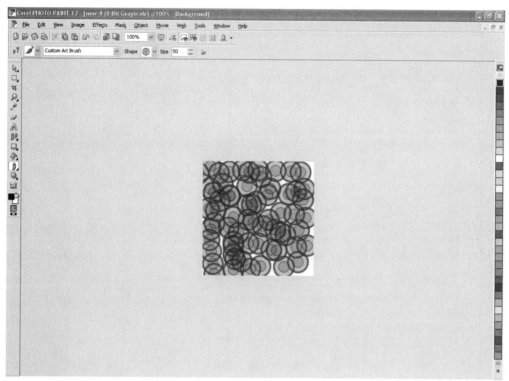

**Figure 8.10**
Drag across the page to apply the brush.

As Type drop-down arrow and scroll until you can select BMP – Windows Bitmap. Now give your file a name: call this heightmap2.bmp, and then click the Save button.

## Creating Heightmaps with Effects

There are really hundreds of different ways to create a heightmap using effects in Photo-Paint. What's the key to creating a cool heightmap with effects? Experiment. After you've followed these instructions, go ahead and experiment on your own with different combinations of effects. First launch Photo-Paint and then follow these steps:

1. Click the New icon. If the Welcome screen doesn't appear, or if you are already in Photo-Paint, just click File > New. A new document dialog box will now appear where you can set the parameters for your heightmap.

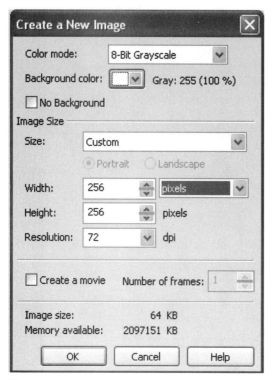

**Figure 8.11**
Enter your image settings for color, size, and resolution.

2. Take a look at Figure 8.11 and make sure that your settings are the same. In a nutshell, you want the Color mode to be 8-bit Grayscale, the width and height to be 256 pixels, and the resolution to be 72 dpi; the background color is white. You'll probably have to change the units of measurement to pixels to be able to enter these numbers. Click OK once you have all the settings entered.

3. Click Effects > Art Strokes > Palette Knife. A dialog box (see Figure 8.12), will appear where you can enter different settings for this effect. Simply accept the defaults and click the OK button. You'll be left with a gray and white image. Now we will smooth things out and make them a little more even.

4. Click Effects > Texture > Relief Sculpture. This will bring open a dialog box (see Figure 8.13) where you can adjust the settings. Enter the following settings and then click OK. Detail: 51, Depth: 23, Smoothness: 37. You will now be left with a useable heightmap.

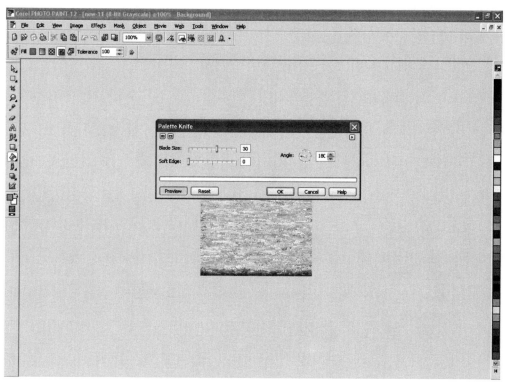

**Figure 8.12**
Accept the default settings by clicking OK.

5. Now that your heightmap is created, it is a good idea to save it. Generally speaking, you should save it as a .bmp file. In Photo-Paint click File > Save As . . . to bring open a dialog box where you can save your file. Click the Save As Type drop-down arrow and scroll until you can select BMP – Windows Bitmap. Now give your file a name: call this heightmap3.bmp, and then click the Save button.

## Creating Textures

Textures can make the difference between a good game and a fantastic game. As mentioned earlier, we'll be using a feature called texture mapping to wrap around our objects. Whether it's a wall, a sky, the ground, or floating objects, most get their "feel" from the textures we create. The good news is that creating your own textures is a breeze, whether you're creating them in Photo-Paint or other graphics applications. In this section, we'll create a variety of different textures for walls, terrains, skies, and other objects. The techniques discussed

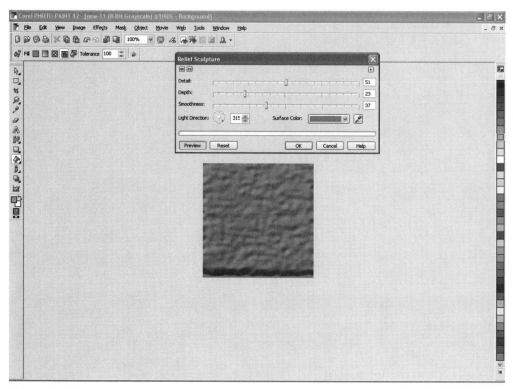

**Figure 8.13**
Enter the settings in the dialog box to adjust the Relief Sculpture effects.

here are not the only options for creating textures, but they will give you a good foundation for creating textures in Photo-Paint. Once you get more familiar with Photo-Paint, experiment with different effects, brushes, and techniques to create your own textures. Start by launching Photo-Paint and clicking New in the Welcome screen. From there, follow any of the following steps to create a texture.

## Walls

How can you create a wall? Let me count the ways. The truth is that Photo-Paint provides you with several dozen options for creating a wall. Below you'll find two samples, but again, I encourage you to experiment on your own to create all types of different walls.

### Brick Walls

There is actually an effect in Photo-Paint that will allow you to instantly create a brick wall.

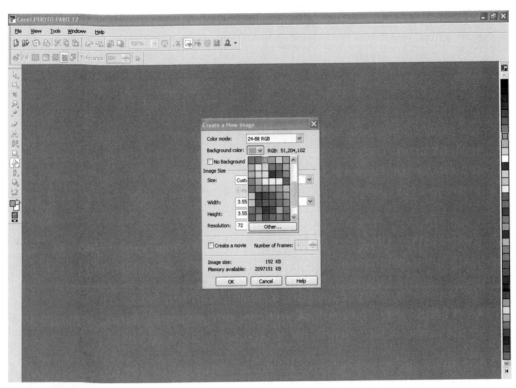

**Figure 8.14**
Choose any color for your brick wall.

1. Set the Color mode to 24-bit RGB and click the Background color drop-down arrow and select a color for your brick wall (see Figure 8.14).

2. For the rest of the settings, take a look at Figure 8.15 and make sure that your settings are the same. In a nutshell, you want the width and height to be 256 pixels and the resolution to be 72 dpi. You'll probably have to change the units of measurement to pixels to be able to enter these numbers. Click OK once you have all the settings entered.

3. Click Effects > Texture > Brick Wall. This will bring up a dialog box (see Figure 8.16), and at the same time you'll be able to preview the effect. You can click and drag the Roughness slider and adjust other settings like the width and height of the brick and grout. Once you've got the brick wall the way you like it, click OK.

4. Now that your brick wall is created, it is a good idea to save it. Generally speaking, you should save it as a .jpg file. In Photo-Paint, click File > Save

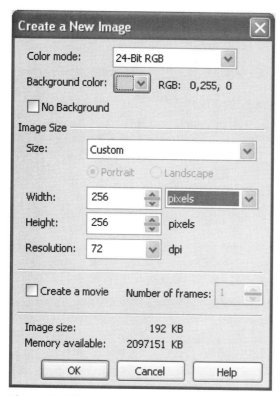

**Figure 8.15**
Enter your image settings for color, size, and resolution.

As . . . to bring open a dialog box where you can save your file. Click the Save As Type drop-down arrow and scroll until you can select JPG – JPEG Bitmaps. Now give your file a name: call this wall1.jpg, and then click the Save button.

### Plaster Wall

You can create the look of a plaster wall by using the same technique used for the brick wall but just applying a different effect.

1. Click the Background color drop-down arrow and select a color for your plaster wall. For the rest of the settings, take a look at Figure 8.17 and make sure that your settings are the same. In a nutshell, you want the Color mode to be 24-bit RGB, the width and height to be 256 pixels, and the

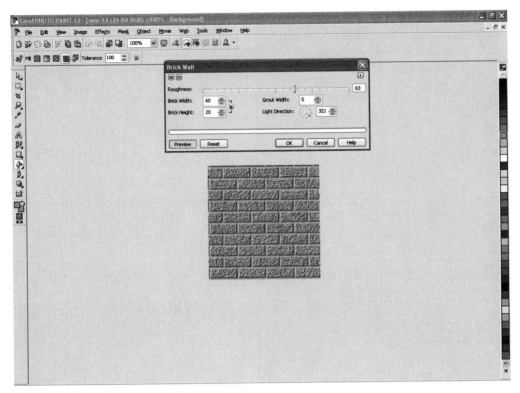

**Figure 8.16**
Drag any of the sliders to adjust the settings.

resolution to be 72 dpi. You'll probably have to change the units of measurement to pixels to be able to enter these numbers. Click OK once you have all the settings entered.

2. Click Effects > Texture > Plaster Wall. This will bring up a dialog box (see Figure 8.18), and at the same time you'll be able to preview the effect. You can click and drag the sliders to adjust the wall. Once you've got the plaster wall the way you'd like it, click OK.

3. Now that your plaster wall is created, it is a good idea to save it. Generally speaking, you should save it as a .jpg file. In Photo-Paint, click File > Save As . . . to bring open a dialog box where you can save your file. Click the Save As Type drop-down arrow and scroll until you can select JPG – JPEG Bitmaps. Now give your file a name: call this wall1.jpg, and then click the Save button.

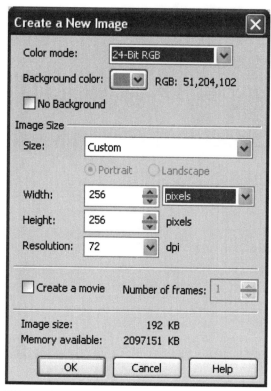

**Figure 8.17**
Enter your image settings for color, size, and resolution.

**Note**

**Why Not Photos?**

Rather than having to create textures, terrains, and skies from scratch, you can always use your own photos when texture mapping. Imagine that you wanted to create a realistic looking building in your game. Why not take a photo of a building and wrap it around a stretched cube. A great resource for finding photos of different objects is the Image search on Google. Just keep in mind that most images are copyrighted, so if you plan on distributing your game, make sure you have permission to use the images.

## Terrains and Skies

A terrain is typically the ground that your players will walk, run, race, or drive on. Again, there are a variety of different ways you can create awesome looking terrains in seconds in Photo-Paint.

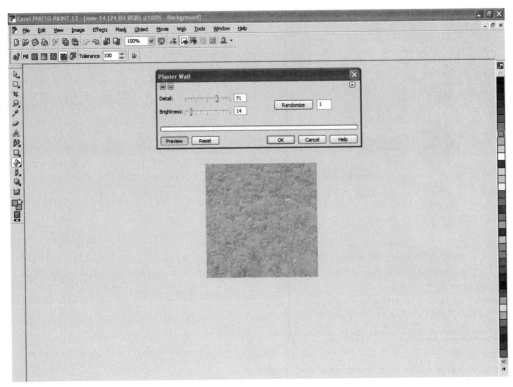

**Figure 8.18**
Adjust the sliders to change the effect.

## Creating Terrains with Texture Fills

The best way to create a realistic looking terrain is to use the Texture fill option in Photo-Paint. There is a complete library of different terrains you can select from and modify.

1. Take a look at Figure 8.19 and make sure that your settings are the same. In a nutshell, you want the Color mode to be 24-bit RGB, the width and height to be 256 pixels, and the resolution to be 72 dpi. You'll probably have to change the units of measurement to pixels to be able to enter these numbers. Click OK once you have all the settings entered.

2. Press the Ctrl key and the Backspace key at the same time. This will bring open the Fill dialog box (see Figure 8.20).

3. At the bottom of the dialog box you will see a row of buttons with little pictures on them. Click the button on the far right called Texture Fill.

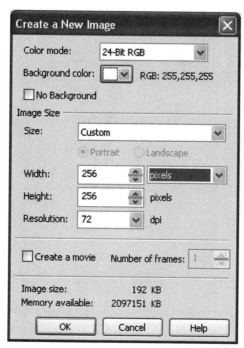

**Figure 8.19**
Enter your image settings for color, size, and resolution.

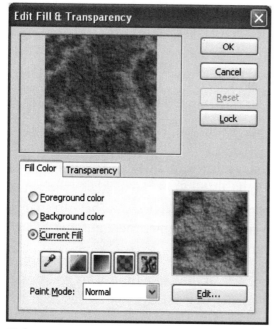

**Figure 8.20**
Click the Edit button to choose a texture for you heightmap.

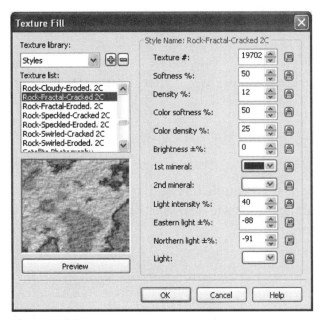

**Figure 8.21**
There are dozens of patterns to choose from.

4. Now click the Edit button. This will bring open a dialog box where you can choose a texture for your heightmap.

5. Scroll through the different textures and click on a texture name to see a preview of it. The textures are grouped into seven different categories. You can change categories by clicking on the Texture Library drop-down arrow. There are dozens of different textures to choose from (see Figure 8.21) with millions of combinations. You can also adjust the colors in the texture by clicking on the drop-down arrow beside the color boxes. Just make sure you click the Preview button to see your changes. Following are some of the best textures you can use for terrains.

Under the Styles Texture library, there are a variety of textures that begin with the word Rock that are perfect to use:

- Rock-Cloudy-Cracked 2C

- Rock-Cloudy-Eroded, 2C

- Rock-Fractal-Cracked 2C

- Rock-Fractal-Eroded, 2C

- Rock-Speckled-Cracked 2C

- Rock-Speckled-Eroded, 2C

Under the Samples 7 Texture library, there are a variety of textures that are great for terrains:

- Drylands

- Polar Surface

For creating sky textures, there are a couple fills that are perfect. You'll have to change the colors to blue, but the results will be perfect. These two options can be found in the Sample 6 Texture library:

- Cotton Candy

- Exhaust Fume

6. Once you find a pattern that you like, you can click the OK button to return to the last dialog box. You'll have to click OK again to be returned to Photo-Paint where you will now see your heightmap. As you make your decision on a heightmap, keep in mind again that the darker an area is, the flatter it will be, while the lighter an area is, the more it will be raised

7. Now that your texture is created, it is a good idea to save it. Generally speaking, you should save it as a .jpg file. In Photo-Paint, click File > Save As . . . to bring open a dialog box where you can save your file. Click the Save As Type drop-down arrow and scroll until you can select JPG – JPEG Bitmap. Now give your file a name, and then click the Save button.

## Wood

There are several bitmap fills that beautifully emulate the real-life wood from which you can create textures. These are applied slightly differently from texture fills.

1. Start by clicking the New button or by clicking File > New. Take a look at Figure 8.22 and make sure that your settings are the same. In a nutshell, you want the Color mode to be 24-bit RGB, the width and height to be 256 pixels, and the resolution to be 72 dpi. You'll probably have to change the units of measurement to pixels to be able to enter these numbers. Click OK once you have all the settings entered.

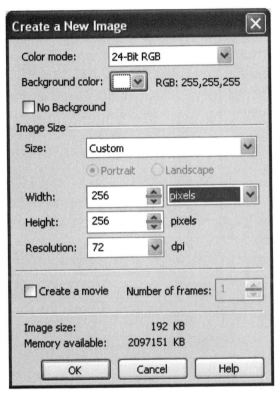

**Figure 8.22**
Enter your image settings for color, size, and resolution.

2. Press the Ctrl key and the Backspace key at the same time. This will bring open the Fill dialog box.

3. At the bottom of the dialog box, you will see a row of buttons with little pictures on them. Click the second to last button on the far right called Bitmap Fill.

4. Now click the Edit button. This will bring open a dialog box (see Figure 8.23) where you can choose a texture for your heightmap.

5. Click the down arrow to see a list of bitmap fills, and scroll to the bottom. At the bottom, you'll find several textures that resemble wood. Click on the one you would like to apply and then click OK. (See Figure 8.24)

6. Click OK in the original dialog box, and your new texture will be created.

7. Now that your texture is created, it is a good idea to save it. Generally speaking, you should save it as a .jpg file. In Photo-Paint click File > Save

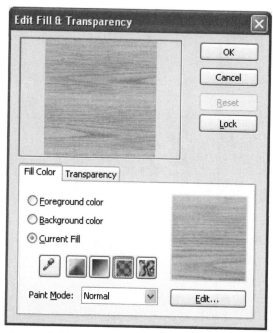

**Figure 8.23**
By clicking the Edit button, you can change the fill.

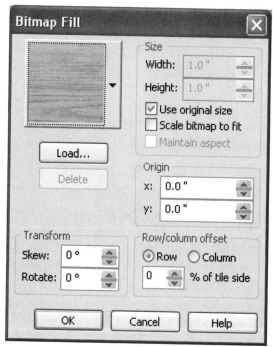

**Figure 8.24**
Choose a fill that looks like wood.

As . . . to bring open a dialog box where you can save your file. Click the Save As Type drop-down arrow and scroll until you can select JPG – JPEG Bitmap. Now give your file a name, and then click the Save button.

## Creating Terrains with Effects

Another option for creating terrains is to use the built-in effects of Photo-Paint. The following three textures are great to use for terrains, walls, or other objects.

### Cobblestone

The Cobblestone effect in Photo-Paint is the perfect way to emulate a desert floor. Here's how you do it.

1. Click the Background color drop-down arrow and select a color for your wall. For the rest of the settings, take a look at Figure 8.25 and make sure

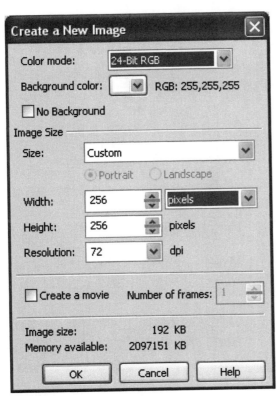

**Figure 8.25**
Enter your image settings for color, size, and resolution.

that your settings are the same. In a nutshell, you want the Color mode to be 24-bit RGB, the Background color should be a light brown, the width and height need to be 256 pixels, and the resolution should be 72 dpi. You'll probably have to change the units of measurement to pixels to be able to enter these numbers. Click OK once you have all the settings entered.

2. Click Effects > Texture > Cobblestone. This will bring up a dialog box, and at the same time you'll be able to preview the effect. You can click and drag the sliders to adjust the cobblestone settings (see Figure 8.26). The larger you slide the Size option, the more realistic the desert floor will look. Once you've got the effect the way you like it, click OK.

3. Now that your desert floor is created, it is a good idea to save it. Generally speaking, you should save it as a .jpg file. In Photo-Paint, click File > Save As . . . to bring open a dialog box where you can save your file. Click the Save As Type drop-down arrow and scroll until you can select JPG – JPEG Bitmaps. Now give your file a name, and then click the Save button.

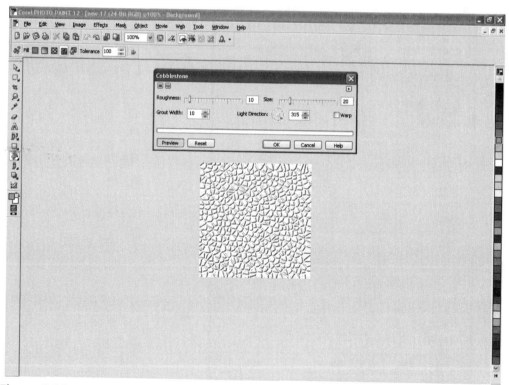

**Figure 8.26**
Drag any of the sliders to adjust the effect.

### Mosaic Tile

From the bottom of pools to bathroom backsplashes to church floors, mosaic tiles are everywhere. You can nicely emulate a real mosaic tile to apply to walls, floors, or ceilings.

1. Click the Background color drop-down arrow and select a color for your wall. For the rest of the settings, take a look at Figure 8.27 and make sure that your settings are the same. In a nutshell, you want the Color mode to be 24-bit RGB, the Background color should be a light brown, the width and height need to be 256 pixels, and the resolution should be 72 dpi. You'll probably have to change the units of measurement to pixels to be able to enter these numbers. Click OK once you have all the settings entered.

2. Click Effects > Creative > Mosaic. This will bring up a dialog box (see Figure 8.28) and at the same time you'll be able to preview the effect. You can click and drag the slider to adjust the size of the tiles. Once you've got the effect the way you like it, click OK.

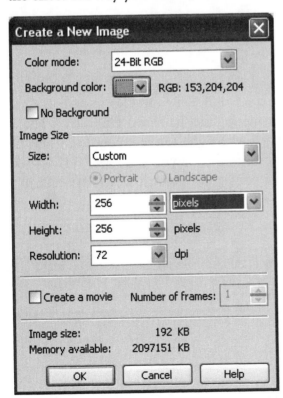

**Figure 8.27**
Enter your image settings for color, size, and resolution.

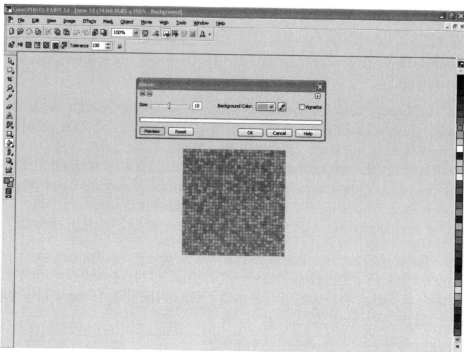

**Figure 8.28**
Drag the slider to change the size of the tiles.

3. Now that your mosaic tile is created, it is a good idea to save it. Generally speaking, you should save it as a .jpg file. In Photo-Paint, click File > Save As . . . to bring open a dialog box where you can save your file. Click the Save As Type drop-down arrow and scroll until you can select JPG – JPEG Bitmaps. Now give your file a name, and then click the Save button.

**Note**

**Now You Try**

In this chapter you've created a variety of different textures. Take what you learned in the last chapter and apply some of the textures you've created to some basic shapes as seen in Figure 8.29.

# Information Screens

Most games have at least one or two information screens that provide the user with, well, information. This information usually includes direction on how to use the game or what is going on at that moment. Typical examples of

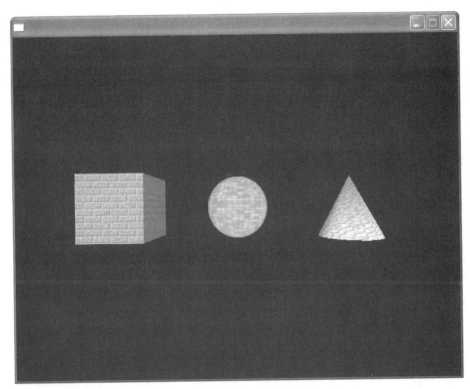

**Figure 8.29**
Create these shapes and apply a texture to them as seen here.

information screens are Welcome screens, Pause screens, and Exit screens. In this section, we'll create a Welcome screen and Pause screen using CorelDRAW. I won't turn you into a graphic designer, but I will show you some cool design tricks. Once you get the hang of things, I suggest you experiment on your own creating different game screens.

## Welcome Screen

The Welcome screen that we'll create will include the name of our game and instructions on how to control the game. We will actually use this Welcome screen in the final game that we create in this book. After the Welcome screen is created, we will export it to a format that can be understood by Blitz3D.

1. Launch CorelDRAW and click New in the Welcome screen that appears. The first thing that we need to do is change the units of measurement to pixels. In the Units drop-down menu in the Property bar, select Pixels, as in Figure 8.30.

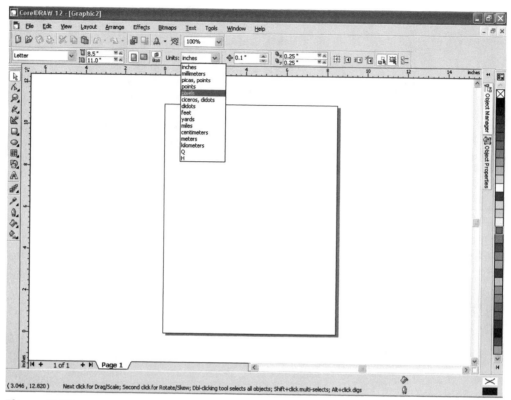

**Figure 8.30**
Change the units to pixels.

2. Select the Rectangle tool from the toolbox on the left side of the screen and click and drag a rectangle onto the page. It doesn't matter how big you make the rectangle since we are going to adjust this momentarily.

3. In the Property bar, change the dimension of your rectangle to 1024 by 768, as in Figure 8.31. This will ensure that our Welcome screen will take up the entire screen when we later import it into our game.

4. With the rectangle still selected, click on the color Yellow in the Colors palette on the right side of the screen. The rectangle should now be yellow. Press Shift+F2 to zoom in to the rectangle.

5. Select the Text tool (the letter A button) from the toolbox on the left side of the screen and click anywhere inside the rectangle. A cursor should begin flashing inside the rectangle. Click the Font Size list drop-down menu from the Property bar and select 48, as in Figure 8.32.

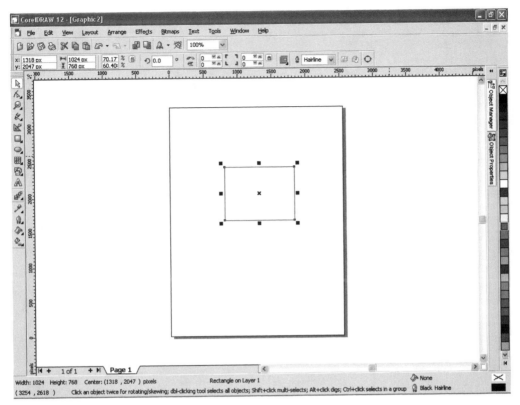

**Figure 8.31**
Adjust the size of the rectangle to be 1024 by 768.

**Note**

**Font**

In addition to changing the font size, you can also change the font face by clicking on the Font list drop-down menu in the Property bar and selecting a different font. For this particular Welcome screen, a thicker font will work better.

6. Type the words "3D Gallery" and then select the Pick tool (the white arrow at the top of the Tools palette on the left side of the screen.) A series of black boxes called *handles* will appear around the word, as seen in Figure 8.33.

7. Position the mouse pointer over the x in the middle of the word and click and drag it until it is positioned as in Figure 8.33.

8. Click on the Interactive Fill tool (the bottom tool in the toolbox.) Position the mouse pointer at the top of the G in "Gallery" and click and drag

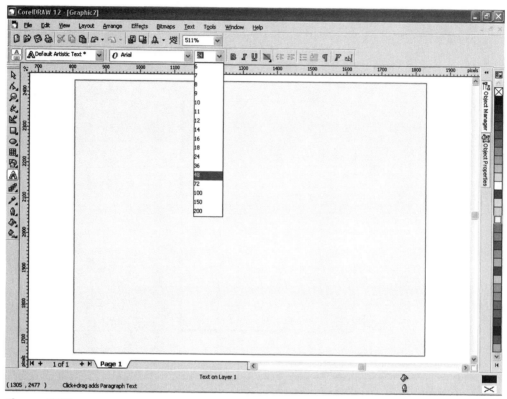

**Figure 8.32**
Select size 48 from the drop-down menu.

downward until you reach the bottom of the G. Two little colored boxes should appear—one at the top and one at the bottom of the G, as seen in Figure 8.34.

9. In the Property bar you should notice two Fill drop-downs: one that is black and another that is white. Click on the Fill drop-down list on the left and select a dark blue from the menu that appears. Click on the Fill drop-down list on the right and select a light-blue color, as seen in Figure 8.35.

10. Now we will make the text seem three-dimensional by using the Perspective effect. Click Effects > Add Perspective from the Menu bar. A red grid will appear around your text. Position your mouse pointer over the black handle in the top right corner of the grid and click and drag it upward slightly. Now position the mouse pointer over the black handle in the bottom right

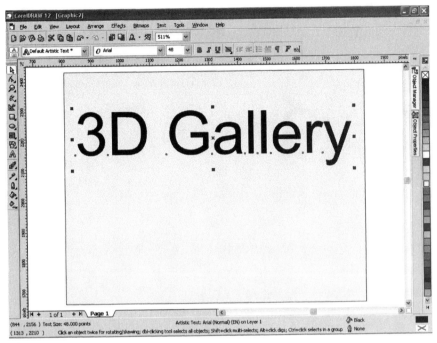

**Figure 8.33**
Position the words "3D Gallery" in the top third of the rectangle as seen here.

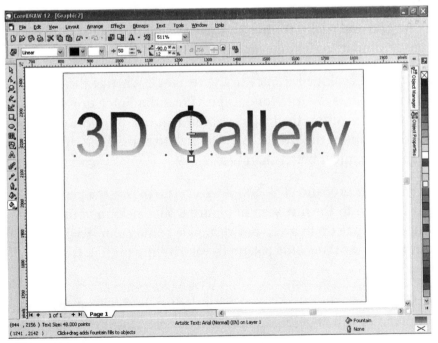

**Figure 8.34**
Click and drag from the top of the G to the bottom using the Interactive Fill tool.

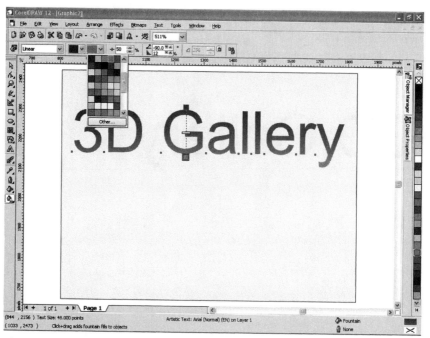

**Figure 8.35**
Select the two colors for your text from the Fill drop-down menus.

corner of the grid and click and drag downward slightly. You should be left with an image similar to the one you see in Figure 8.36.

11. Click the Text tool again, click once in the rectangle, change the font size to 12, and choose your favorite font. Type "Press the Enter or Return Key to Start" and then position the text as seen in Figure 8.37. Notice too that I've changed the font of the words "3D Gallery" to something thicker, and the text stands out much better than before.

12. Select the Rectangle tool and click and drag a rectangle on the page, similar in size and position to the one seen in Figure 8.38. Click on your favorite color in the Color palette to give your rectangle some color. Right-click on the x in the top of the Color palette to remove the outline from the rectangle.

13. Select the Shape tool (the second tool from the top in the Tools palette). Four black handles will appear around the rectangle. Position your mouse pointer over any of these black handles and click and drag inward to round the corners of the rectangle, as seen in Figure 8.39.

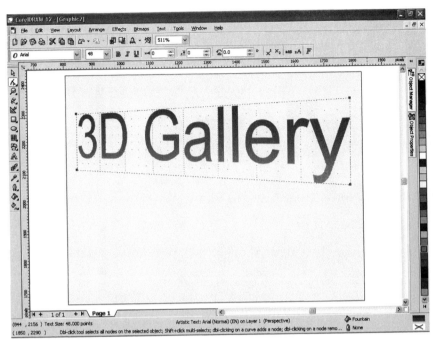

**Figure 8.36**
Make the text appear as if it is jumping off the page by using the Perspective feature.

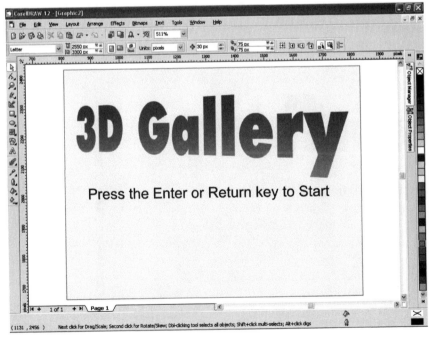

**Figure 8.37**
Position the text you created as seen here.

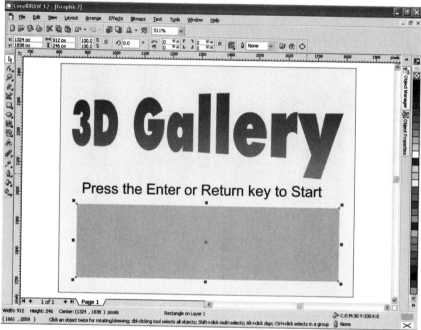

**Figure 8.38**
Create a rectangle similar to the one seen here.

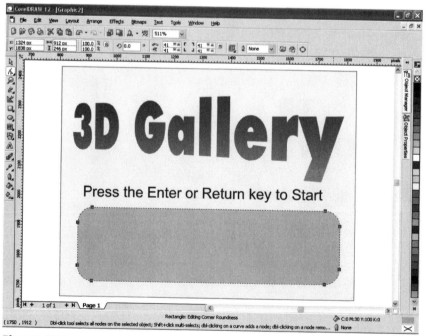

**Figure 8.39**
Round the corners of the rectangle using the Shape tool.

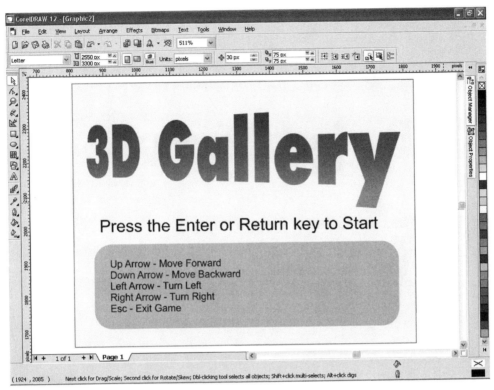

**Figure 8.40**
Position the text you created on the left side of the rectangle.

14. Select the Text tool again and click within the rectangle you just created. Change the font size to 7. Type the following: "Up Arrow – Move Forward." Press the Enter key, and then type "Down Arrow – move Backward." Continue adding the following new lines of text: "Left Arrow – Turn Left," "Right Arrow – Turn Right," and "Esc – Exit Game." Select the Pick tool and move the text to the left side of the rectangle, as seen in Figure 8.40.

15. Repeat Step 14 to create another block of text that includes the following: "Space Bar – Fire," "P – Pause Game," "Mouse Button – Continue," "R – Reload," "V – Hover." Position this new block of text as seen in Figure 8.41

16. Now it's time to export our image to a format that Blitz3D can understand. In this case, we will convert our drawing into a .bmp image, but we could just as easily save it as a .jpeg or .gif. Click File > Export to bring up the Export dialog box. Click the Save As Type drop-down arrow and scroll until you can select BMP – Windows Bitmap. Now give your file the name "welcome," and then click the Export button.

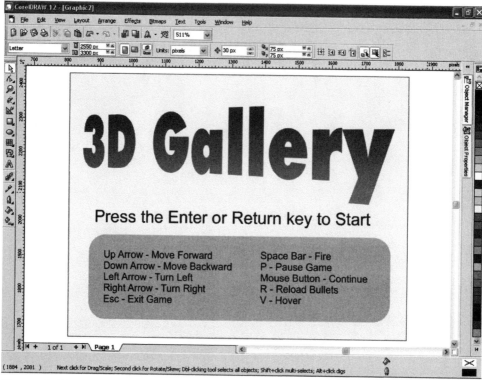

**Figure 8.41**
Position the remaining text as seen here.

17. In the Convert to Bitmap dialog box that appears, enter 1024 in the width box and 768 in the height box. Make sure the resolution is 96 dpi and the Color mode is set to Paletted (8-bit), as seen in Figure 8.42. Click OK and another dialog box will appear. Click OK in this dialog box, and your file will be exported.

## Pause Screen

When the player pauses the game, typically a Pause screen appears letting him know how he can restart the game. We will create a Pause screen that incorporates some design elements from the final game that we'll be creating in this book.

1. Launch CorelDRAW and click New in the Welcome screen that appears. The first thing that we need to do is change the units of measurement to pixels. In the Units drop-down menu in the Property bar, select Pixels.

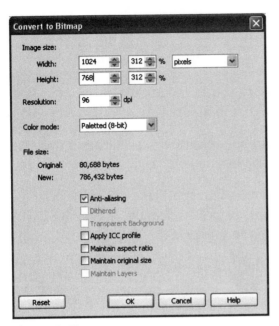

**Figure 8.42**
Ensure that these settings are entered.

2. Select the Rectangle tool from the toolbox on the left side of the screen and click and drag a rectangle onto the page. It doesn't matter how big you make the rectangle since we are going to adjust this momentarily.

3. In the Property bar, change the dimension of your rectangle to 1024 by 768. This will ensure that our Welcome screen will take up the entire screen when we later import it into our game.

4. With the rectangle still selected, click on the color blue in the Colors palette on the right side of the screen. The rectangle should now be blue. Press Shift+F2 to zoom in to the rectangle.

5. Select the Text tool (the letter A button) from the toolbox on the left side of the screen and click anywhere inside the rectangle. A cursor should begin flashing inside the rectangle. Click the Font Size list drop-down menu from the Property bar and select 24. You can also choose any font face you'd like.

6. Click on the color dark blue in the Color palette and right-click on the color white. This will give the text you are about to type a dark blue fill and a white outline.

7. Type the words "Game Paused" and then select the Pick tool (the white arrow at the top of the Tools palette on the left side of the screen.) A series of black boxes called *handles* will appear around the words.

8. Position the mouse pointer over the x in the middle of the word and click and drag it until it is positioned as in Figure 8.43.

9. Click on the Outline tool flyout and select the 1-point outline as seen in Figure 8.44. This will thicken the outline.

10. Click and hold the button *under* the Text tool (letter A) in the toolbox. This will bring open a flyout of different tools. Select the Interactive Distortion tool, the third button in, as seen in Figure 8.45.

11. Click the Twister option from the Property bar. Position the mouse pointer over the middle of "P" in "Paused" and ever so slightly click and drag upward to twist the words, as seen in Figure 8.46.

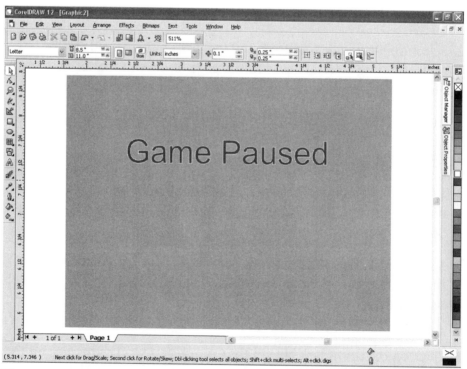

**Figure 8.43**
Position the word "Game Paused" about one third of the way down.

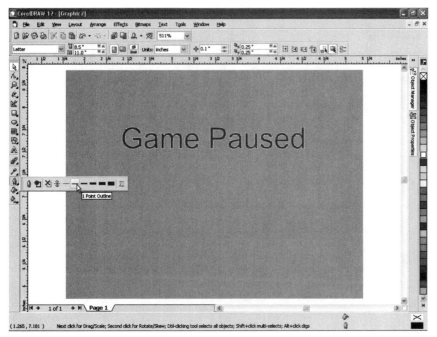

**Figure 8.44**
Change the outline thickness to 1 point as seen here.

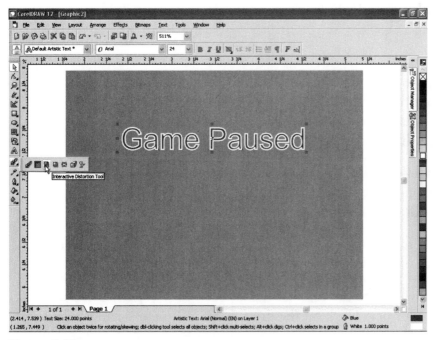

**Figure 8.45**
Select the Interactive Distortion tool as seen here.

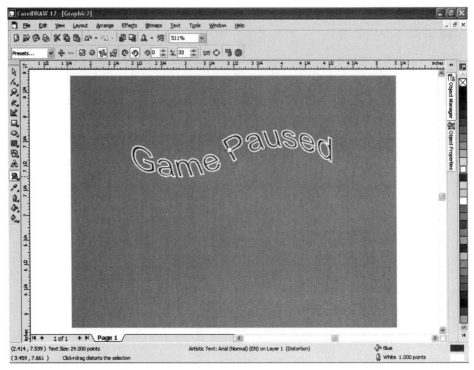

**Figure 8.46**
Twist the text using the Twister option.

12. Click the Text tool, click once in the rectangle, change the font size to 12, and choose your favorite font. Type "Press the Mouse Button to," press Enter, and then type "Resume Play." Press Ctrl+E to center the text, and then select the Pick tool and position the text as seen in Figure 8.47.

13. Click and hold the button *under* the Text tool (letter A) in the toolbox. This will bring open a flyout of different tools. Select the Interactive Drop Shadow tool, the fourth button in.

14. From the Presets drop-down menu, choose Medium Glow, as seen in Figure 8.48. The text will now have a black glow.

15. We will now change the color of the glow. In the Property bar is a Drop Shadow Color box. Click on the drop-down button and choose the color white. The glow color will now change to white as seen in Figure 8.49.

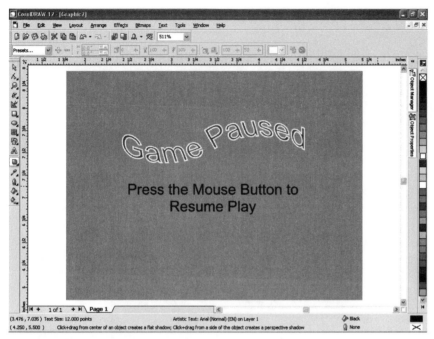

**Figure 8.47**
Position the text you created as seen here.

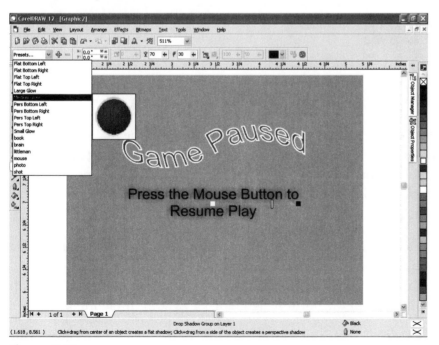

**Figure 8.48**
Select Medium Glow from the Presets drop-down menu.

**Figure 8.49**
Change the glow color to white.

16. Click File > Import to open the Import dialog box so that we can import an image of a 3D duck into our image. Navigate to the CD folder and click on the file called duck.cdr. Click the Import button. The dialog box will close and the mouse pointer will change into two lines connected at a right angle. Click once on the page to import the duck and it will appear. Using the Pick tool, position the duck in the bottom left corner of the rectangle as seen in Figure 8.50.

17. With the duck still selected, press Ctrl+D to make an exact duplicate of the duck. Position the mouse pointer over any of the corner handles of the duplicate duck and click and drag inward slightly to reduce its size. Position the duplicate duck in the bottom right corner as seen in Figure 8.51.

18. Click and hold the button *under* the Text tool (letter A) in the toolbar. This will bring open a flyout of different tools. Select the Interactive Blend tool, the first button in, as seen in Figure 8.52.

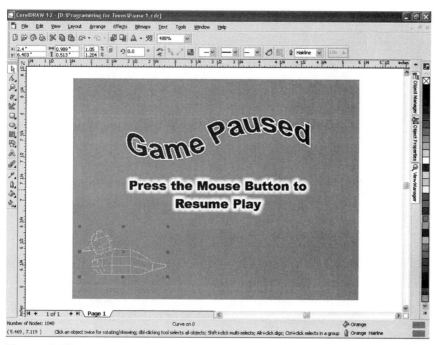

**Figure 8.50**
Position the duck you just imported in the bottom left corner.

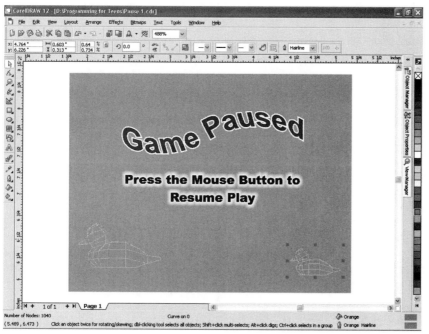

**Figure 8.51**
Position the duplicate duck in the bottom right corner and slightly reduce its size.

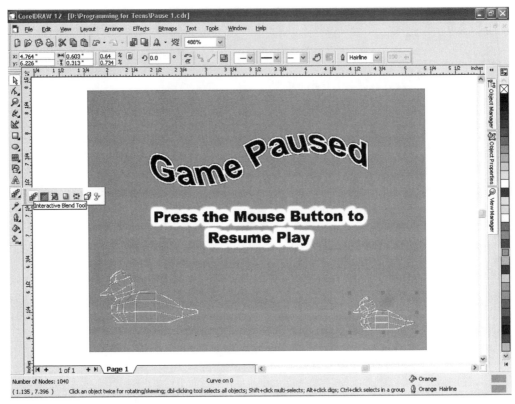

**Figure 8.52**
Select the Interactive Blend tool.

19. Click on the small duck on the right and drag until the mouse pointer is over the larger duck on the left. When you release the mouse button, 20 copies of the ducks will appear between the first and the last as seen in Figure 8.53.

20. In the Property bar, change the number of transition steps from 20 to 4 (see Figure 8.54). There will now be four ducks between the first and the last. Also click the Counterclockwise Blend button to change the color of the ducks within the blend.

21. Click and hold the button right above the Text tool in the toolbox. A flyout of different tools will appear. Click the Star Shapes option.

22. From the Property bar, click the Perfect Shapes button and select the five-sided star as seen in Figure 8.55. Click and drag a star onto the rectangle and then click on the color red in the color palette to fill the star.

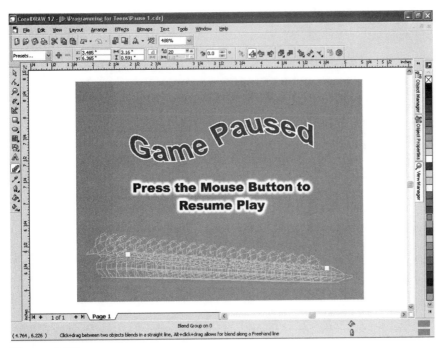

**Figure 8.53**
Using the Interactive Blend tool, blend the two ducks.

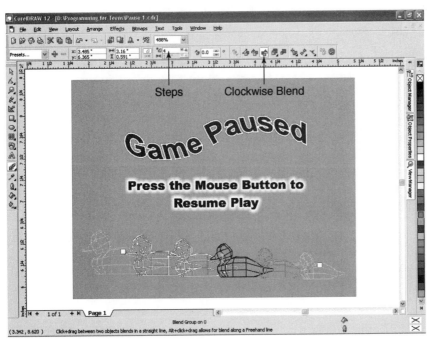

**Figure 8.54**
Change the number of blend steps to 4 and then click the Counterclockwise Blend button.

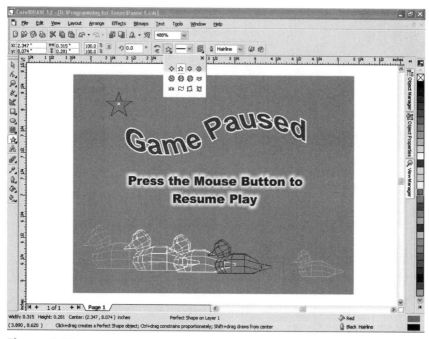

**Figure 8.55**
Create a star similar to the one seen here.

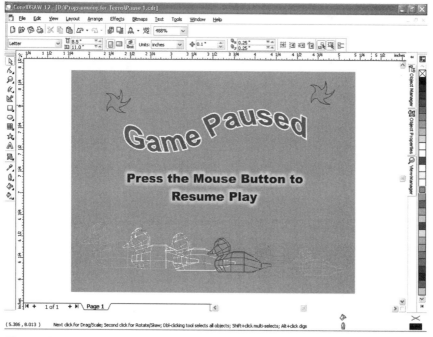

**Figure 8.56**
Twist the stars and then position them as seen here.

23. Using the technique you used in Steps 9 and 10, apply a slight twister to the star. Duplicate the star by pressing Ctrl+D. Position the two stars as seen in Figure 8.56. You are now ready to export your file to a format that Blitz3D can understand. Follow Steps 16 and 17 from the last section, this time saving the file as pause.bmp.

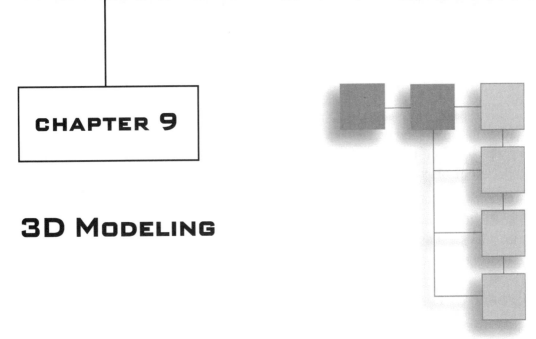

# CHAPTER 9

# 3D MODELING

In Chapter 7, "Shapes and Objects," you learned how to create a few basic objects. Truth be told, to make your game a little more appealing, you'll probably want to create some out of the ordinary, wild, and interesting shapes. To do this, you'll need to use one of the 3D modeling software packages available on the market. In this book you'll be using a program called Autodesk 3ds Max. This package is one of the gaming industry's standards for 3D modeling and has all the tools necessary for creating all types of 3D objects. Keep in mind that 3ds Max is not the only package available; dozens of other programs are used, including one called Maya that is also quite popular. I chose 3ds Max for several reasons. First of all, it allows you to export objects to a file format that can be opened in Blitz3D. In many other 3D programs, you can't save your file formats to something that Blitz3D will understand. However, there are many third-party programs (programs by other companies) that will convert the files for you. Another advantage of 3ds Max is that you can also try it out for free for 30 days. Finally, the skills you learn in 3ds Max can be transferred to other 3D modeling packages.

The purpose of this chapter is to give you an introduction to creating shapes in 3ds Max. As you'll see just by opening the program, there is a lot there! There are thousands of different combinations of filters, effects, and objects that you can apply and create, and it would take several books to cover all the features. My goal is not to teach you everything about 3D modeling and 3ds Max, but to give you a jump-start into learning the program and creating a few objects. If you are interested in pursuing 3D modeling further, I suggest you start by reading *Game Art for Teens* by Les Pardew, published by Thomson Course Technology.

Rather than showing you each tool and describing it, we will take a project-based approach. I'll show you how to create several objects, but then I encourage you to experiment on your own and go out and learn more about this and other 3D modeling packages.

The CD that came with this book has the 30-day trial version of 3ds Max that you must first install before going any further in this chapter. If, for some reason, you don't have the CD, you can download the trial from usa.autodesk.com.

## Creating a Bottle

This project will take you through the steps necessary to create a bottle and then export it to a format that Blitz3D will understand. The primary tool we will be using in this project is the Lathe tool. If you've ever taken woodworking, you know that a lathe is a machine that spins an object (usually a piece of wood or metal). By using a tool like a chisel on the object as it spins you can create interesting shapes or patterns. The Lathe modifier in 3ds Max allows you to create objects that look like they have been through a lathe.

### Creating the Outline

To begin with, we'll create an outline of a bottle in two dimensions, which we will later convert to 3D.

1. Click on the window labeled Left. A yellow outline will appear around the window.

2. Click the Maximize Viewpoint toggle button (see Figure 9.1). This will expand the Left window so that it takes up the entire screen.

3. Click the Create button at the far right side of the screen. It looks like a mouse pointer with a white star behind it.

4. Click the Shapes button. This will bring up a list of different object types from which you can select.

5. Click Line. The box will turn yellow to indicate that it is selected.

6. Position the mouse pointer about ten grid squares up on the middle line and click once to start the line (see Figure 9.2).

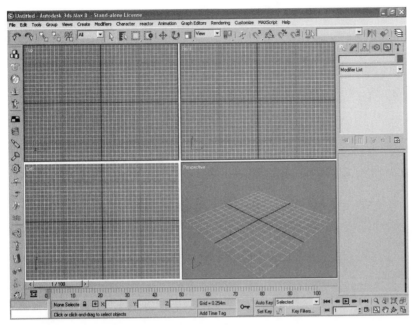

**Figure 9.1**
By clicking the Maximize Viewpoint toggle button, you can maximize the currently selected view.

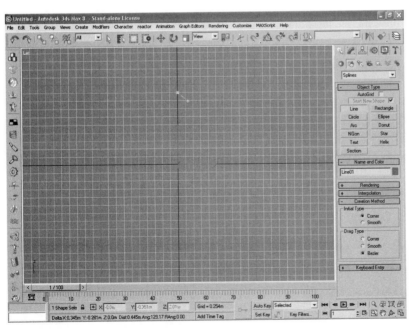

**Figure 9.2**
Click once about 10 squares up from the center to start the line.

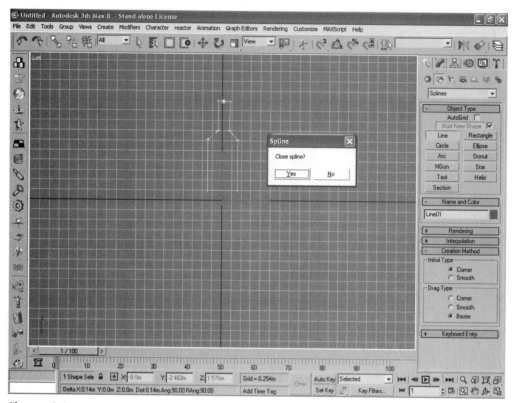

**Figure 9.3**
Click Yes in the dialog box that appears after you've finished creating the bottle shape.

7. Move the mouse pointer to the right on the grid square and click again.

8. Continue moving the mouse and clicking in the designated spots until you've created the outline of a bottle. When you click the point where you started, a dialog box will appear.

9. Click Yes in the Spline dialog box that appears (see Figure 9.3).

## Lathing the Bottle

Now the fun part—we get to convert our two-dimensional bottle into a 3D object. We do this by using the Lathe modifier.

1. Click the Maximize viewport toggle button. This will return you to the main screen where you can see all views.

2. Click the Modify button. The Modify button looks like a blue quarter oval.

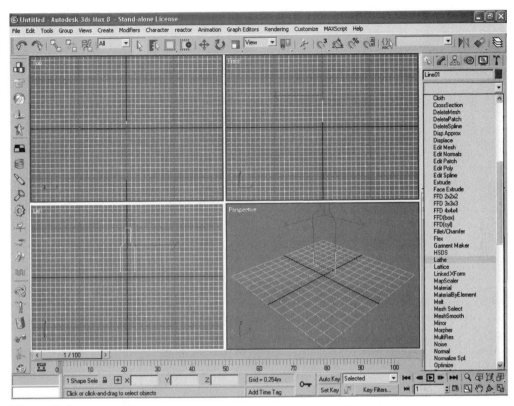

**Figure 9.4**
Choose Lathe from the Modifiers list.

3. Click the Modifiers list drop-down arrow to see a list of different modifiers (see Figure 9.4).

4. Scroll through the list and click Lathe (see Figure 9.5). Ta da! You've just created a 3D bottle!

## Exporting the Bottle

Now we need to convert the bottle into a format that Blitz3D can understand. Before we do that, the bottle needs to be resized since it is currently huge.

1. Click the Select and Uniform Scale button. It looks like a square within a square. A series of yellow shaded triangles will appear around your bottle.

2. Position the mouse pointer over the middle of the yellow triangle in the Perspective window (see Figure 9.6).

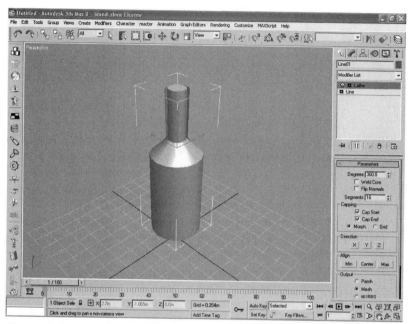

**Figure 9.5**
You should be left with an object that looks like a bottle as seen here.

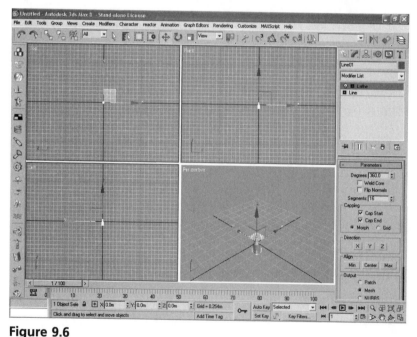

**Figure 9.6**
After you've selected the Select and Uniform Scale button, drag downward on the inner yellow triangle that appears.

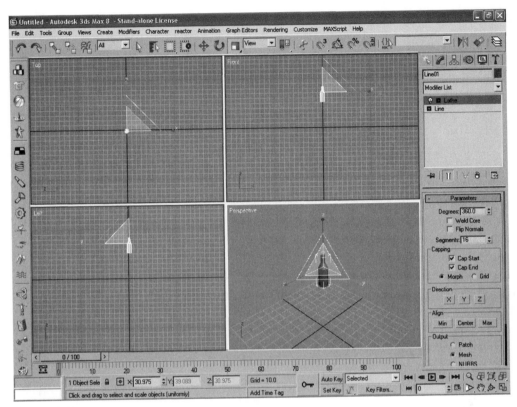

**Figure 9.7**
When you shrunk the bottle, it became off center.

3. Click and drag downward. As you drag, the bottle will shrink (see Figure 9.7). Doing this also moves the bottle off center, so we'll now move it back.

4. Click the Select and Move button from the toolbar. A yellow rectangle and several axes will appear around your object.

5. Position the mouse pointer over the middle of the yellow rectangle in the Perspective window.

6. Click and drag the bottle until it is in the middle of the grid (see Figure 9.8). Alternatively, you can just enter 0 in the X, Y, and Z fields at the bottom of the screen.

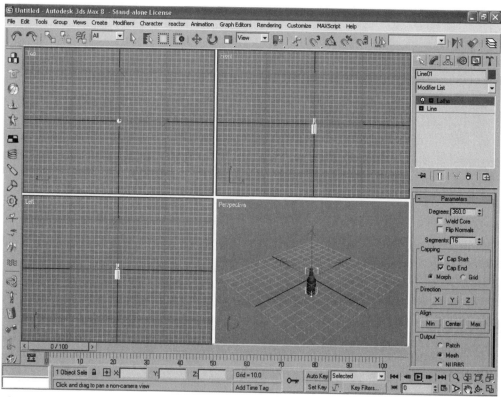

**Figure 9.8**
Position the bottle in the middle of the screen.

### Note

**Object Position**

It's very important that you move your object to the middle of the grid before you export it. When you insert the object into your program, Blitz3D will remember its location from the point where it was exported. If the object was not in the center of the grid, you'll have a hard time positioning it within your game.

7. Click File > Export Selected. The Select File to Export dialog box will appear.

8. Click the Save As Type drop-down arrow and choose 3D Studio (*.3ds). This will save your file to the .3ds format, which can be read by Blitz3D.

9. Navigate to the folder where you would like to save the file, give it a name, and then click Save (see Figure 9.9). You've now successfully saved the file so that it can be used in Blitz3D.

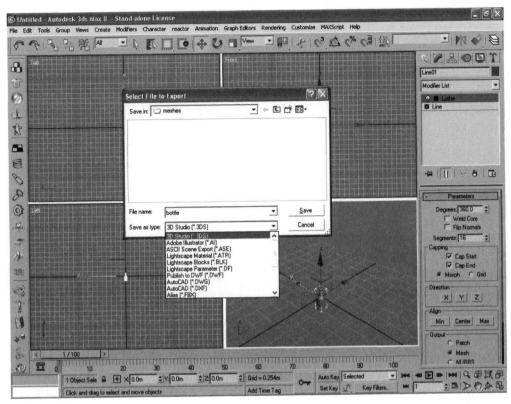

**Figure 9.9**
Save your file to the .3ds format that Blitz3D can easily understand.

# Creating a Missile

In most good 3D video games, it's all about the weapons. How many you have, what kind of weapons, and how much damage they can do. In this section we are going to use 3ds Max to create a weapon that we can use over and over in our games: a missile. The missile itself is made from only a few basic shapes that we will manipulate and combine in order to get our final image. Although there are only a few shapes used in this image, working in the 3ds environment can be a little tricky, especially if you are new to the program, so follow each instruction carefully and make sure not to skip any steps.

## Creating the Missile Body

The main body of our missile is simply a long cylinder to which we will later add different parts. For most of this drawing we will use the Perspective viewport so we can actually see our final image as we draw.

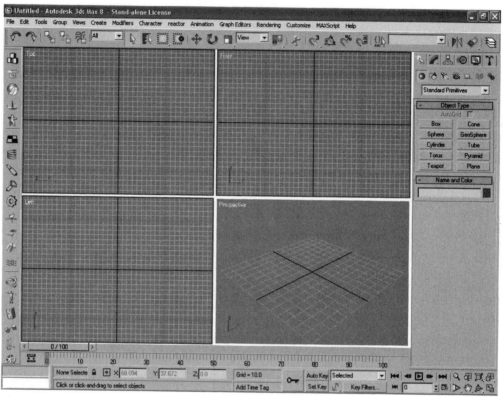

**Figure 9.10**
Maximize the Perspective window.

1. Click anywhere in the Perspective viewport to select this window. A yellow border will appear around the window. Click on the Maximize viewport toggle button to maximize this viewport and hide the others, as seen in Figure 9.10.

2. Click Create > Standard Primitives > Cylinder. You can now set certain parameters for your cylinder.

3. Expand the Parameters panel by clicking on the + beside the word "parameters" if it is not already expanded.

4. Enter 5 for both the Height Segments and Cap Segments as seen in Figure 9.11, This is a very important step; if you don't do this, you'll have trouble later on.

5. Click and drag a circle across the screen It doesn't matter what size it is; we'll adjust this later. When you release the mouse button you'll be able to

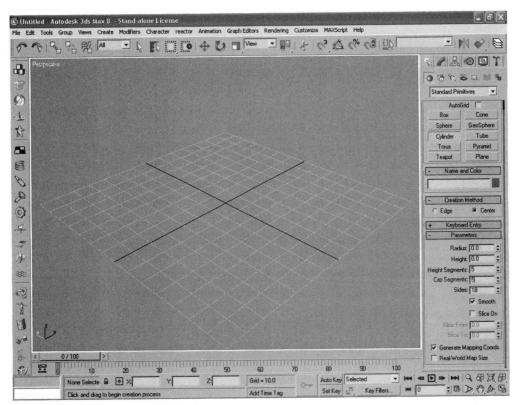

**Figure 9.11**
Make sure that you enter a 5 in the Cap Segments portion of the Parameters panel.

adjust the height of the cylinder. Drag upwards to extend the cylinder, and then release the mouse button. You should now have a cylinder similar to the one in Figure 9.12.

6. Now we are going to taper off the peak of the cylinder to make it look like a missile head. We'll do this by converting the cylinder into an editable poly and stretching out the peak of the cone. Click on the Modify panel if it's not already selected.

7. Right-click on the word "cylinder" and select Editable Poly from the menu that appears (see Figure 9.13).

8. Click on the Select and Move button in the toolbar. In the Selection panel, click on the Vertex button (three red dots). You should now see a series of dots appear all around the cylinder, as in Figure 9.14. We'll manipulate these dots in order to change the shape of the cylinder.

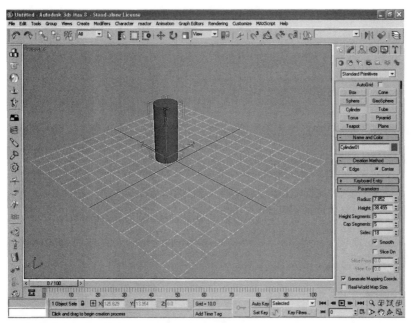

**Figure 9.12**
Try to create a cylinder similar in size to the one seen here.

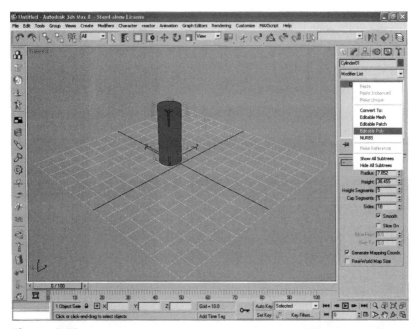

**Figure 9.13**
In the Modify panel, right-click on the word "cylinder" and select Editable Poly.

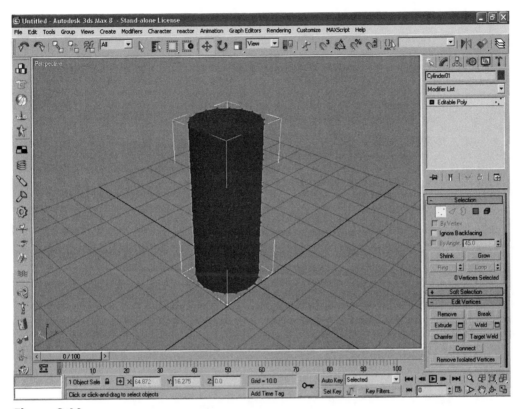

**Figure 9.14**
When you select the Vertex button, a series of dots will appear around the cylinder.

9. Click Vertex in the very middle of the cylinder. It should turn red, and three arrows should appear around it as in Figure 9.15. You may have to zoom in to accomplish this. You can zoom in by selecting the Zoom tool (the magnifying glass at the bottom right of the screen) and clicking and dragging upwards. You can then pan to the top of the cylinder by using the Pan tool (the little white hand).

10. Expand the Soft Selection panel if it is not already expanded. In this panel, click the check box labeled Use Soft Selection. In the Falloff box, enter the number 20. The vertexes on top of the cylinder should be orange and yellow.

11. Position your mouse pointer over the blue z arrow and click and drag upwards until the cylinder has a cone peak as in Figure 9.16.

12. Click on Editable Poly in the Modifier list. It will turn from yellow to gray, and the vertexes will no longer appear on the cylinder.

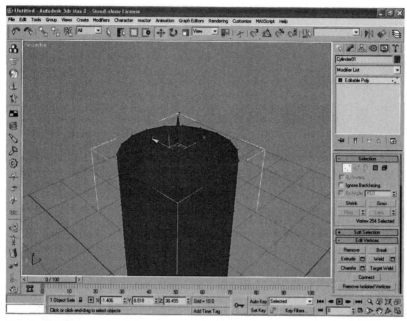

**Figure 9.15**
Select the center vertex and a series of arrows will appear around it.

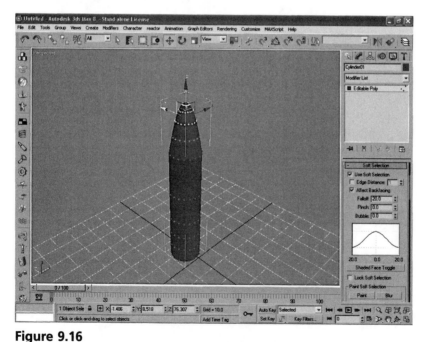

**Figure 9.16**
After you've created a 20-unit soft selection, click and drag upwards on the blue z arrow to create a peak out of the top of the cylinder.

## Creating the Wings

To create the wings that control the flight path of the missile, we will create and modify a box. We'll then duplicate the manipulated cube several times and place it in different locations around the missile.

1. Click Create > Standard Primitives > Box. The Parameter panel should appear on the right side of the screen. Make sure that the Length, Width, and Height boxes all have the number 1 in them.

2. Click and drag a rectangle across the screen. Try to make it about the size of the rectangle in Figure 9.17 in relation to the missile. When you release the mouse button, you'll be able to adjust the height of the box. Drag upwards to extend the box and then release the mouse button. You should now have a box similar to the one in Figure 9.17.

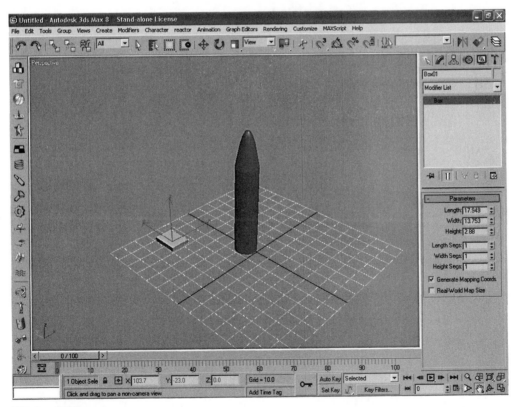

**Figure 9.17**
Create a box similar in size to the one seen here.

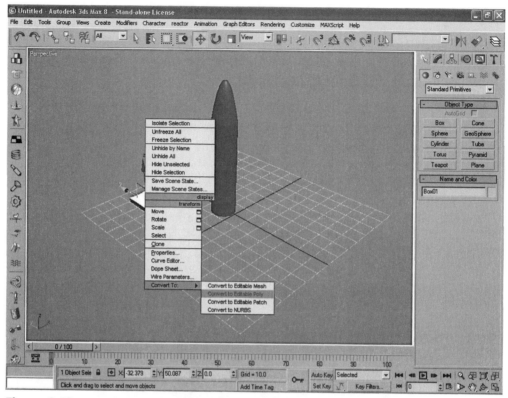

**Figure 9.18**
Convert the image to an Editable Poly by right-clicking on the box.

3. Right-click on the box to bring up a menu of different options. Click on the Convert To option and then select Convert to Poly (see Figure 9.18).

4. In the Selection panel, click on the Vertex button. You should now see a series of dots appear around the edges of the box. Position the mouse pointer to the outside of one of the corners of the box. Click and drag around the corner vertexes. As you drag, a marquee (see Figure 9.19) should appear surrounding both of the vertexes in the corner. When you release the mouse button, the corner vertexes should appear red. Green, blue, and red arrows should appear around the box.

5. Click and drag the green arrow upwards to bring in the corner of the box. Release the mouse button when the shape looks like the one in Figure 9.20.

6. Repeat Steps 4 and 5 for the vertexes on the other side. You should be left with the shape you see in Figure 9.21.

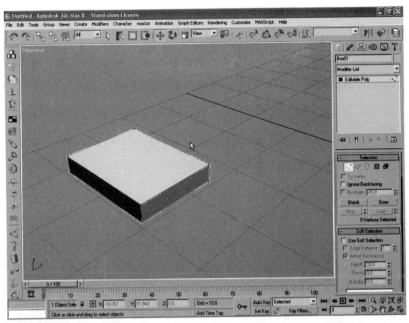

**Figure 9.19**
Drag the marquee around the corner of the box to select both the top and bottom corner nodes.

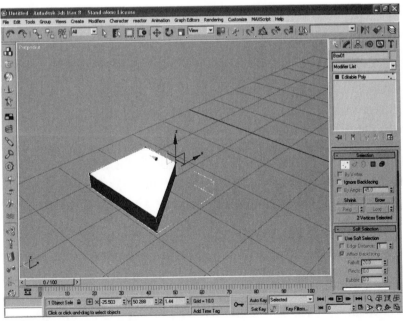

**Figure 9.20**
Drag the green arrow to bring in the two selected vertexes and create the shape you see here.

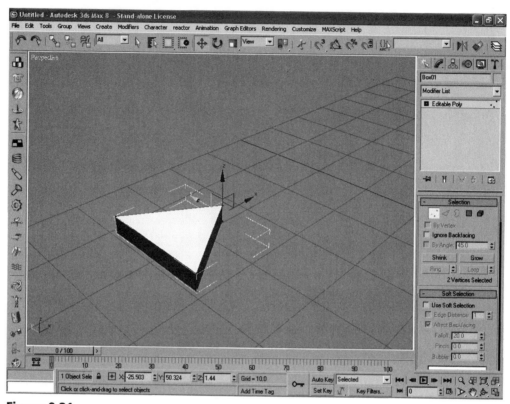

**Figure 9.21**
Using the same technique, bring in the other side.

7. Click on Editable Poly in the Modifiers list. It will turn from yellow to gray, and the vertexes will no longer appear on the box.

8. Click on the Select and Rotate button. At the bottom of the screen, enter **–90** in the Y box to rotate the wing (see Figure 9.22).

9. Click on the Select and Move button in the toolbox. Position the mouse pointer around the point where the three arrows meet. You'll know you're in the right place when a yellow transparent square appears. Click and drag the arrow until it is at the bottom of the cylinder.

10. You may need to resize the wing to make it fit in perspective with the rest of the missile. Click the Select and Uniform Scale button in the toolbar. Position the mouse pointer over the point where the three arrows meet. A yellow triangle will appear when you are in the right place. Click and drag up or down to increase or decrease the size of the wing as necessary. We've slightly enlarged our triangle, as seen in Figure 9.23.

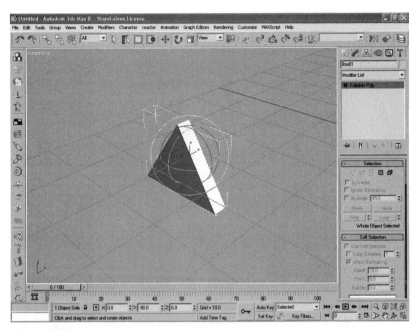

**Figure 9.22**
By entering −90 in the Y field, you can "stand up" your 3D triangle.

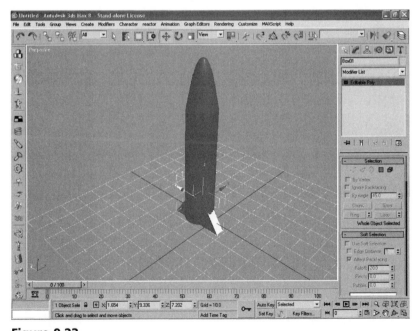

**Figure 9.23**
Using the Select and Uniform Scale button, resize and reposition the triangle so that it looks similar to the one seen here in relation to the cylinder.

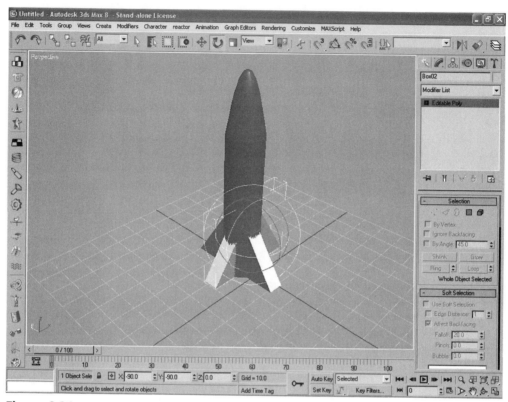

**Figure 9.24**
Flip the cloned triangle by entering −90 in the X and Y boxes at the bottom of the screen.

11. Click Edit > Clone to make an exact copy of the wing. A dialog box will appear from which you should click the Copy option and then click OK.

12. We are now going to rotate this wing. Click the Select and Rotate button from the toolbox. A series of circular arrows will appear around the wing. At the bottom left of the screen, enter −**90** in the X and Y boxes. This will flip the copy of the wing, as seen in Figure 9.24.

13. Click Edit > Clone to make another exact copy of the wing. A dialog box will appear from which you should click the Copy option and then click OK.

14. Click the Select and Move button in the toolbar. Three colored arrows will appear around the wing. Position the mouse pointer over the blue z arrow, and click and drag upwards until the wing is halfway up the missile as seen in Figure 9.25.

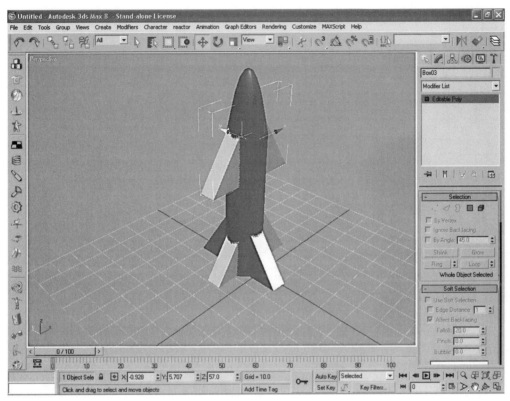

**Figure 9.25**
Move the cloned triangle about halfway up the cylinder.

15. The middle wing is a little too big, so we are going to change its size. Click the Select and Uniform Scale button in the toolbar. Position the mouse pointer over the point where the three arrows meet. A yellow triangle will appear when you are in the right place. Click and drag down to decrease the size of the wing, as seen in Figure 9.26.

## Exporting the Missile

We now need to convert the missile into a format that Blitz3D can understand. In this case, we'll export it to the .3ds format.

1. Resize, rotate, and reposition the missile to be in the middle of the grid as seen in Figure 9.27. Remember from earlier that Blitz3D will remember the size, location, and direction of your objects when they are imported, so take the time to get them into their final position before exporting.

2. Click File > Export. The Select File to Export dialog box will appear.

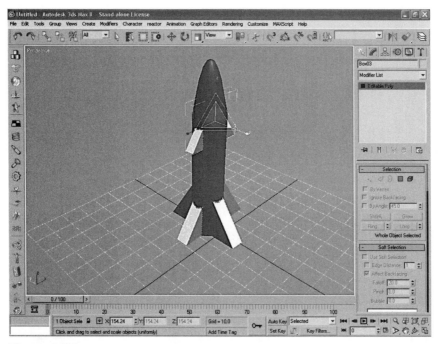

**Figure 9.26**
Resize the middle triangle to the approximate dimension you see here.

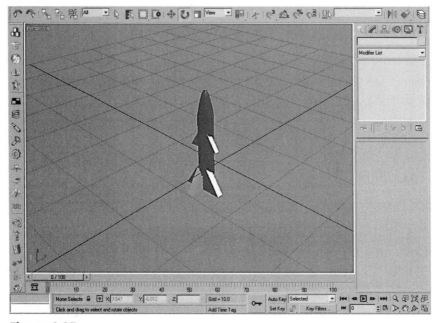

**Figure 9.27**
We've reduced the size of the image to get it ready for export.

3. Click the Save As Type drop-down arrow and choose 3D Studio (*.3ds). This will save your file to the .3ds format, which can be read by Blitz3D.

4. Navigate to the folder where you would like to save the file, give it the name "missile," and then click Save. You've now successfully saved the file so that it can be used in Blitz3D.

### Note

**Getting Models**

If you're not comfortable or if you don't have the patience or time to master 3ds, you have other options for getting 3D models. Dozens of Web sites offer free downloads of 3D models that you can use in your games. Open Google in your Internet browser and search for "Free 3D Models" to see hundreds of different Web sites from which you can download files.

## Importing Models into Blitz3D

Creating your 3D models is only the first step. They won't do you any good if you can't bring them into your programs. That's what we'll take care of now by using the LoadMesh function. Once the object is imported, you can apply a texture to it like any other.

Create the following blank program, save it with any name, and make sure that the files "missile.3ds" and "missile.jpg" are in the same folder where you saved the program.

```
; Missile
; ------------------

Graphics3D 640,480
SetBuffer BackBuffer()

; Create camera
camera=CreateCamera()

; Creating a light
light=CreateLight()

RenderWorld
While Not Keydown(1)
Flip

Wend

End
```

Now it's time to actually load our 3D model using the LoadMesh command. We'll also apply a texture to it, resize it, and position it at the same time by adding the following code (in bold):

```
; Missile
; ---------------------

Graphics3D 640,480
SetBuffer BackBuffer()

; Create camera
camera=CreateCamera()

; Creating a light
light=CreateLight()

missile=LoadMesh ("missile.3ds")
tex=LoadTexture ("missile.jpg")
EntityTexture missile,tex
PositionEntity missile, 1,0,5
ScaleEntity missile, .07,.07,.07
While Not Keydown(1)

RenderWorld
Flip

Wend

End
```

Now run the program, and you should see the missile that you created in 3ds Max, as seen in Figure 9.28.

Let's break down the code to see how we did it:

**missile=LoadMesh ("missile.3ds")** – Using this line of code, we loaded up the 3D model. We gave the model the identifier "missile."

**tex=LoadTexture ("missile.jpg")** – This is the texture to be applied to the missile after it has been imported.

**EntityTexture missile,tex** – This applies the texture to the missile.

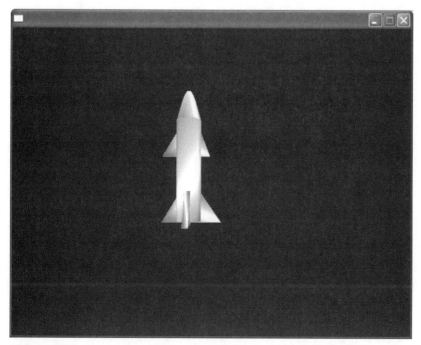

**Figure 9.28**
Import your file into Blitz3D using the LoadMesh command.

**ScaleEntity missile, 0.07,0.07,0.07** – Typically, the models that you import from 3ds Max will be quite large when imported. You can see here that we needed to resize the missile quite a bit in order to see it.

**PositionEntity missile, 1,0,5** – Here we simply positioned the missile in front of the camera so that we could see it.

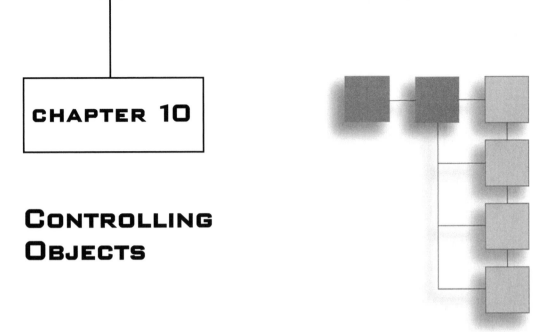

# CHAPTER 10

# CONTROLLING OBJECTS

What's the difference between watching a video and playing a video game? In a video game you have a certain amount of control over your players, the environment, and certain objects, but while watching a video you just watch the events unfold. This chapter is all about control—controlling the objects you create by moving them around the screen. You have a variety of choices when it comes to moving your objects. You can decide along which axis you want them moved, by what increments, and what controls will be used to navigate your objects. This chapter will also explore rotating objects and creating pivots.

## Moving Objects

Now that you know how to create objects, we're going to have some fun and start moving them around the screen. We'll start off by taking a simple object (a sphere with the brick texture map applied to it) and create controls so that by using our keyboard we can move it around the screen. First, open the file called moving a sphere.bb from the CD, or enter the following code. Save the file to a new folder and copy the file called brick.jpg to that folder.

```
; Moving a Sphere
; --------------------

Graphics3D 640,480
SetBuffer BackBuffer()
```

```
; Create camera
camera=CreateCamera()

; Creating a light
light=CreateLight()

; This is the code creating the sphere
sphere=CreateSphere(16)
PositionEntity sphere,0,0,5

; Creating the texture
tex=LoadTexture( "brick.jpg" )
ScaleTexture tex, .5,.5
EntityTexture sphere,tex

; This following code moves our sphere:
While Not KeyDown( 1 )

If KeyDown(30) TranslateEntity sphere,0,-.3,0
If KeyDown(44) TranslateEntity sphere,0,.3,0
If KeyDown(203) TranslateEntity sphere, -0.3,0,0
If KeyDown(205) TranslateEntity sphere, 0.3,0,0
If KeyDown(200) TranslateEntity sphere,0,0,0.3
If KeyDown(208) TranslateEntity sphere,0,0,-0.3

RenderWorld
Flip

Wend

End
```

Run the program now, and what you see on the screen should look similar to Figure 10.1.

Now take a closer look at the part of the program that actually controls the movement:

```
; This following code moves our sphere:
While Not KeyDown( 1 )

If KeyDown(30) TranslateEntity sphere,0,-.3,0
If KeyDown(44) TranslateEntity sphere,0,.3,0
If KeyDown(203) TranslateEntity sphere, -0.3,0,0
```

**Figure 10.1**
When you run the program you can now use the arrow keys and the A and Z keys to move this sphere around the screen.

```
If KeyDown(205) TranslateEntity sphere, 0.3,0,0
If KeyDown(200) TranslateEntity sphere,0,0,0.3
If KeyDown(208) TranslateEntity sphere,0,0,-0.3
```

Let's examine this section of code piece by piece to see what is going on.

**While Not KeyDown( 1 )** – This basically means: as long as the Esc key (designated as key number 1) is not pressed down, do the following.

**If KeyDown(30) TranslateEntity sphere,0,-.3,0** – This line is saying that when the letter Z is pressed on the keyboard (designated by the number 30), move the object down the y axis by 0.3 units. The command that tells Blitz3D to actually move the object is TranslateEntity. The rest of the lines basically say the same thing, but using different keys and designating different movements along the x, y, and z axes.

## Rotating Objects

Rotating your objects is similar to moving them in that you need to define which keys you want to use to rotate your objects and on which axis you'd like to rotate them. The axis for the rotation will determine how your objects will spin. Rotation can occur along the x axis, the y axis, or the z axis (see Figures 10.2, 10.3, and 10.4).

# Pitch

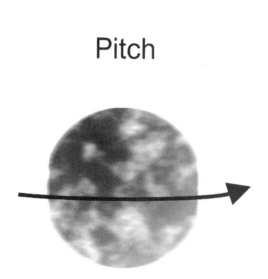

**Figure 10.2**
Rotation along the x axis.

# Yaw

**Figure 10.3**
Rotation along the y axis.

# Roll

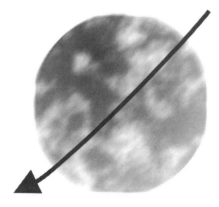

**Figure 10.4**
Rotation along the z axis.

The code we are about to use works a little differently. You have to enter what are called if. . .then statements. I'll talk about these types of statements in Chapter 16, "Programming Fundamentals," but basically what these statements say is that if something happens (like a keyboard key is pressed), then do something (like rotate an object.)

Using the same program as above, let's add the following code above the RenderWorld line to add rotation controls:

```
; Change rotation values depending on the key pressed
If KeyDown( 49 )= True Then pitch#=pitch#-1
If KeyDown( 50 )=True Then pitch#=pitch#+1
If KeyDown( 51 )=True Then yaw#=yaw#-1
If KeyDown( 52 )=True Then yaw#=yaw#+1
If KeyDown( 45 )=True Then roll#=roll#-1
If KeyDown( 46 )=True Then roll#=roll#+1

; Rotate sphere using rotation values
RotateEntity sphere,pitch#,yaw#,roll#
```

Now run the program and you'll see that, by pressing the keys M, N, Comma, Period, X, and C, you can rotate your object along the different axes. Here's a breakdown of the code that we just entered:

If KeyDown (49)= True means that when the letter "n" is pressed on the keyboard, then do the following. Pitch#=pitch#+1 basically says that the pitch of the object should change positively (in other words, rotate clockwise) on the x axis by one unit. The rest of this section of code is the same but changes the values positively and negatively for pitch, yaw, and roll.

The next section tells Blitz3D what to rotate:

```
RotateEntity sphere,pitch#,yaw#,roll#
```

Here we are telling Blitz3D to rotate the object called sphere by the amount we defined in the previous section of code.

## Rotating Objects on Their Own

In the previous section, you learned how you could rotate an object via keyboard commands. What if you wanted to just have an object rotate on its own? To do this, you just have to slightly modify the code you used in the last section. Here is the code for a program that contains a single cube that rotates on its own:

```
; Rotate Cube
; ──────────────────

Graphics3D 640,480
SetBuffer BackBuffer()
camera=CreateCamera()
light=CreateLight()
cube=CreateCube()
PositionEntity cube,0,0,5

; Creating the rotation
While Not KeyDown( 1 )
pitch#=pitch#-3
RotateEntity cube,pitch#,yaw#,roll#

RenderWorld
Flip

Wend

End
```

Basically, the program we just created is a simple cube with one element of code that makes it rotate:

```
While Not KeyDown( 1 )
pitch#=pitch#-1
RotateEntity cube,pitch#,yaw#,roll#
```

The While Not KeyDown(1), as usual, says that as long as the Esc key isn't pressed, do the following. The code pitch#=pitch#-1 controls the speed, direction, and angle of rotation for your cube. The value of the pitch will always be changing because we entered this code within the game loop. This way, it will continue to rotate on its own. Because we didn't define a starting speed, the pitch will start at 0. After the first loop of the game, the pitch will be −1, after the second loop, it will be −2, and so on. To slow down the rotation, you would enter an integer between 0 and 1, and to speed it up, enter a number greater than 1. For example, if you used pitch#=pitch#=+0.2, the rotation would be extremely slow, while using pitch#=pitch#=+5 would create an extremely fast rotation. If the number you enter is negative, the rotation will be toward you, and a positive number means the rotation will be away from you.

## Note

### Don't Forget the + and −

You have to enter a + or − sign before the speed of rotation number or the code won't work. For example, pitch#=pitch#1 wouldn't work because there is no plus or minus sign in front of the 1. It would have to be either pitch#=pitch#-1 or pitch#=pitch#+1 because we are decreasing or increasing it by one unit.

In this example, we rotated the cube along the x axis. If we wanted to rotate the cube on the y or z axis, we would have entered yaw#=yaw#-1 or roll#=roll#-1 instead of the pitch#=pitch#-1.

## Note

### Rotate Around Multiple Axes

You are not restricted to rotating around one axis at a time. You can have your objects rotate around the x, y, and z axes individually or with any combination of the three. For example, if I wanted the cube in the last section to rotate around all three axes, I would have entered the following code in the run section:

```
While Not KeyDown( 1 )
pitch#=pitch#-1
yaw#=yaw#=+1
roll#=roll#-1
RotateEntity cube,pitch#,yaw#,roll#
```

## Note

### Now You Try

Experiment with different rotation speeds, angles, and directions until you're comfortable with it. It's always a good idea to apply a texture to your object before you start rotating it so that you can really see the effects of the rotation.

# Orbiting (a.k.a. Pivoting)

What's the difference between rotating and pivoting? Let's look to the galaxies for our answer. Think of how the earth orbits around the sun. While the earth is rotating, it is also orbiting (in the case of Blitz3D we'll call this pivoting) around the sun. The sun is set as the pivot point, and the earth orbits around it. Let's

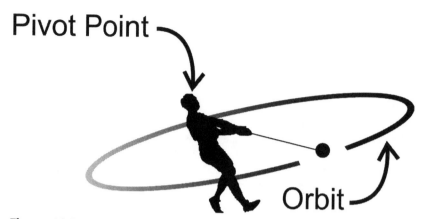

**Figure 10.5**
The athlete is the pivot and the ball twirling around him is the orbit.

recreate this scene and combine both rotating and orbiting using Blitz3D. To make our scene look a little more realistic, we'll add a texture map to both the sun and the earth. On the CD you'll find the two textures that were used, sunskin.jpg and earthskin.jpg, but rather than using those, why not put the skills you learned in the last chapter to use and create your own textures?

The key to this program is the item called the *pivot*. Think of the pivot item as an invisible anchor that sets the point of rotation. Have you ever seen someone do the discus or hammer throw at the Olympics? The athlete stays in one spot and spins as the hammer or discus "orbits" around him until he lets go. If we were to compare this to Blitz3D code, the athlete, who acts as the center of the rotation, would be the "pivot." Take a look at Figure 10.5, which provides an illustrated example of a pivot.

Before we get to the code of this little program, I should warn you: You might get a little confused. There are a lot of concepts in this program, and I combine a few different elements, so if you are a little confused, don't worry; I'll break it down nicely afterward and give you plenty of help.

Here's the code we use to create the program:

```
; Orbiting
; ------------------

Graphics3D 640,480
SetBuffer BackBuffer()
camera=CreateCamera()
PositionEntity camera,0,0,-10
```

```
light=CreateLight()
RotateEntity light,90,0,0

; Creating the Sun
sun=CreateSphere (16)
ScaleEntity sun, 2,2,2
PositionEntity sun, 2,3,1
tex=LoadTexture( "sunskin.jpg" )
EntityTexture sun,tex

; Create a pivot.
pivot=CreatePivot()
PositionEntity pivot,2,3,1

; Create the planet earth. Make the pivot the parent of the earth.
earth=CreateSphere(16,pivot)
tex1=LoadTexture( "earthskin.jpg" )
EntityTexture earth, tex1

; Position planet so that it is offset from the sun
PositionEntity earth,5,0,0
While Not KeyDown(1)

; Turn pivot, making planet orbit around the pivot point.
TurnEntity pivot,0,1,0

; Rotate the earth.
pitch#=pitch#+1
RotateEntity earth,pitch#,yaw#,roll#

RenderWorld
Flip

Wend

End
```

Now take a close look, and I'll explain the important parts of the above code:

```
; Creating the Sun
sun=CreateSphere (16)
ScaleEntity sun, 2,2,2
PositionEntity sun, 2,3,1
tex=LoadTexture( "sunskin.jpg" )
EntityTexture sun,tex
```

There's nothing in this code that you haven't seen already. We simply created the sun by making a sphere and then applied the texture sunskin.jpg to it. The line you should take note of is the position of the sun at 2,3,1. We offset the sun on purpose, to illustrate that the pivot we create later in the program will have to be located in the same spot to make it look as if the sun is the center of the orbit.

```
; Create a pivot.
pivot=CreatePivot()
PositionEntity pivot,2,3,1
```

With this code, we name our pivot—in this case we were very original and called it pivot. This is followed by the actual command to create the pivot: CreatePivot(). In the next line we position the pivot. We put it in the exact same location (2,3,1) that we put the sun so that it will appear as if the planet we create is orbiting the sun. The truth is that the planet will actually be orbiting the pivot point. If you deleted the sun, the planet we created would still orbit the same location.

```
; Create the planet earth. Make the pivot the parent of the earth.
earth=CreateSphere(16,pivot)
tex1=LoadTexture( "earthskin.jpg" )
EntityTexture earth, tex1
```

The creation of the earth is fairly straightforward, but you are seeing a piece of code that you have not seen before. In the first line, notice the word pivot after the 16:

```
earth=CreateSphere(16,pivot)
```

By doing this we are making the pivot the *parent* of the earth. A parent is a piece of code that will tie the two objects together. Anything that we do to the parent—in this case, the pivot—will also affect the child, which in this case, is the earth. Parents are awesome—you may not think so in real life, but in Blitz3D, they can save you a lot of time and effort. I'll talk a little more about parents later in the book and you'll see how they can benefit you.

```
; Position planet so that it is offset from the sun
PositionEntity earth,5,0,0
```

Here we are just placing the earth on the screen, a little away from the sun. Next we enter the code that actually makes the program run:

```
While Not KeyDown(1)
```

```
; Turn pivot, making planet orbit around the pivot point.
TurnEntity pivot,0,1,0

; Rotate the earth.
pitch#=pitch#+1
RotateEntity earth,pitch#,yaw#,roll#

RenderWorld
Flip

Wend

End
```

We've discussed While Not KeyDown(1) already in this book. Again, it says that as long as the Esc key is not pressed, do the following. TurnEntity pivot 0,1,0 tells the program to continually orbit the pivot (this also includes the earth because we made the pivot the parent of the earth) around the y axis. If you wanted the orbit to go around the x axis, you would've entered 1,0,0 and if you wanted it to orbit around the z axis you would have used 0,0,1. You could have also changed the direction of the pivot by making the pivot value a negative number.

The earth doesn't just orbit around the sun; it also rotates as it is orbiting. To set the rotation, we used the same code you learned in the last section, but we just took out the If statement. Without the If statement, the earth spins continually.

**N o t e**

**Now You Try**

Create a replica of an atom with protons orbiting around the nucleus, as seen in Figure 10.6. Give the protons a different color. Once you've tried this, compare it to the actual code used. Keep in mind that we used the texture sunskin.jpg for the nucleus and orbit.jpg for the orbits. You can use those or create your own.

```
; Atom
; ─────────────────

Graphics3D 640, 480
SetBuffer BackBuffer()
camera=CreateCamera()
PositionEntity camera,0,0,-10
light=CreateLight()
RotateEntity light,90,0,0
```

**Figure 10.6**
Your final program should look something like this.

```
; Creating the nucleus.
nucleus=CreateSphere (16)
PositionEntity nucleus, 0,0,1
tex=LoadTexture( "sunskin.jpg" )
EntityTexture nucleus,tex

; Create a pivot for each orbit.
pivot=CreatePivot()
PositionEntity pivot,0,0,1
pivot2=CreatePivot()
PositionEntity pivot2, 0,0,1
pivot3=CreatePivot()
PositionEntity pivot3, 0,0,1

; Creating each orbit.
orbit=CreateSphere(16,pivot)
tex1=LoadTexture( "orbit.jpg" )

EntityTexture orbit, tex1
ScaleEntity orbit, 0.3,0.3,0.3
PositionEntity orbit,4,0,0
```

```
orbit2=CreateSphere(16,pivot2)
tex2=LoadTexture("orbit.jpg")
EntityTexture orbit2, tex1
ScaleEntity orbit2, 0.3,0.3,0.3
PositionEntity orbit2, 0,0,4

orbit3=CreateSphere(16, pivot3)
tex2=LoadTexture("orbit.jpg")
EntityTexture orbit3, tex1
ScaleEntity orbit3, 0.3,0.3,0.3
PositionEntity orbit3, 4,0,0

While Not KeyDown(1)

; Turn pivots, making atome orbit around the nucleus.
TurnEntity pivot,0,3,0
TurnEntity pivot2, 3,0,0
TurnEntity pivot3, 0,0,3

; Spinning the nucleus.
pitch#=pitch#+3 yaw#=yaw#+3 roll#=roll#+3
RotateEntity nucleus,pitch#,yaw#,roll#

RenderWorld
Flip

Wend

End
```

Run the program now, and what you see on your screen should look similar to Figure 10.6.

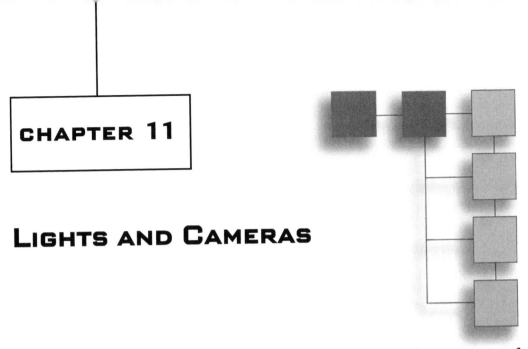

# CHAPTER 11

# LIGHTS AND CAMERAS

As you've seen from the previous chapters, two of the essential components of your Blitz3D programs are lights and cameras. In fact, in every program we've created so far, we've created at least one light and one camera by entering the following code:

```
camera=CreateCamera()
light=CreateLight()
```

Blitz 3D allows you to do so much with both lights and cameras. You can change the type of lights, their strength and position; you can tie the camera to objects, add multiple cameras, and rotate and move the camera, among other things. In this chapter, you'll be using some of the techniques you learned in the previous chapters on creating and moving objects, so just be sure you have a good grasp on those chapters before you move on.

## Working with Cameras

The camera acts as the eyes for the player of the game. Where you place the camera or cameras will directly determine the action that the player sees. Blitz3D makes it easy to manipulate the location, angle, and zoom level of our cameras. Most of the camera settings we will apply in this chapter will be performed on a simple cylinder. Before continuing, either open the program called "cylinder_camera" or enter the following code:

```
; Lighting and Cameras
; ————————————

Graphics3D 640,480
SetBuffer BackBuffer()

; Create camera
camera=CreateCamera()

; Creating a light
light=CreateLight()

; This is the code for creating the cylinder
cylinder=CreateCylinder()
PositionEntity cylinder,0,0,5
EntityColor cylinder, 0,26,125

; This following code makes our program run
While Not KeyDown(1)

RenderWorld
Flip

Wend

End
```

When you run this program, you should see a cylinder (see Figure 11.1).

## Creating and Positioning a Camera

You've actually created a camera several times already by using the CreateCamera() command. Just like with creating shapes you need to give your camera a name. Typically when coding a camera you should give the camera a generic name like camera or camera1 to make things easier. For example, if we wanted to create and name a camera called camera1, we would enter the following code:

```
camera1=CreateCamera()
```

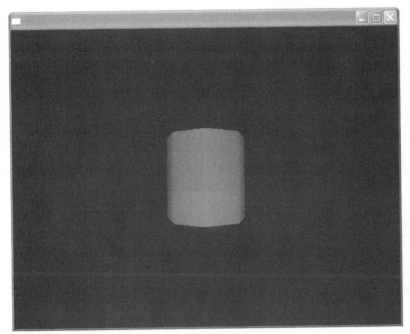

**Figure 11.1**
You can "see" the cylinder because we created the camera using the `CreateCamera()` command.

The next step is to position your camera. Cameras can be positioned like most other objects using the `PositionEntity` command. You simply need to specify where on the screen you would like the camera to be.

For this example, remove the existing code under `; Create Camera` in the cone_camera.bb program and replace it with this:

```
; Create camera
camera1=CreateCamera()
PositionEntity camera1, 1,-3,-1
```

Now when you run the program, it may seem as though the cylinder has moved, but it hasn't (see Figure 11.2). What has actually happened is that you've moved the location of your camera, and the cylinder is actually in the same spot it always was.

## Rotating a Camera

Just like other objects, you can rotate a camera to change the angle of your view. By using the `RotateEntity` command, you can specify the axis on which you want the rotation to occur. To test this out, we're going to place a camera on top of our

**Figure 11.2**
The cylinder hasn't really moved, just the location of the camera.

shape and rotate it so that it is facing downward. Replace the code under ; Create camera with the following:

```
; Create camera
camera1=CreateCamera()
PositionEntity camera1,0,5,5
RotateEntity camera1,90,0,0
```

After you run the program, you'll notice that you now have a view of the cylinder, as if you were on the ceiling looking down (see Figure 11.3).

Let's take a closer look at the code to see how we created this.

PositionEnitity camera1, 0,5,5 moved the camera along the y and z axes so that the camera was directly over the cylinder (remember the cylinder is at position 0,0,5). If you ran the program at this point, you wouldn't see anything because the camera is pointing straight ahead instead of downward at the cylinder. To correct this, we rotate the camera by entering this code:

```
RotateEntity camera1,90,0,0
```

The 90,0,0 rotated the camera 90 degrees along the x axis.

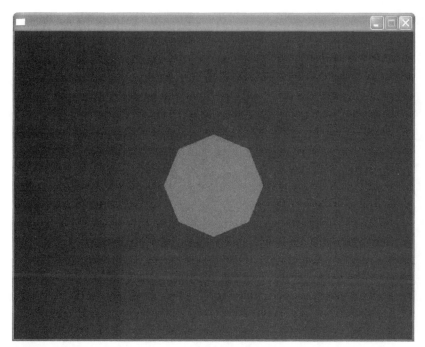

**Figure 11.3**
A view of the cylinder from the top.

## Using Two Cameras

Normally when you watch television you sit back, relax, and let the show entertain you. While you're sitting there relaxing, there's a lot of hard work going on, especially in the TV director's control room. Whether it's a sporting event, a sitcom, the local news, or a soap opera, there are typically three or more cameras that are continuously being switched by the director.

In the following example, we will create two cameras around our cylinder and then switch to each one, using the HideEntity and ShowEntity commands. While the program is running we'll switch each camera as if we were big-time television directors!

The first thing we'll do is create two cameras:

```
; Create camera
camera1=CreateCamera()
PositionEntity camera1,0,5,5
RotateEntity camera1,90,0,0
camera2=CreateCamera()
PositionEntity camera2,0,0,0
```

**Figure 11.4**
The view would be from camera2 because it's the last one created.

If we ran the program right now, the view would be from camera2 because it was the last one created, as seen in Figure 11.4.

Now we have to create the code to control the program while it is running.

```
; The following code makes our program run
While Not KeyDown( 1 )
RenderWorld

If KeyHit(2) HideEntity camera2
If KeyHit(3) ShowEntity camera2
Flip

Wend

End
```

The following two lines of code are the ones that control the camera:

```
If KeyHit(2) HideEntity camera2
If KeyHit(3) ShowEntity camera2
```

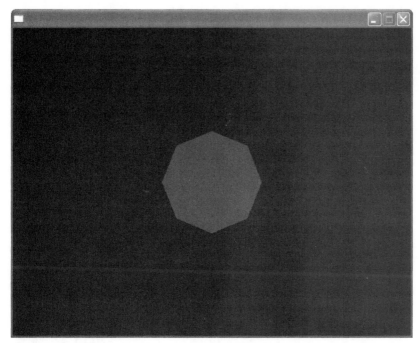

**Figure 11.5**
When you press the numbers 1 and 2, the second camera is activated or deactivated.

The first line, If KeyHit(2) HideEntity camera2, says that if you press the number 1 on the keyboard (designated by KeyHit(2)), then the camera will be hidden. When the camera is hidden with the HideEntity command, the view will default to the other camera, camera1. To show camera2 again, we use the ShowEntity command by using the number 2 on the keyboard, as seen in Figure 11.5.

## Switching Cameras Virtually

While switching cameras is one way of changing the viewpoint, another easier to apply method is to simply move or reposition a camera when an event occurs. In the following example, we'll change the position of the camera when certain keys are hit. Enter the following code to create a simple cylinder:

```
; Lighting and Cameras
; --------------------

Graphics3D 640,480
SetBuffer BackBuffer()
```

```
;Create camera
camera=CreateCamera()

; Creating a light
light=CreateLight()

; This is the code for creating the cylinder
cylinder=CreateCylinder()
PositionEntity cylinder,0,0,5

; This following code makes our program run
While Not KeyDown( 1 )

RenderWorld
Flip

Wend

End
```

If you run the program now, you should just see a cylinder as in Figure 11.6.

**Figure 11.6**
The code you created should produce this cylinder.

Now enter the following code in bold that will move the camera when certain keys are pressed:

```
; This following code makes our program run
While Not KeyDown( 1 )
RenderWorld

If KeyDown(2) PositionEntity camera, 0,-1,0
If KeyDown(3) PositionEntity camera, 0,1,0
If KeyDown(4) PositionEntity camera, 1,0,0
If KeyDown(5) PositionEntity camera, 0,0,0
Flip

Wend

End
```

When you run the program, pressing the keys 1 through 4 will change the viewpoint (see Figures 11.7–11.10).

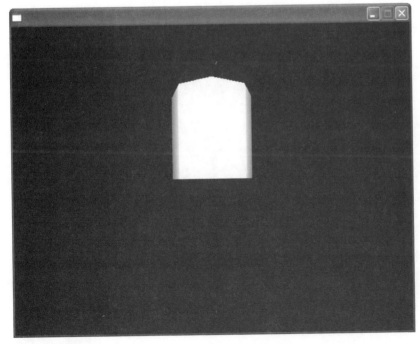

**Figure 11.7**
View 1.

**Figure 11.8**
View 2.

**Figure 11.9**
View 3.

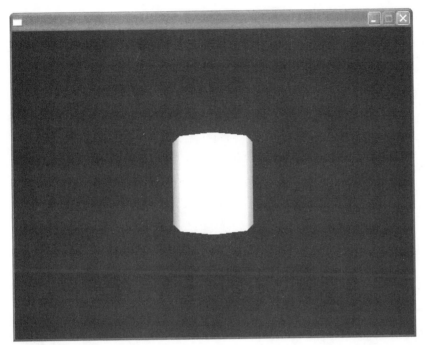

**Figure 11.10**
View 4.

## Splitting Views

Another option you have when working with cameras is to use a split screen. When you have more than one camera, you can split the screen in two so that you can see the view from both cameras at once. To split the screen, you use the `CameraViewport` command. Start by entering the following code to create a program with two cameras:

```
; Lighting and Cameras
; --------------------

Graphics3D 640,480
SetBuffer BackBuffer()

; Create camera
camera1=CreateCamera()
PositionEntity camera1,0,5,5
RotateEntity camera1,90,0,0
camera2=CreateCamera()
PositionEntity camera2,0,0,0
```

```
; Creating a light
light=CreateLight()

; This is the code for creating the cylinder
cylinder=CreateCylinder()
PositionEntity cylinder,0,0,5


; This following code makes our program run
While Not KeyDown( 1 )

RenderWorld
Flip

Wend

End
```

Now we'll create the split screens using the `CameraViewport` command by entering the following code in bold:

```
; This is the code for creating the cylinder
cylinder=CreateCylinder()

PositionEntity cylinder,0,0,5


; Using CameraViewport
CameraViewport camera1,0,0,GraphicsWidth(),GraphicsHeight()/2
CameraViewport camera2,0,GraphicsHeight()/2,
  GraphicsWidth(),GraphicsHeight()/2
```

Now when you run the program, you'll see the screen split in two. The top section is a view of the cylinder from the top, and the bottom section is a face-on view, as seen in Figure 11.11.

Okay, this code is made up of a bunch of different numbers and text, so let's break it down step by step.

`CameraViewport camera1` – This creates the split screen portion for `camera1`.

`,0,0` – This tells you the x and y coordinates (starting from the top left corner of the screen) for this section of the split screen.

`GraphicsWidth()` – This tells you how wide this section of the split screen should be in relation to the entire screen. Let's say you wanted the width of this split to be half the size of the screen. You would enter `GraphicsWidth()/2` in this section of

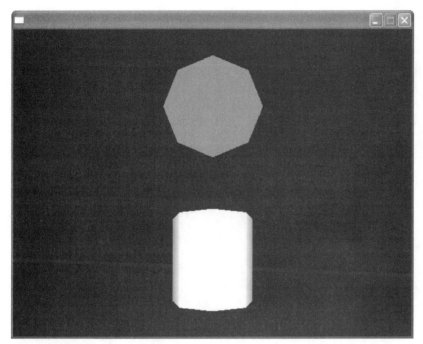

**Figure 11.11**
The view is now split.

code. The "divided by 2" code "/2" tells Blitz3D to divide the width of the screen in two.

`GraphicsHeight()/2` – This indicates what the height of the split screen should be. In this case the "/2" divides the screen in two horizontally so we have one split screen at the top of the screen and the one at the bottom.

**Note**

**Now You Try**

In the last example, the screen was split horizontally through the middle. Try on your own to create a split vertically down the middle of the screen with a cone. Once you are done, compare your code with the actual code used to create Figure 11.12.

```
; Vertical Splitscreen
; ——————————————

Graphics3D 640,480
SetBuffer BackBuffer()
```

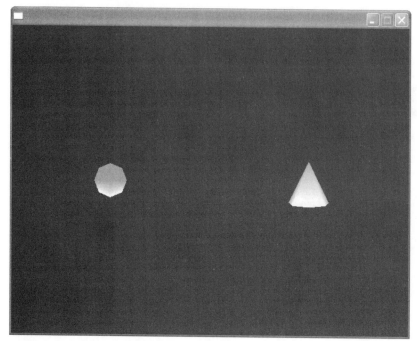

**Figure 11.12**
Try to recreate this vertical split.

```
; Create camera
camera1=CreateCamera()
PositionEntity camera1,0,5,5
RotateEntity camera1,90,0,0
camera2=CreateCamera()
PositionEntity camera2,0,0,0

; Creating a light
light=CreateLight()

; This is the code for creating the cone
cone=CreateCone()
PositionEntity cone,0,0,5
EntityColor cone, 0,26,125

; Using CameraViewport
CameraViewport camera1,0,0,GraphicsWidth()/2,GraphicsHeight()
CameraViewport camera2,GraphicsWidth()/2,0,GraphicsWidth()/2,
  GraphicsHeight()
```

```
; This following code makes our program run
While Not KeyDown( 1 )

RenderWorld
Flip

Wend

End
```

## Zooming

Rather than having to move a camera to get closer or further away from an object, you can take advantage of Blitz3D's camera zooming capabilities. In this exercise, we'll create a sphere that seems far off in the distance and then give the player the ability to zoom in and out using the CameraZoom command.

Start by creating a program that contains only a simple sphere as designated by the following code. Alternatively, if you want to save a little time typing, open the program called simplesphere.bb.

```
; Simple Sphere
; ———————————————

Graphics3D 640,480
SetBuffer BackBuffer()

; Create camera
camera=CreateCamera()

; Creating a light
light=CreateLight()

; This is the code for creating the sphere
sphere=CreateSphere()
PositionEntity sphere,0,0,9
ScaleEntity sphere,.2,.2,.2
EntityColor sphere, 0,26,125

; This following code makes our program run
While Not KeyDown( 1 )

RenderWorld
```

```
Flip

Wend

End
```

The program should look like Figure 11.13 when it is run.

Now that we have a camera and a simple sphere far off in the distance, we can add some parameters that will allow us to zoom. The first thing that we do is set the starting zoom values. The zoom value, or zoom level, is represented in the code by zoom#. You can set the zoom value to any number you want. The number 1 represents no zoom at all, any number that is greater than 1 will zoom you in, and any number less than 1 will zoom you out. For our program, we'll set the default zoom level at 30 to test out the zoom by entering the code below in bold.

```
; Create camera
camera=CreateCamera()

; Setting the default zoom level
zoom# = 30
```

**Figure 11.13**
The sphere looks like it is off in the distance.

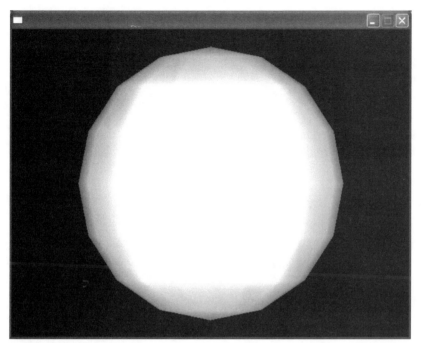

**Figure 11.14**
With the zoom level at 30, the sphere looks much, much closer.

The next step is to apply the `CameraZoom` command to our camera:

```
; Applying the zoom
CameraZoom camera,zoom#
```

Go ahead and run the program now. You'll see that the sphere that was previously so far away is now in your face (see Figure 11.14) because we zoomed in so strongly.

While setting a default zoom level of 30 and applying the zoom is a great way to illustrate how to use zooming, it doesn't have a lot of practical applications. For our next step, we'll change the default zoom level to 1, but add controls so that we can change the zoom level as the program is running. Start by changing the default zoom code to 1 instead of 30, so that there is no zoom when the program starts:

```
; Setting the default zoom level
zoom# = 1
```

Next we have to create controls so that when certain keys are pressed, the zoom level will change. This code (in bold) should be entered in the program running section of the code:

```
; This following code makes our program run
While Not KeyDown( 1 )
RenderWorld


If KeyDown( 208 )=True Then zoom#=zoom#-0.5
If KeyDown( 200 )=True Then zoom#=zoom#+0.5


; Applying the zoom
CameraZoom camera,zoom#
Flip


Wend


End
```

What this code says is that if the down arrow is pressed (If KeyDown( 208 )=True), then the zoom level (zoom#) should decrease by 0.5 units (=zoom#-0.5). The opposite is true for the up arrow. Notice also that we moved the section called ; Applying the zoom after these controls. It has to be placed after the controls or the zoom won't work. Go ahead and test out your new zoom technique by changing the zoom increments (in this case our increments were –0.5 and +0.5) to see how it affects the zoom level.

## Camera Movement

Like just about any other object, the camera that you create can be moved around and rotated to either follow the action or survey your surroundings. In this example, we will work with a file we created earlier in the book called atom.bb—a file that has some protons and electrons floating around a spinning nucleus. We will create a camera that can be moved around and rotated so that you can navigate through the atom. First we'll add controls that will allow us to turn and pivot the camera. Add this code before the RenderWorld line near the end of the program:

```
;Moving the Camera
If KeyDown(205) TurnEntity camera,0,1,0
If KeyDown(203) TurnEntity camera,0,-1,0
If KeyDown(200) MoveEntity camera,0,0,1
If KeyDown(208) MoveEntity camera,0,0,-1
```

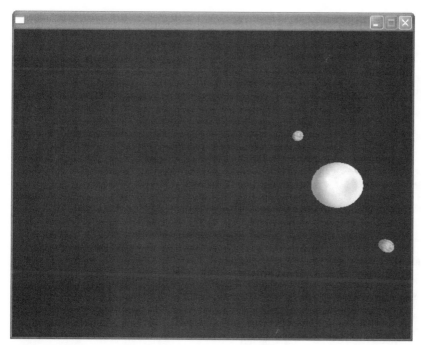

**Figure 11.15**
Camera view 1.

Basically what we've done is set the camera to turn by an increment when the arrow keys are pressed. The MoveEntity command moves the physical location of the camera, while the TurnEntity command turns it by an increment on the axis specified. You can enter different numbers and different increments to see how the camera will react. You can also specify other keys to have the camera move and turn on a different axis.

By using the arrow keys, you can change the viewpoint by moving the camera (see Figures 11.15 and 11.16).

## Following an Object

Having a camera follow an object automatically is a common technique used by 3D video games. Whether it's a race car, plane, or character, being able to automatically follow an object as it moves is the key to game play in certain programs. The goal of this chapter is to give you the groundwork for creating, moving and switching cameras. There are several methods for having a camera follow an object, all of which are quite involved and are beyond the scope of this

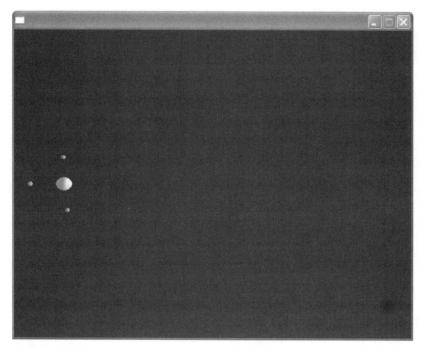

**Figure 11.16**
Camera view 2.

chapter. We'll attack this challenge a little later on in the book in Chapter 15, "Almost There."

## Light

If you have read the Old Testament, you probably know the importance of light and you may even recall that the first words ever uttered by God were "Let there be light." Whether you believe in the Old Testament or not, there is one truth you can be certain of: If you don't create light in your Blitz3D programs, you'll be left in darkness! Every Blitz program that you create requires at least one light. You can change the type, position, and effect of your lights by altering the codes.

## Types of Lights

Unlike your local Home Depot that has thousands of different varieties of lights, Blitz3D offers you only three different light types. Take a look at the code used to create a light:

```
light = CreateLight()
```

The first part of the code `light=` is just the name that you give to your light, it can really be called anything you like—you can name your lights after your pets, brother, or cousins if that's what you prefer. The next part of the code `CreateLight` actually creates the light, and, finally, the brackets `()` tell Blitz3D what type of light to create. You can specify one of three different types of lights:

- **Directional Light** created by the code `light = CreateLight()` or `light = CreateLight(1)`. Everything that faces the light will be equally lit (see Figure 11.17).

- **Point Light** created by the code `light = CreateLight(2)`. This type of light starts strong at a specific point and fades out the further you get away from the light (see Figure 11.18).

- **Spot Light** created by the code `light = CreateLight(3)`. Think of spot light as holding a flashlight on an object (see Figure 11.19).

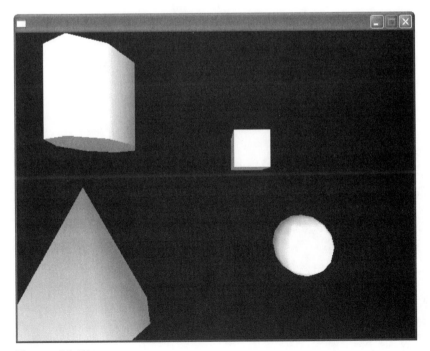

**Figure 11.17**
Directional lighting.

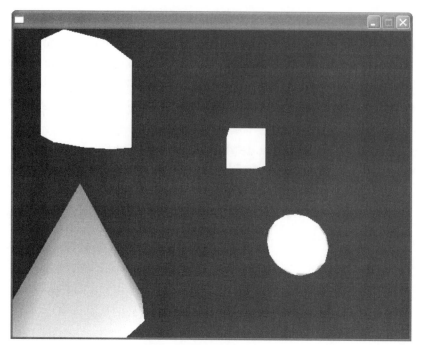

**Figure 11.18**
Point lighting.

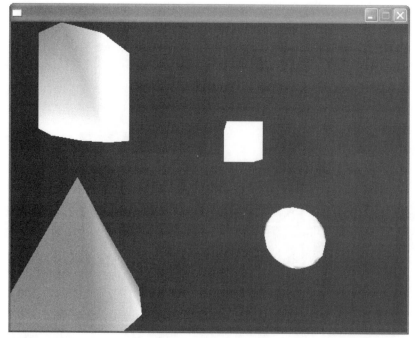

**Figure 11.19**
Spot lighting.

**Note**

**Now You Try**

Create a program with a cone or sphere. Try each variety of light to see how the light affects the object.

## Light Range

You can control how "strong" a light is by adjusting its range. The stronger the range is, the further it will reach. In the next example, we'll create a sphere that is far off in the distance and is lit by a spotlight. We'll then change the light range to see how it affects our image. The code used to adjust the range is LightRange followed by the name of the light and the amount of range. Open the file called light_sphere.bb or enter this code:

```
; Lighting
; ------------------

Graphics3D 640,480
SetBuffer BackBuffer()

; Create camera
camera=CreateCamera()

; Creating a light
light=CreateLight(3)

; This is the code for creating the sphere

sphere=CreateSphere()
PositionEntity sphere,0,0,9
ScaleEntity sphere,0.5,,5,0.5
EntityColor sphere, 0,26,125

; This following code makes our program run
While Not KeyDown( 1 )

RenderWorld
Flip

Wend

End
```

**Figure 11.20**
This is what the object looks like with default lighting.

**Figure 11.21**
This is what the object looks like with stronger lighting created with the LightRange command.

When you run the program, you should see a sphere, as in Figure 11.20.

Now we are going to adjust the range of the light to make it stronger by adding this code in the Creating a light section. We'll increase the range to 50.

```
; Creating a light
light=CreateLight()
LightRange light, 50
```

You'll now see that the object appears brighter (see Figure 11.21) because we've increased its intensity using this code.

**Note**

**Now You Try**

Experiment with this code, adjusting the intensity (currently set at 50) to see the results you get by changing the range of a light.

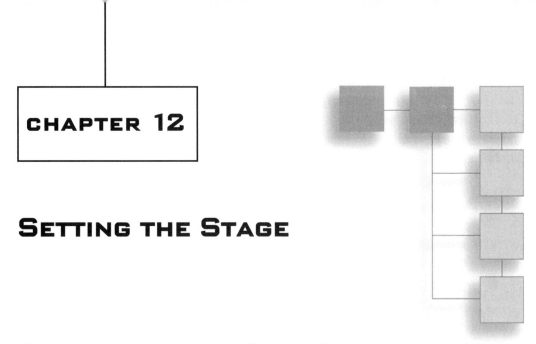

# CHAPTER 12

# SETTING THE STAGE

The environment of your game is really the world in which the events of the game take place. The type of world that you create will depend heavily on the type of game that you are creating. An adventure game may include buildings that your character walks through, a race game may have a track, a tank battle game may take place on a field. Regardless of the type of game you are creating, Blitz3D gives you all the tools necessary to create the "stage" on which your game takes place.

There are many different components that you can choose to create for your world, but several are fairly common throughout most games, including the ground, the sky, and buildings. Beyond that, the options are endless. Here we will explore creating those basic elements as well as some of the other options available to you. The techniques you use can vary from creating basic shapes to act as components in your world to using advanced techniques available in Blitz3D.

## Creating a Terrain

One of the quickest ways to create a terrain (or the ground) for your games is to use the programming code called CreateTerrain. This code allows you to create and specify a size for the terrain (again, think of this as the ground) of your game. In this example, we'll add a terrain to an empty program. Start by entering the following code or simply open the file called empty.bb.

```
; Empty Program
;_____

Graphics3D 640,480
SetBuffer BackBuffer()

; Create camera
camera=CreateCamera()

; Creating a light
light=CreateLight()

; The following code makes the program run
While Not KeyDown( 1 )

RenderWorld
Flip

Wend

End
```

If you ran this program now, you would see only a blank, black screen. We are now going to add the code to create a terrain for this program. Add the following code under the "Creating a Light" section to create the terrain:

```
; Creating the terrain
ground=CreateTerrain(512)
```

If you ran this program right now, you'd see nothing because the camera isn't looking at the terrain (see Figure 12.1). We'll fix that in a moment, but for now let's take a closer look at the code we just entered. The first part `ground` is just the name we are giving to the terrain. `CreateTerrain` is the code that creates the terrain, and the number in parentheses (512) is how far the terrain extends along the x and z axes.

## Positioning a Terrain

To actually see the terrain, you have two options. You can either reposition your camera, or you can change the location of your terrain. The following sections will cover both methods.

**Figure 12.1**
Oh no! There's nothing on the screen. That's OK, the terrain is actually there—it's just out of the view of the camera.

### Repositioning the Camera

We need to change the position of the camera. The terrain begins at position 1 on the y axis, and in this case, our terrain extends to the position 512,1,512. Since the default camera is at position 0,0,0, we need to bring it up to 0,1,0 so that we can see the terrain. Add the following lines to the camera code to position it so that we can see the terrain:

```
; Create camera
camera=CreateCamera()
PositionEntity camera,0,1,0
```

If you run the program right now you'll see the beginning of the terrain we created. Not much of a terrain yet—just a gray box (see Figure 12.2).

Let's now add some controls so that we can navigate around the terrain with our arrow keys.

```
; The following code makes the program run
While Not KeyDown( 1 )
```

**Figure 12.2**
There's our terrain. Beautiful, isn't it? You can move the terrain or the camera to get a better view.

```
If KeyDown( 205 )=True Then TurnEntity camera,0,-1,0
If KeyDown( 203 )=True Then TurnEntity camera,0,1,0
If KeyDown( 208 )=True Then MoveEntity camera,0,0,-0.05
If KeyDown( 200 )=True Then MoveEntity camera,0,0,0.05

RenderWorld
Flip

Wend

End
```

Now run this program and use the arrow keys to move the camera around so that you can navigate around your terrain (see Figure 12.3).

### Repositioning the Terrain

Rather than changing the position of the camera in order to see the terrain, you can simply reposition the terrain. To do this, we make use of the `PositionEntity` command.

**Figure 12.3**
By adding code that allows us to move the camera, we can get a better view of our terrain.

```
; Creating the terrain
ground=CreateTerrain(512)
PositionEntity ground, 0,-1,0

; The following code makes the program run
While Not KeyDown( 1 )

If KeyDown( 205 )=True Then TurnEntity camera,0,-1,0
If KeyDown( 203 )=True Then TurnEntity camera,0,1,0
If KeyDown( 208 )=True Then MoveEntity camera,0,0,-0.05
If KeyDown( 200 )=True Then MoveEntity camera,0,0,0.05

RenderWorld
Flip

Wend

End
```

**Figure 12.4**
The terrain above is positioned at -500,-1,-500.

We've lowered the plane so that it is now below the camera and can be seen. Here we chose a position of 0,-1,0, but you can choose any starting position that you'd like. In fact, try the same program above but replace the position of the terrain with -500,-1,-500 (see Figure 12.4).

## Changing the Terrain Color

By default, the terrain you created was gray in color. You can change the color of a terrain just as you would any other object by using the EntityColor command. Let's change the color of our terrain by adding the following code in bold:

```
; Create terrain
ground=CreateTerrain(512)
EntityColor terrain, 125,36,32
```

## Applying a Texture to a Terrain

More often than not, rather than coloring a terrain, you'll probably want to apply a texture to it. You can apply a texture to a terrain just as you would any other entity. Before you continue, open the file called terrain_texture.bb and make

**Figure 12.5**
A grassy texture has been applied to the terrain.

sure that the file grass1.jpg is in the same folder as the program. Add the following code (in bold) to apply a grass texture to our terrain.

```
; Creating the terrain
ground=CreateTerrain(512)
texture=LoadTexture ( ''grass1.jpg'' )
EntityTexture ground, texture
```

Go ahead and run the program now and you'll see that your terrain now has the grass texture applied to it (see Figure 12.5).

## Changing the Size of a Terrain

We'll use the ScaleEntity command to change the size of a terrain. In the example we've been using, we'll scale the terrain by 15 times on the y axis and 10 times on the x and z axes by adding the following code (in bold):

```
; Creating the terrain
ground=CreateTerrain(512)
PositionEntity ground, -500,0,-500
ScaleEntity ground, 10,15,10
```

Using the ScaleEntity command, you can increase or decrease the size of your playing field.

## Creating a Plane

One of the easiest ways to make a "playing field" for your game is to create a plane. A *plane* is an endless surface that continues on and on into infinity. The biggest advantage of a plane is that it goes on forever, so there is no chance that your players will fall off the edge of the playing surface. This is a great alternative to creating a terrain.

Creating a plane is quite simple and can be made as easily as any shape. Planes act much like shapes in that they can be colored or textured. In the following example, we'll add a plane to an empty program.

Start by entering the following code or simply open the file called empty.bb. Once the file is open or you have entered the code, save it with a new name.

```
; Empty Program
;_____

Graphics3D 640,480
SetBuffer BackBuffer()

; Create camera
camera=CreateCamera()

; Creating a light
light=CreateLight()

; The following code makes our program run
While Not KeyDown( 1 )

RenderWorld
Flip

Wend

End
```

Add the following code (in bold) below the "Creating a light" section to create a plane:

```
; Creating a plane
myplane=CreatePlane()
```

**Figure 12.6**
This plane was positioned at 0,-1,0.

The name of the plane we created in this example is "myplane," but we could have called it anything. The actual code that creates the plane is CreatePlane(). If you were to run the program now you wouldn't see anything because the plane is out of sight. Once you have a plane created, you can either adjust the position of the plane (see Figure 12.6) or the position of the camera in order to see it. (See the previous sections called "Repositioning the Camera" and "Repositioning the Terrain" to learn how to move the camera or the plane.) Just as with a terrain, a plane can be colored or textured.

## Applying a Heightmap

You may have noticed something peculiar about the terrain you created in the last section—it was flat. If you want the terrain to have a more realistic look to it, you can load a heightmap. A heightmap defines the landscape of your terrain. In other words, it informs the program where any bumps, mountains, and valleys should occur. Heightmap images are made in Grayscale mode, which means that there is no color in them, just 256 shades of gray. Anything that is fully white in the heightmap represents the highest peak, while anything that is completely black represents the lowest point. The shades of gray in between will make up the valleys and mountains in your terrain. Look at Figure 12.7 to see how the heightmap would convert into actual terrain.

I discussed the creation of heightmaps earlier in this book in Chapter 8, "Getting Graphic." There, we created a heightmap, but we didn't actually apply it using any code. You can refer back to that chapter to learn how to actually create a heightmap.

Once you have a heightmap created, you can simply load it using the LoadTerrain command and then apply a texture to it. In the following example, we will start by creating a program with nothing at all in it and then apply three different heightmaps so that you can get a good idea of how they would look in the games you create. Start by opening the file called empty.bb or entering the following code. Save the file to a new folder, give it a new name, and make sure that the files spikey.jpg, valley.jpg, highmountain.jpg and greenery.jpg are in the same folder. Notice in the code how we've positioned the camera 15 units above the ground so that we can get a good view of our landscape once it is created.

```
; Empty Program
;_____

Graphics3D 640,480
SetBuffer BackBuffer()

; Create camera
camera=CreateCamera()
PositionEntity camera,0,15,0

; Creating a light
light=CreateLight(3)

; The following code makes the program run
While Not KeyDown( 1 )

RenderWorld
Flip

Wend

End
```

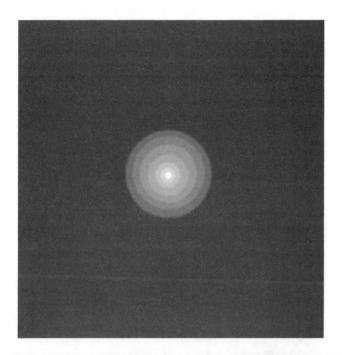

**Figure 12.7**
The heightmap on the top was used to create the terrain on the bottom.

Now we'll enter the code to add our heightmap, scale it, and apply a texture to it. I'll introduce a few new lines of code here, each of which will be discussed individually. Add this code after the "Creating a light" section:

```
; Loading the heightmap
terrain=LoadTerrain ( "highmountain.jpg" )
ScaleEntity terrain,5,100,5
PositionEntity terrain,-500,0,-500
tex=LoadTexture( "greenery.jpg" )
ScaleTexture tex, 50,50
EntityTexture terrain,tex
```

Run the program now, and with any luck your screen should be similar to the one shown in Figure 12.8.

Let's take a look at each line individually to see what we have done.

**terrain=LoadTerrain ( "highmountain.jpg" )** – This code creates a terrain called terrain by loading up the heightmap file called highmountain.jpg.

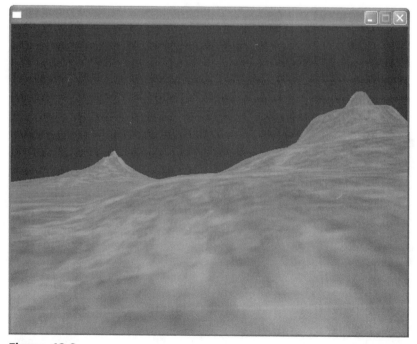

**Figure 12.8**
The heightmap highmountain.jpg has been loaded, and the texture greenery.jpg has been applied.

**ScaleEntity terrain,5,100,5** — This is a very important piece of code when working with heightmaps. The heightmap file that we created is saved as a very small file format to save processing time. When we apply it to our terrain, we need to stretch it out. In order to retain the shape of our mountains, we need to ensure that the y axis is stretched out much more than the x and z axes. In this case, we enlarged the y axis by 100 times and enlarged the x and z axes by 5 times. You can experiment with these numbers to see how it will affect your terrain.

**PositionEntity terrain,-500,0,-500** — With this code, we positioned the terrain at the 0 mark on the y axis and at −500 along the x and z axes.

**tex=LoadTexture( "greenery.jpg" )** — This code creates a texture that we called tex from the file greenery.jpg.

**ScaleTexture tex, 50,50** — Because we scaled our terrain, it's a good idea to stretch out our texture so that it retains the original look that we intended. Remember that a texture is a two-dimensional image that we apply to a three-dimensional object, so it has only x and y coordinates to adjust. In this case we have scaled the x and y coordinates by 50 times.

**EntityTexture terrain,tex** — This command applies the texture we created, called tex to the terrain.

Before we run the program, let's add the following code (in bold) to the run section so that we can navigate through our terrain using the arrow keys:

```
; The following code makes the program run
While Not KeyDown( 1 )

If KeyDown( 205 )=True Then TurnEntity camera,0,-1,0
If KeyDown( 203 )=True Then TurnEntity camera,0,1,0
If KeyDown( 208 )=True Then MoveEntity camera,0,0,-1
If KeyDown( 200 )=True Then MoveEntity camera,0,0,1

RenderWorld
Flip

Wend

End
```

Go ahead and run the program now and use the arrow keys to navigate through the 3D world that you have created.

**Figure 12.9**
The valley.jpg heightmap.

**Now You Try**

In the code that you just created, replace the file highmountain.jpg with valley.jpg and then spikey.jpg to see how those heightmaps will look when applied to a game. Look at Figures 12.9 and 12.10 to see the results.

## Shapes as Environments

Simple shapes will play an important part in the creation of your 3D worlds. You can use them in combination with your terrains or on their own to create entire environments or elements of your environment including the sky, ground, buildings, walls, and much more. Earlier in the book, you learned how to create simple shapes like spheres, cubes, and cylinders. Blitz3D gives you the ability to use any shape as the environment for your games. You can create a huge shape, such as a sphere or rectangle, and then have your game take place inside that sphere. You can then apply a texture to that shape and turn the texture inside out using the FlipMesh command so that you can see the texture when you are inside that shape. Does that sound confusing? The best way to clarify things is to take it piece by piece and learn by doing, as in the following sections.

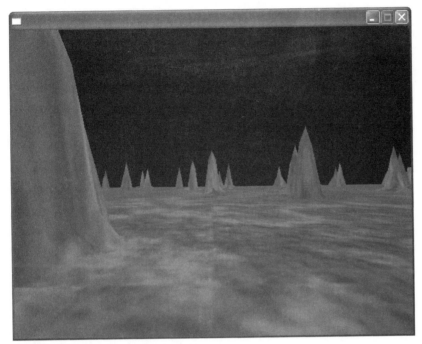

**Figure 12.10**
The spikey.jpg heightmap.

## Going Inside Shapes

The process of creating a shape to use as your 3D world isn't very difficult. You simply have to create a large version of the desired shape and then add a few commands to make things work. There are three new commands that we'll use in this section of code, including FitMesh, FlipMesh, and EntityFX. I'll discuss each of these after we've entered the code.

We'll start by creating an "empty" program that includes camera controls that will allow us to turn the camera up and down and right and left, so we can look around after we have completed our world. Open the program called empty_controls.bb or enter the following code. Now save this file with a new name to a new folder and ensure that the file called wall.jpg is also placed in that file.

```
; Empty Program
;_____

Graphics3D 640,480
SetBuffer BackBuffer()
```

```
; Create camera
camera=CreateCamera()
PositionEntity camera, 0,+50,0

;Create light
light=CreateLight()

;The following code makes the program run
While Not KeyDown( 1 )

If KeyDown( 205 )=True Then TurnEntity camera,0,-1,0
If KeyDown( 203 )=True Then TurnEntity camera,0,1,0
If KeyDown( 208 )=True Then TurnEntity camera,-1,0,0
If KeyDown( 200 )=True Then TurnEntity camera,1,0,0

RenderWorld
Flip

Wend

End
```

If you ran the program now, you wouldn't see anything because we haven't created any objects. Add the following code after the "Create light" section to create your cube world:

```
;Creating our Cube World
cubeworld=CreateCube()
FitMesh cubeworld,-250,0,-250,500,500,500
FlipMesh cubeworld
tex=LoadTexture( "wall.jpg" )
ScaleTexture tex, 0.5,0.5
EntityTexture cubeworld,tex
EntityFX cubeworld,1
```

Run the program now and have a look around by pressing the arrow keys. You'll notice that you are now inside your cube world that looks like a room made of hardwood walls, ceiling, and floor as in Figure 12.11.

Now let's look at the code you just entered line by line to figure out exactly how we did what we did.

**Figure 12.11**
Navigate around your wooden room using the arrow keys.

`cubeworld=CreateCube()` – This code creates a standard cube at the default size. In this case, we called our cube `cubeworld`. You don't have to specify a size or location for the cube because you do so in the next command.

`FitMesh cubeworld,-250,0,-250,500,500,500` – The `FitMesh` command creates a mesh that will fit inside the cube that we created. After the `FitMesh` command, you need to specify the location of the mesh on the x, y, and z axes and the dimensions. The first three numbers specify the position of the mesh. In this case, it is at position –250 on the x axis, 0 on the y axis, and –250 on the z axis. The next three numbers specify the width, height, and depth of the mesh. In this case, we've made all three 500.

`FlipMesh cubeworld` – When we apply a texture to an object, that texture is wrapped around the outside of the object, not the inside. If you were to go inside an object that has a texture applied to it, it would appear dark. Think of the example of a box that is covered in gift wrapping. If you were inside the box, you would be in the dark because the wrapping paper is on the outside. Blitz3D has a function called `FlipMesh` that allows you to turn the wrapped object inside out so that the wrapping paper appears on the inside. That's exactly what we've done in this step. We've told Blitz3D that anything we wrap around the object `cubeworld` should be wrapped around the inside, not the outside.

`tex=LoadTexture( "wall.jpg" )` – This is the command we have used many times already to load a texture. In this case we are using the image called wall.jpg as the texture that we are calling `tex`.

`ScaleTexture tex, 0.5,0.5` – We will reduce the scale of our texture by half by adding this command.

`EntityTexture cubeworld,tex` –This applies the texture to the cube. Remember, because we created a FlipMesh, the texture will be on the inside of the cube.

`EntityFX cubeworld,1` – It would be very dark inside our box if we didn't have a way of brightening the inside. To do this, we use the `EntityFX` command. The `EntityFX` command has several different effects. In this case, the number 1 indicates that the area should be filled with full brightness. Run the program without this code and you'll notice that the walls inside your cube are much darker.

## Using Shapes with Terrains

What's better than chocolate mixing with peanut butter? How about terrains mixing with shapes? Maybe that's not quite as good, but combining a terrain with a shape is how many 3D games create their environments. Typically, the terrain will make up the ground, and the shapes will make up the sky and other objects within the game. In the following example, we'll create a sky using a shape and apply it to a standard. Start by opening the file called terrain_sky.bb or entering the following code. Save the file with a new name into a new folder and make sure that the files called greenery.jpg and sky2.jpg are copied to that folder.

```
; Terrain_Sky
;_____

Graphics3D 640,480
SetBuffer BackBuffer()

; Create camera
camera=CreateCamera()
PositionEntity camera,0,1,0
```

```
; Creating a light
light=CreateLight()

; Creating the terrain
ground=CreateTerrain(512)
PositionEntity ground, -500,0,-500
ScaleEntity ground, 10,15,10
tex=LoadTexture( "greenery.jpg" )
EntityTexture ground, tex

; The following code makes the program run
While Not KeyDown( 1 )

If KeyDown( 205 )=True Then TurnEntity camera,0,-1,0
If KeyDown( 203 )=True Then TurnEntity camera,0,1,0
If KeyDown( 208 )=True Then MoveEntity camera,0,0,-0.5
If KeyDown( 200 )=True Then MoveEntity camera,0,0,0.5

RenderWorld
Flip

Wend

End
```

Run the program now and you should be able to see a green terrain and nothing (black) as the sky (see Figure 12.12). We are going to change all that by creating a sphere to act as the sky. We will make the sphere extremely large, apply a texture to it, and then use the FlipMesh function we learned earlier to put the texture on the inside of the sphere. Enter this code after the "Creating the terrain" section.

```
;Creating the sky
sky = CreateSphere (40)
FlipMesh sky
ScaleEntity sky, 100,100,100
PositionEntity sky, 0,50,0
sky_tex = LoadTexture ( "sky2.jpg" )
EntityTexture sky,sky_tex
EntityFX sky,1
```

Run the program now to see the sky as in Figure 12.13.

I have described in detail all of the previous code in earlier sections of this chapter. Here we are just adding it to the code of an existing terrain. If you run

**Figure 12.12**
The program at this point has terrain and a black sky.

**Figure 12.13**
We've now added a bright, beautiful sky to our terrain.

the program now, you'll see both the terrain and the sky. We've actually done something pretty cool here, and I want you to see how it works. We haven't really created a "sky"—we've just created a sphere that takes up most of the screen so that it looks like a sky. Want to see what I mean? Run the program and hold down the down arrow. You'll move backwards and backwards until you can see that your sky was simply a sphere. You wouldn't actually want this to happen in a real game, so there are measures that we can take to avoid having our "fake" sky from being discovered. First of all, in a real game we would make the sphere much bigger. Rather than having it scaled at 100 times (as we did with this line of code: ScaleEntity sky, 100,100,100), we would scale it much larger and we would create a "parent" so that as our player moved, the sphere that made up the sky would also move. You'll learn more about parents later in the book. You'll also notice that if you hold down the up arrow, you'll move toward the sky and eventually be able to go through it. In an actual game, setting up a "collision" would prevent this. You'll learn more about collisions in the next chapter.

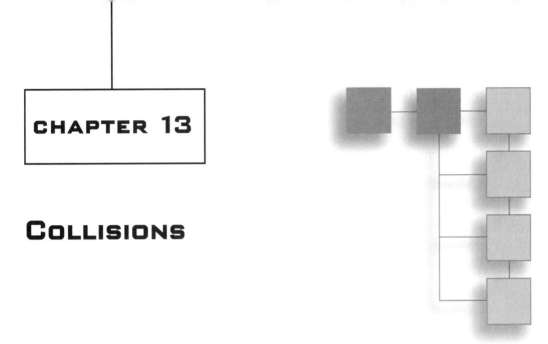

# CHAPTER 13

# COLLISIONS

What's the first thing you think of when someone says the word "collision"? I think of two cars hurtling down the road at one another and then smashing head-on in an impressive display of fireworks, flying metal, and screeching tires. Thankfully, in my vision nobody gets hurt! In Blitz3D, collisions control how two or more objects react with one another. Collisions are an important part of any game since they allow you to control whether your players can bump into walls or go through them. They also prevent players from falling off the edge of the screen, and they tell the computer what type of reaction should happen when two objects meet. By default, when you move one object into another using Blitz3D, the objects will pass right through each other. You have the ability to control both the method in which two objects collide and the response of the collision.

A very important concept that you must understand when defining collisions is that of *types*. Types are basically a way of grouping different objects that share similar qualities. Think of a type as a "team"—you can assign different objects to that team and then define the type of collisions for the team. For example, let's say in your 3D game you have created hundreds of different enemy invaders. Rather than having to program the collisions for each enemy invader, you can assign each invader to a team and then define the collisions for that team. The collision parameters you apply to the "team" (the type) will all apply to all members of the team—in this case all the enemy invaders. When you create a type, you assign a number for your team. The number you choose isn't important; it's just important that you assign it a number.

## Creating a Collision

The Collisions command is used in Blitz3D to define how objects will collide with one another. There are five different things that you must specify when creating collisions:

- **Source Type.** The source type tells Blitz3D which object it should watch for that might collide into something else. Typically, this is the player or players in your game. In the example we are going to use below, we will create a sphere that will collide with a cone. In this example, the sphere would be the source type.

- **Destination Type.** This is the object that is being collided into. In the example, the cone acting as our object to smash into will be the destination type.

Figure 13.1 illustrates the difference between a Source type and a Destination type.

- **Entity Radius.** Imagine a really skinny cat trying to walk into the open entrance of your house. The cat could probably do it with no problem at all. Now imagine an 800-pound elephant trying to get through the same door—it'd probably get stuck. In Blitz3D, you have to define how "fat" or "skinny" your objects are so that the program knows whether or not a collision should occur when two objects get close to one another. You have to define

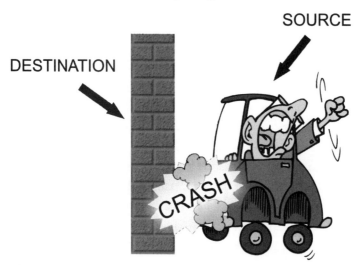

**Figure 13.1**
The difference between a Source and a Destination type.

this by setting an entity radius for each source object. Keep in mind that creating a large or small entity radius doesn't actually change the shape or size of an object; it just tells Blitz3D how close or far objects need to be to one another for a collision to be registered. Figures 13.2 and 13.3 illustrate how the radius of an object works.

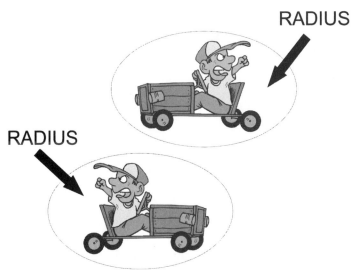

**Figure 13.2**
In this example, a collision wouldn't occur because the radii of the two objects don't collide.

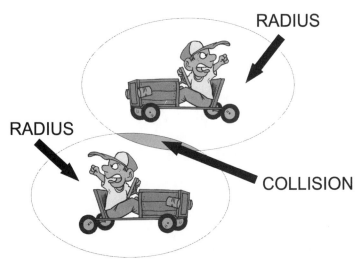

**Figure 13.3**
In this example, a collision occurs because the radii of the two objects collide.

- **Method**. This controls the detection method for the collisions. Your choices are:

ellipsoid-to-ellipsoid = 1

ellipsoid-to-polygon = 2

ellipsoid-to-box = 3

- **Response**. This tells the program how you want an object you are moving to react when it hits another object. You can have it stop, slide sideways, or slide upwards. Different numbers indicate the type of response you want as follows:

Stop = 1

Slide Sideways = 2

Slide Upwards = 3

## Collision Code

Above you learned the parts of the collision code. Let's look at the actual code you use to create a collision. We'll use this code in the next section to create our collision:

```
Collisions type_player,type_obstacle,2,2
```

Let's look at the individual parts of this code:

`Collisions`—This is the actual code that tells Blitz3D that we are about to define a collision.

`type_player`—This is the name of the source object that will be doing the colliding. In this case, we've called our type "player," but you can give your types any names you wish. Keep in mind that the types have to be defined before this code is entered. In the next section you'll be shown how to define the types.

`,type_obstacle,`—This is the name of the object that your source will be colliding into. In this case we've called the type `obstacle`, but again, you can give your types any names you wish.

`2,2`—The first number defines the method, and the second number defines the response. The list of different methods and responses can be found in the previous section.

## Colliding Objects

Now that we know what is required to define a collision, let's create one in a simple program. The following program contains two simple objects: a sphere that will be our player that we move, and a cone that will be the object we smash into. Open the file collide.bb or enter the following code:

```
; Collide
;_____

Graphics3D 640,480
SetBuffer BackBuffer()

; Create camera
camera=CreateCamera()

; Creating a light
light=CreateLight()

; Creating a sphere
sphere=CreateSphere()
ScaleEntity sphere, 0.5,0.5,0.5
PositionEntity sphere, -3,0,5

; Creating a cone
cone=CreateCone()
PositionEntity cone, 1,0,5
ScaleEntity cone, 1.5,1.5,1.5

; This following code makes our program run
While Not KeyDown( 1 )
x#=0
y#=0
z#=0

If KeyDown( 203 )=True Then x#=-0.1
If KeyDown( 205 )=True Then x#=0.1
If KeyDown( 208 )=True Then y#=-0.1
If KeyDown( 200 )=True Then y#=0.1
MoveEntity sphere,x#,y#,z#

RenderWorld
Flip

Wend

End
```

Go ahead and run the program and use the arrow keys to move the sphere around. You can see that when the sphere gets to the cone, it goes right through. We'll now create a collision so that the sphere won't be able to go through the cone. The first thing we'll do is create the types. In this instance we'll create two types—one for the sphere, which we'll call player, and the other which we'll call "obstacle." Enter the following code under the "SetBuffer" section to create the types. If you ran the program now (see Figure 13.4), the sphere could go through the cone.

```
; Creating the types
type_player=1
type_obstacle=2
```

The number that we chose for the two different types (1 and 2) don't have any importance. We could have selected any numbers; it's just important that they have a number assigned to them.

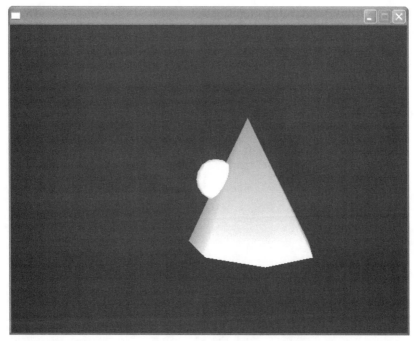

**Figure 13.4**
At this point the sphere can go right through the cone because no collisions have been set up.

Next we have to assign the objects that we created to our types. Add the following code (in bold) to assign the two objects to the different teams:

```
; Creating a sphere
sphere=CreateSphere()
ScaleEntity sphere, 0.5,0.5,0.5
PositionEntity sphere, -3,0,5
EntityType sphere,type_player

; Creating a cone
cone=CreateCone()
PositionEntity cone, 1,0,5
ScaleEntity cone, 1.5,1.5,1.5
EntityType cone,type_obstacle
```

Now we will create the collision itself. Add the two lines of code in bold below in the specified locations:

```
Collisions type_player,type_obstacle,2,2

; This following code makes our program run
While Not KeyDown( 1 )
x#=0
y#=0
z#=0

If KeyDown( 203 )=True Then x#=-0.1
If KeyDown( 205 )=True Then x#=0.1
If KeyDown( 208 )=True Then y#=-0.1
If KeyDown( 200 )=True Then y#=0.1
MoveEntity sphere,x#,y#,z#
UpdateWorld

RenderWorld
Flip

Wend

End
```

Let's take a close look at the code to see what we have just done.

*Collisions type_player,type_obstacle,2,2*—This is the code that creates the collision and defines the methods and response for the collision.

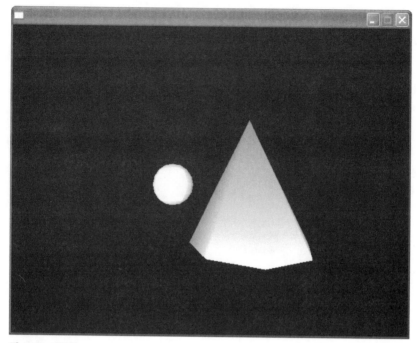

**Figure 13.5**
Deflector shields up! Your sphere can't get close to the cone because you've created a collision.

**UpdateWorld**—This line is very important because it checks for collisions.

Now go ahead and run the program and you should see that your objects can't get close, as in Figure 13.5.

## Collision Radius

You'll notice from the last section that the sphere couldn't get close to the cone. You can specify how close or far you can get to an object by specifying a radius using the EntityRadius command. You specify the radius for the individual objects. Let's continue with the same program we were using in the last section. If you've closed it, open the file called collide_radius.bb. Enter the following code in bold below:

```
; Creating a sphere
sphere=CreateSphere()
ScaleEntity sphere, 0.5,0.5,0.5
PositionEntity sphere, -3,0,5
EntityType sphere,type_player
EntityRadius sphere, 0.2
```

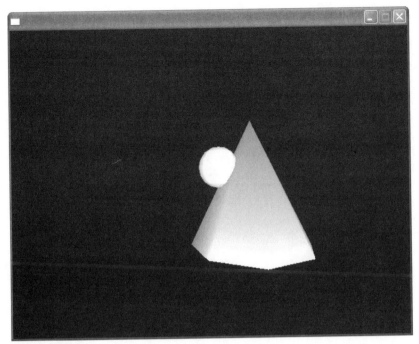

**Figure 13.6**
You can now get much closer to the cone. In fact, you can get half way through the cone before the collision occurs.

Go ahead and run the program now, and you'll see that you can get a lot closer to the object because you've entered a radius less than 1 (see Figure 13.6).

If you entered a radius greater than 1, you wouldn't be able to get as close to the cone.

**Note**

**Now You Try**
Practice entering different radius values between 0 and 1 and then greater than 1 to see how it affects how close your sphere can get to the cone.

## Shields Down!—Clear Collisions

You can remove the collisions command permanently or temporarily using the ClearCollisions command. Continue using the code you used in the last section; otherwise, open collide_clear.bb.

Add the following code in bold below:

```
; This following code makes our program run
While Not KeyDown( 1 )
x#=0
y#=0
z#=0

If KeyDown( 203 )=True Then x#=-0.1
If KeyDown( 205 )=True Then x#=0.1
If KeyDown( 208 )=True Then y#=-0.1
If KeyDown( 200 )=True Then y#=0.1
MoveEntity sphere,x#,y#,z#
While KeyHit( 57 ) ClearCollisions
Wend
UpdateWorld

RenderWorld
Flip

Wend

End
```

Run the program now, and when you press the space bar, the collisions are cleared as in Figure 13.7.

The code that we entered basically says that when the space bar is pressed, turn off the collisions. Go ahead and run the program now. You'll see that you can still move around the object, but as soon as you press the space bar, collisions will be turned off. What if you wanted the ability to turn collisions on and off as you please? Let's add one more line of code that will turn the collisions on again when you press the number 1. Add the following line in bold:

```
If KeyDown( 200 )=True Then y#=0.1
MoveEntity sphere,x#,y#,z#

While KeyHit( 57 ) ClearCollisions
Wend

While KeyHit( 2) Collisions type_player,type_obstacle,2,2
Wend
UpdateWorld
```

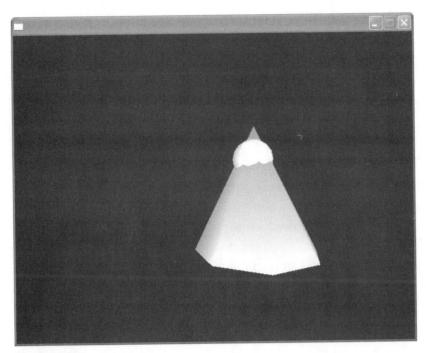

**Figure 13.7**
Once the space bar is pressed, the collisions are cleared and the sphere can once again go through the cone.

```
RenderWorld
Flip

Wend

End
```

When you run the program, you can turn collisions off or on. Pressing the space bar will turn the collisions off, while pressing the number 1 will turn them back on.

**Note**

> Another collision you'll typically want to add is one with the terrain and one with the sky so that your players don't fall through the terrain or over the edge.

## Collision Effects

Not only can collisions prevent objects from going through one another, you can create all sorts of effects when two objects collide with one another. When two cars collide or a bullet hits an object, you don't just want them to slide off one another; you want them to explode, leave a mark, or disappear. In this section, we will examine different collision effects that we can create when two objects collide. To create our collision effects, we'll use the CountCollisions command. This command will count how many times an object you specify has collided with another object.

## Poof! Now You See It, Now You Don't

One type of collision you'll want to create often is having one object disappear when it hits another. This is perfect when you create things like bullets that hit enemies, since you'll want the enemies to disappear. We'll keep things simple in this example. We'll have one object (a cone) disappear when it is hit by a sphere. Start by opening the file hide_collisions.bb, and save it with a new name. This program controls a sphere that can collide with a cone. When you run the program, you'll see that you can control the sphere, but it can't go through the cone since a collision has been created. Now enter the following code in bold:

```
; This following code makes our program run
While Not KeyDown( 1 )
x#=0
y#=0
z#=0

If KeyDown( 203 )=True Then x#=-0.1
If KeyDown( 205 )=True Then x#=0.1
If KeyDown( 208 )=True Then y#=-0.1
If KeyDown( 200 )=True Then y#=0.1
MoveEntity sphere,x#,y#,z#
If CountCollisions (sphere)=True Then HideEntity cone
UpdateWorld

RenderWorld
Flip

Wend

End
```

Run the program now and, when the sphere hits the cone, the cone will disappear as in Figure 13.8.

**Figure 13.8**
Poof! The cone disappears when it is hit by the sphere.

Run the program now and see what happens. When the sphere hits the cone, it disappears. Let's take a close look at the one line of code we added to create this effect. The first part uses the CountCollision command. As mentioned earlier, Blitz3D counts how many times one object has collided with another. The CountCollision command will tell you how many collisions have occurred. When we add the code If CountCollisions (sphere)=True we are basically saying that if there are any collisions of the sphere at all, then do the following HideEntity cone which will hide the cone.

The problem with the code above is that if you want other objects to disappear when they are hit by the sphere, you would have to create a HideEntity command for each object that is hit. Rather than having to do that, we can use the Collision Entity command. This command will tell Blitz3D which object was involved in a collision.

Start by opening the file Collision_Entity.bb, and save it with a new name. This file has a sphere that you can control and two cones. Collisions are currently set up so that the sphere can't go through the cones. Let's add the following code in bold that will make any object that the sphere collides with disappear.

```
; This following code makes our program run
While Not KeyDown( 1 )
x#=0
y#=0
z#=0

If KeyDown( 203 )=True Then x#=-0.1
If KeyDown( 205 )=True Then x#=0.1
If KeyDown( 208 )=True Then y#=-0.1
If KeyDown( 200 )=True Then y#=0.1
MoveEntity sphere,x#,y#,z#

If CountCollisions (sphere)
crash=CollisionEntity (sphere,1)
HideEntity crash
EndIf
UpdateWorld

RenderWorld
Flip

Wend

End
```

Run the program now and you'll see that any object the sphere encounters will disappear. Now let's take a close look at the code we used to get this effect.

**If CountCollisions (sphere)** – This part of the code says that if the sphere has registered any collision at all, then do the following.

**crash=CollisionEntity (sphere,1)** – Here we create an entity called crash (which we could have called any name we chose) and we assign the Collision Entity command to it. The collision entity has two parameters in parentheses: the first is sphere and the second is 1. This basically tells Blitz to remember what the sphere has crashed into and call it crash.

**HideEntity crash** – This will hide the entity called crash, which is whatever the sphere has crashed into.

**EndIf**– This ends the If statement.

## Chameleon Colors

One effect you may want to add to your collisions is to have your objects change colors. Have you ever played the classic game Pac-Man? In it, if Pac-Man ate a Power Pellet, the ghost in the game would change colors. Here you'll learn how to create a similar effect using Blitz3D. When two objects collide, not only can you change the color of the objects that collide, you can change the colors of other objects.

Start by opening the file called Collision_color.bb and save it with a new name. Add the following code in bold to the existing code:

```
; This following code makes our program run
While Not KeyDown( 1 )
x#=0
y#=0
z#=0

If KeyDown( 203 )=True Then x#=-0.1
If KeyDown( 205 )=True Then x#=0.1
If KeyDown( 208 )=True Then y#=-0.1
If KeyDown( 200 )=True Then y#=0.1
MoveEntity sphere,x#,y#,z#
If CountCollisions (sphere)
EntityColor sphere1, 123,255,212
EntityColor sphere2, 123,255,212
EntityColor sphere3, 123,255,212
EntityColor sphere4, 123,255,212
EndIf
UpdateWorld

RenderWorld
Flip

Wend

End
```

When you run the program now, you'll notice that as soon as the sphere collided with the cone, all of the spheres in the corners changed colors. Looking at the code, we see that all we did was use the EntityColor command instead of the

HideEntity command that we had used earlier, and we changed the colors of each of the spheres in the corners.

```
; This following code makes our program run
While Not KeyDown( 1 )
x#=0
y#=0
z#=0

If KeyDown( 203 )=True Then x#=-0.1
If KeyDown( 205 )=True Then x#=0.1
If KeyDown( 208 )=True Then y#=-0.1
If KeyDown( 200 )=True Then y#=0.1
MoveEntity sphere,x#,y#,z#
If CountCollisions (sphere)
EntityColor sphere1, 123,255,212
EntityColor sphere2, 123,255,212
EntityColor sphere3, 123,255,212
EntityColor sphere4, 123,255,212
EntityColor cone, 123,255,212
EndIf
UpdateWorld

RenderWorld
Flip

Wend

End
```

# Blowing Up Stuff

Have you ever heard the saying, "There are many ways to skin a cat"? That saying means that there are different methods to accomplish a specific task, and nowhere is that more true than in creating explosions in Blitz3D. I'm going to show you a simple way to create the illusion of an object blowing up. It will require quite a few lines of code, but I'll break it down into pieces in order to make it easier to understand.

Imagine a bullet (in this case the bullet will be a simple sphere) hitting an object and causing that object to shatter into a few pieces that fly away. We would accomplish this in a few different steps. The first thing that we would do is have the object (in our example the object will be a cone) disappear when it is hit by the bullet. In the last section, you learned to do this by using the HideEntity command when a collision occurred. The next thing we'll do is have three tiny spheres appear where the cone once stood and simultaneously have those fly in different directions so that it appears that they are particles from the exploding cone.

Start by opening the file called Explosion.bb and saving it with a new name. This program contains a cone, which we will "blow up," and a sphere that will act as our bullet. Collision groups have already been set up for these objects.

We will start by making the cone disappear as soon as it is hit by the sphere. This was covered in the last section, so try doing it on your own first and then review the code below in bold which we added:

```
While Not KeyDown( 1 )
x#=0
y#=0
z#=0

If KeyDown( 203 )=True Then x#=-0.1
If KeyDown( 205 )=True Then x#=0.1
If KeyDown( 208 )=True Then y#=-0.1
If KeyDown( 200 )=True Then y#=0.1
MoveEntity sphere,x#,y#,z#

If CountCollisions (sphere)
HideEntity cone
UpdateWorld
```

```
RenderWorld
Flip

Wend

End
```

Please review the previous section if the code in bold doesn't make sense to you. The next thing we need to do is create the pieces that will make up the shattered cone. These pieces will be simple spheres. We have two options here: We can create the spheres within the If CountCollision statement, or we can create Global variables. I'll discuss global variables in further detail in Chapter 16, "Programming Fundamentals," but here I'll explain why we would want to use them. Let's say in our game we want to create many explosions. Rather than having to create particles for our exploded objects every time they are destroyed, we can create a global variable. These global variables can be included in any function. Although we are not using functions here, you'll see how valuable they are when they are covered in Chapter 16. In this case we will create a global variable that creates a sphere. That way, every time an explosion occurs, we won't have to use the CreateSphere command; we'll only have to reference our global variable. Sound confusing? It will become quite a bit clearer in a moment when you put it in use. Add the following three global variables at the beginning of the program just underneath the line SetBuffer BackBuffer().

```
; Hide Collision
;_____

Graphics3D 640,480
SetBuffer BackBuffer()
Global particle=CreateSphere()
Global particle1=CreateSphere()
Global particle2=CreateSphere()
```

Here we have created four spheres. The beauty of making them global variables is that whenever we need a sphere to act as part of an explosion, we don't have to create new spheres; we can just call on any of these three. As it stands, these spheres are a little big to be particles in an explosion, so in the next step we'll reduce their size and color them. Add the following code in bold:

```
Global particle=CreateSphere()
ScaleEntity particle, 0.2,0.2,0.2
```

```
EntityColor particle, 235,125,23
Global particle1=CreateSphere()
ScaleEntity particle1, 0.2,0.2,0.2
EntityColor particle1, 125,125,125
Global particle2=CreateSphere()
ScaleEntity particle2, 0.2,0.2,0.2
EntityColor particle2, 235,1,234
```

So with this code we've given each particle in the explosion a different color and we've reduced the size of the spheres. Now it's on to the code that will create the explosion. Basically, when the collision between the sphere and the cone takes place, we want to place the three spheres at the exact location of the cone, and then we will scatter those spheres. Let's enter the following code in bold and then dissect it:

```
While Not KeyDown( 1 )
x#=0
y#=0
z#=0

If KeyDown( 203 )=True Then x#=-0.1
If KeyDown( 205 )=True Then x#=0.1
If KeyDown( 208 )=True Then y#=-0.1
If KeyDown( 200 )=True Then y#=0.1
MoveEntity sphere,x#,y#,z#
If CountCollisions (sphere)
PositionEntity particle, EntityX(cone),EntityY(cone), EntityZ(cone)
PositionEntity particle1, EntityX(cone),EntityY(cone), EntityZ(cone)
PositionEntity particle2, EntityX(cone),EntityY(cone), EntityZ(cone)
HideEntity cone
End If
UpdateWorld

RenderWorld
Flip

Wend

End
```

By adding this code, we are saying that when a collision with the sphere occurs, put the three spheres at the exact location of the cone. If we looked at the location of the cone in the code (which happens to be at 3,0,5), we could have just entered that location rather than EntityX(cone),EntityY(cone), EntityZ(cone). We entered that code because it will enter a value of the exact location of the cone, even if the cone was moving. In many games, our target will be moving, so we won't always know its exact location. Entering this code will always tell you the exact location of an object.

We need to enter one more valuable piece of code to this text. In the next section, we will send those three spheres flying. Before we do that, we need to create a variable saying that the collision has happened and that the three particles have been put in place. You can create absolutely any variable you want—it makes no difference as long as we have a variable we can call on in the next section. In this instance, we are going to create the variable called explosion and make its state ready by entering the following code in bold:

```
If CountCollisions (sphere)
PositionEntity particle, EntityX(cone),EntityY(cone), EntityZ(cone)
PositionEntity particle1, EntityX(cone),EntityY(cone), EntityZ(cone)
PositionEntity particle2, EntityX(cone),EntityY(cone), EntityZ(cone)
explosion=ready
HideEntity cone
End If
```

Adding explosion=ready may not make much sense right now, but you'll see why we had to add it in the next section. Again, it's important to know that this variable could have been anything. As long as there is an equal sign, any variable would have been valid, including monkeys=flyoutmybutt, cow=jumpoverthemoon, or darth=vader.

Finally, we have to send our spheres flying. We'll do so by adding the following If statement in bold:

```
While Not KeyDown( 1 )
x#=0
y#=0
z#=0

If KeyDown( 203 )=True Then x#=-0.1
If KeyDown( 205 )=True Then x#=0.1
If KeyDown( 208 )=True Then y#=-0.1
If KeyDown( 200 )=True Then y#=0.1
MoveEntity sphere,x#,y#,z#
If CountCollisions (sphere)
```

```
PositionEntity particle, EntityX(cone),EntityY(cone), EntityZ(cone)
PositionEntity particle1, EntityX(cone),EntityY(cone), EntityZ(cone)
PositionEntity particle2, EntityX(cone),EntityY(cone), EntityZ(cone)
HideEntity cone
explosion=ready
End If

If explosion=ready
MoveEntity particle, -.3,.5,0
MoveEntity particle1, +.5,.5,0
MoveEntity particle2, .5,-.5,0
End If
UpdateWorld

RenderWorld
Flip

Wend


End
```

This If statement is quite straightforward. It says that when the variable explosion=ready is true, then move the spheres in the following directions. Even though this is a separate If statement, it is part of the main loop of the program, so it will continue over and over, meaning those particles will keep moving to infinity and beyond. If we had added it to the same loop that positioned the three spheres, then the three spheres would have only moved once by a small increment and wouldn't fly off the screen.

Here's the magic moment. Go ahead and run the program and crash the sphere into the cone. Ta da! You should have your explosion.

As I mentioned in the beginning of this section, there are many ways to skin a cat, and there are a variety of ways we could've created this type of explosion. While the code we've created here creates an explosion, there are some potential problems that may arise—for example, what about the flying debris? Does it go on forever? What if I have other objects that collide with the bullet? Will they create an explosion? Later in the book, when you learn about functions, you'll see how you can group code together to combine common tasks, which will certainly help in creating exploding objects. Another way you can solve potential problems with this collision is to use some timing.

## Other Collision Commands

Before leaving collisions, there are a few other pieces of code that you should become familiar with. Throughout this chapter, we have been using the CountCollisions command to detect when a collision occurs, but there are other collision commands that you can use as well:

EntityCollided(entity,type) – This command will tell Blitz3D what other object was involved with the entity that you specified.

CollisionX(entity,index), CollisionY(entity,index), CollisionZ(entity, index) – These commands will produce the x, y, and z coordinates for the location of a collision.

CollisionEntity – This command will tell Blitz3D what other object was involved with the entity that you specified.

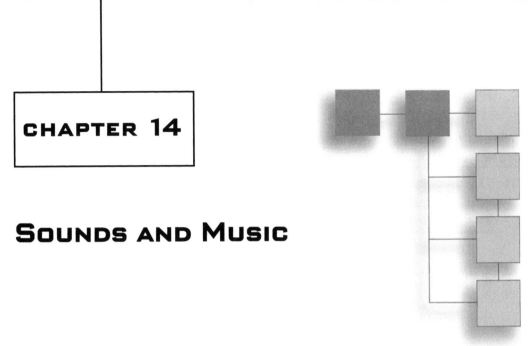

# CHAPTER 14

# SOUNDS AND MUSIC

I want you to do some homework. Don't worry; it'll be fun. Go out and rent a DVD—an action movie or a horror flick. A good movie to rent would be any in the *Star Wars* series. Turn on the closed captioning feature (which runs the dialog across the bottom of the screen) and then turn the volume off. Now watch the movie. You'll notice that even though you can follow the story, it won't seem to have the same emotion, feel, tension, and suspense that it will have when you watch it with the sound on. Music and sounds don't only play a critical role in movies, they can make a huge difference in your games. From explosions to shooting to aliens to background music, you can add all types of sounds and music to your games using Blitz3D. What's the difference between sounds and music? For our purposes, a sound is something that plays as a result of something happening in the game (for example, a bullet hits an opposing player), while music just plays in the background, no matter what is happening.

In this chapter, we'll explore most of the sound and music features that you can control in Blitz3D—and believe me, there are lots of controls. You can control things like the volume, the direction, the channels, the pitch, the pan, and many other musical controls.

## Sounds

I remember the first time I watched the movie *Star Wars* and recall being so amazed by the sound that was made whenever a blaster was fired. Later I remember watching a documentary that showed that the blaster sound was made by tapping on wires. We'll actually be using a blaster sound similar to the one used in the movie later in this section. Regardless of the sounds you decide to use, Blitz3D makes them easy to load.

**Note**

**Audio File Formats**

Digital audio files come in a variety of different formats, many of which are supported by Blitz3D. These include .raw, .mod, .s3m, .xm, .it, .mid, .rmi, .wav, .mp2, .mp3, .ogg, .wma, and .asf.

## Loading and Playing Sounds

To get a sound file into your program, you first need to load it. After it is loaded, you can assign it to play at specific times. The following code will load a sound:

```
; Loading a sound
sound = LoadSound (filename)
```

Obviously, you would replace `filename` with the actual name of your sound file. For example, if your filename was blaster.wav, the command would read `LoadSound (blaster.wav)`. The `sound` part of the code is just a name we gave our sound, and you can call your sounds anything you'd like.

Open the file called sound.bb and save it to a new folder. Make sure that the file called blaster.wav is in the same folder. Add the following code in bold under the "Create Cube" section.

```
blaster = LoadSound (blaster.wav)
```

The game that we have loaded contains a sphere and a cube, where the sphere can be controlled by moving the left and right arrow keys. Now that we have a sound loaded into the game, we need to create a certain event that will trigger the sound. In the case of this game, we will play the blaster sound whenever the sphere hits the cube. Add the following code in bold to create the event that will play the sound.

```
While Not KeyDown( 1 )

x#=0
y#=0
z#=0

If KeyDown( 203 )=True Then x#=-0.1
If KeyDown( 205 )=True Then x#=0.1
If KeyDown( 208 )=True Then y#=-0.1
If KeyDown( 200 )=True Then y#=0.1
```

```
If KeyDown( 44 )=True Then z#=-0.1
If KeyDown( 30 )=True Then z#=0.1

MoveEntity sphere,x#,y#,z#

; Collision Sound
If CountCollisions (sphere)
PlaySound blaster
EndIf
```

Let's take a look at the code we created. We created an If statement that basically says that whenever a collision occurs involving the sphere, play the blaster sound. The code CountCollisions(sphere) says to Blitz3D, let me know if there have been any collisions involving the sphere, and tell me how many have taken place since the last UpdateWorld. The next piece of code, PlaySound blaster, tells Blitz3D to play the sound that we loaded earlier called blaster. Finally, the EndIf code ends the If statement.

### Note

**Now You Try**

Add a piece of code to the existing program that will play the blaster sound whenever the space bar is pressed. When you're done trying, compare your code to the following code in bold.

```
While Not KeyDown( 1 )

x#=0
y#=0
z#=0

If KeyDown( 203 )=True Then x#=-0.1
If KeyDown( 205 )=True Then x#=0.1
If KeyDown( 208 )=True Then y#=-0.1
If KeyDown( 200 )=True Then y#=0.1
If KeyDown( 44 )=True Then z#=-0.1
If KeyDown( 30 )=True Then z#=0.1
If KeyDown (57)=True Then PlaySound blaster
MoveEntity sphere,x#,y#,z#
```

## Adjusting Volume

When two ships crash in your game, do you want the sound to be an earth-shattering roar? When players are talking behind enemy lines, should their voices be barely heard? You can easily adjust the volume of your sound effects by using

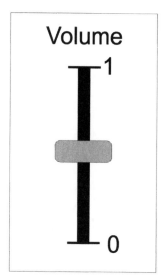

**Figure 14.1**
You can adjust the volume "dial" from 0 to 1 for your sounds.

the SoundVolume command in Blitz3D. You can even manipulate the volume of a sound so that it changes in relation to an object. For example, let's say you have an object far off in the distance. You can have the sound get louder and louder as it approaches your player. Let's start by adjusting the volume of a non-moving object and then get a bit fancier by adjusting the volume of a moving object.

Start by opening the file called volume.bb. It is the same file we used in the last section that has a sphere that plays a sound when it bumps into a cube. To change the volume of a sound, you must enter a value for the volume between 0 and 1 (see Figure 14.1). Entering a value of 1 will produce the loudest sound, while entering 0 will produce no sound at all. You can enter any decimal value in between to adjust the volume level (for example, 0.3, 0.04, 0.9). In this example, we will make the volume half its current level by entering a value of 0.5.

Add the following code in bold to the existing code:

```
;Collision Sound
If CountCollisions (sphere)
PlaySound blaster
SoundVolume blaster, 0.5
EndIf
```

If you run the program now, you'll notice that the volume level is half of what it was when we originally created the program. Now let's look at another example where we will change the volume level depending on how far away an object is to our player. To do this, we will create a variable called vol_level (that's what I've chosen to call it; you can call it anything you want), and we'll change the volume level based on the collision's distance from the camera. Open the file called volume_distance.bb, save it to a new folder, and make sure that the sound file punch is in the same folder. Here we have a sphere that can be moved along the z axis by pressing the up and down arrows and can be moved along the x axis by pressing the left or right arrows. Go ahead and run the program and move the sphere into the wall (a stretched cube) that we've created.

## Adjusting Pitch

Do you know what the difference is between a tenor and a soprano? Tenors have voices that are low, while sopranos have voices that are higher. The level of a person's voice, high or low, is called the pitch. I'm sure you've heard sound effects in which the pitch of someone's voice is set so high that it sounds like they are talking like a chipmunk. Or, perhaps you've heard the pitch of someone's voice lowered to a point that they sound like the devil or a monster.

Pitch is measured in a unit called a Hertz (Hz). In Blitz3D, you can adjust the pitch of a sound by adjusting its Hertz. The range goes from 1 Hz to 44,000 Hz.

Adjusting the pitch is simply a matter of using the SoundPitch code. Let's create an empty program using the following code and then add controls that will play a sound at different pitch levels. Before you start entering the code, save the program to a folder that contains the file hello.wav.

```
; Changing Pitch
;_____

Graphics3D 640,480
SetBuffer BackBuffer()

; Creating a light
light=CreateLight()

; Create camera
camera=CreateCamera()
PositionEntity camera, 0,1,0

;Loading the sound
hello = LoadSound ( "hello.wav" )
```

```
; Running the program
While Not KeyDown( 1 )
pitch#=12000

If KeyDown( 200 )=True Then pitch#= pitch#+500
If KeyDown( 208 )=True Then pitch#= pitch#-500
If pitch# < 1 Then pitch#=2000
If KeyDown( 57 )=True Then SoundPitch hello, pitch# PlaySound hello

RenderWorld
Flip

Wend

End
```

We'll look at the code in a moment, but for now, just run the program. Use the space bar to play the sound and then press the up or down arrows to adjust the pitch, and then press the space bar again.

Now let's look at the code we used to create the sound and adjust the pitch.

**hello = LoadSound ( "hello.wav" )**—This loads the sound into the program. We called our sound hello.

**pitch#=12000**—Here we created a variable and called it pitch#. We could have given the variable any name. We made the initial pitch level 12000 Hz.

**If KeyDown( 200 )=True Then pitch#= pitch#+500**—When the up arrow is pressed, the pitch will go up by 500 Hz.

**If KeyDown( 208 )=True Then pitch#= pitch#-500**—When the down arrow is pressed, the pitch will go down by 500 Hz.

**If pitch# < 2000 Then pitch#=2000**—If the pitch gets too low, you won't be able to hear it, so we will create a safety net that prevents the pitch from falling below 2000 Hz. The code says that if the pitch level (**pitch#**) falls below 2000 then just set it at 2000.

**If KeyDown( 57 )=True Then SoundPitch hello, pitch# PlaySound hello**—This code says that if the space bar is pressed, then set the pitch level and play the sound called hello.

**Note**

**Experiment with Pitch**

Unless you created the sound itself, you won't know what its pitch level is, so you'll have to experiment with different pitch levels if you want to make an adjustment.

## Adjusting Pan

Most computers that have sound have two speakers, one on the left and the other on the right. You can adjust how much of a sound comes out of each speaker. If you are familiar with a car radio or home stereo, adjusting the pan is the same as moving the Balance dial between left and right on your stereo (see Figure 14.2).

By adjusting the pan level, you can create some pretty cool effects because you can enhance the illusion of movement by having a sound play from one speaker to another. Imagine a ship flying across the screen. You could have the sound of the ship move from one speaker to the next as the ship moves.

Pan is applied by using the SoundPan command and setting a pan number. The pan number can be anywhere between –1 and 1. Here's how it works: A negative pan number will put more of the sound out of the left speaker, while a positive pan number puts more sound out of the right speaker. Here are some examples of pan numbers and how the sound would be divided:

- **0.75**—75% of the sound would come from the right speaker, and 25% would come from the left.

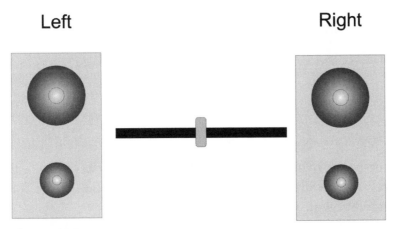

**Figure 14.2**
Pan allows you to adjust the level of sound coming out of each speaker.

■ **−0.25**—25% of the sound would come from the left speaker, and 75% would come from the right.

Get the idea? Let's put it to the test so that you can see how it works. Start by opening the file called pan.bb. Save the file to a new folder and make sure that the file train.wav is in that folder. We are now going to add the following code in bold to adjust the pan.

```
; Loading sound
train = LoadSound ( "train.wav" )

; Running the program
While Not KeyDown( 1 )
x#=0

If KeyDown( 203 )=True Then x#=-0.1
If KeyDown( 205 )=True Then x#=0.1
If x# > 0
pan# = 1
Else
pan# = -1
EndIf

MoveEntity sphere, x#,0,0

If x# <> 0
SoundPan train, pan#
PlaySound train
EndIf
UpdateWorld

RenderWorld
Flip

Wend

End
```

When you run the program and press the right or left arrow keys, you'll notice the sound "move" along with the sphere. Let's take a close look at the code we added to understand how it works.

```
train = LoadSound ( "train.wav" )
```

This loads the sound which we have called `train`.

```
If x# > 0
pan# = 1
Else
pan# = -1
EndIf -
```

This code tells Blitz3D that if the x coordinate of the sphere is greater than 0 (in other words, if it moves to the right), then the music should play out of the right speaker and vice versa for the left.

```
If x# <> 0
SoundPan train, pan#
PlaySound train
EndIf
```

This says that when the sphere moves, the music should begin playing.

## Note

**Looping a Sound**

You can use the code LoopSound ("soundfile.mp3") if you want to have a sound loop over and over. Obviously, you'd replace soundfile.mp3 with the actual file that you want to use.

# All I Want Is Loving You, and Music, Music, Music

That's the line from an old song called "Put Another Nickel In, In The Nickelodeon" that tells of the songwriter's love for a woman and, of course, music. Music can convert your game from a dud into a stud. Even a lame game can come to life with the addition of music.

Blitz3D makes a distinction between music and sounds. Sounds are played for particular events that happen in a game—for example, a button is pressed or a collision occurs—while music plays regardless of the events taking place.

With the exception of when you are using functions, it's a good idea to enter the code that plays the music outside of the game loop code. In the following example, we'll have an mp3 music file play while the game is running. Open the file called music.bb, save it to a new folder, and make sure that the file called med.mp3 is in that folder.

Playing music is accomplished simply by using the PlayMusic command and specifying a song to play.

Enter the following code before the "Running the Program" section.

```
; Playing Music
PlayMusic (''med.mp3'')
```

Go ahead and run the program. You should hear some funky music playing.

## Working with Channels

Imagine that you had a television set that could show you all the channels that were playing on your television all at once. That's how music works in Blitz3D: when you play music, it plays on a channel. You can have different songs playing on different channels, and you can hear them all at once. You can also control individual channels, pausing them, stopping them, adjusting their volume, and so on. To create a channel, you simply have to name a variable and make it PlayMusic.

Look at the following code:

```
backgroundmusic=PlayMusic("song.mp3")
```

Here, the channel is called backgroundmusic. You can create as many channels as you want in order to play as much music as you want.

### Channel Options

Just as with sounds, you can control the volume, pan, and pitch of your music by adding a few lines of code. In the following examples, assume that the channel created is called backgroundmusic.

**ChannelVolume backgroundmusic,1**—This code will adjust the volume of the backgroundmusic channel. Just as with sounds, you can enter a volume level between 0 and 1.

**ChannelPan backgroundmusic,-1**—This code will adjust the strength of the backgroundmusic channel between the left and the right speaker. Just as with sounds, you can enter a pan number between -1 and 1.

**ChannelPitch backgroundmusic,44000**—This code will adjust the pitch of the channel. Just as with sounds, you can enter a pitch value between 0 and 44000. Remember that pitch changes the deepness of the sound—the lower the pitch, the deeper the sound, and vice versa.

### Channel Control

Just as you can control the music playing on your mp3 player, you can stop, pause, and resume play by using the following code. This will come in handy if you want to stop or pause the music at a certain point in the game. Once again, in this example, assume that the channel we created is called backgroundmusic.

StopChannel backgroundmusic—This will stop the music from playing. If you restart the music, it will start from the beginning.

PauseChannel backgroundmusic—This will pause the music. When you restart it, it will start from the point where it was paused.

ResumeChannel backgroundmusic—This will resume play of the music from the point it was paused.

### Note

**Quirky MP3s**

Blitz3D is a little funny when it comes to MP3 files. There are some files that it simply won't play. You'll have to experiment to ensure that your sound file will work in the game you create.

## Looping Music

Depending on the length of your song, it may not be long enough to continue throughout the entire game. To resolve this, you can have the song play over and over by creating a loop. There's no command that allows you to play *music* repeatedly, but there is one for *sound*). Using any program, you can add a loop by creating an If statement like the one that follows.

```
backgroundmusic=PlayMusic("song.mp3")

; Running the program
While Not KeyDown( 1 )
If Not ChannelPlaying (backgroundmusic)
backgroundmusic=PlayMusic ("song.mp3")
EndIf
```

Let's take a look at the code used to create this loop.

```
backgroundmusic=PlayMusic("song.mp3")
```

This code will create a channel called backgroundmusic.

```
If Not ChannelPlaying (backgroundmusic)
backgroundmusic=PlayMusic ("song.mp3")
```

This code says that if the channel background music isn't playing, then it should be played. That means that as soon as the music ends, Blitz3D will notice that there is no song playing and will restart the music.

## Note

**Copyright**

Nothing is more fun than putting your favorite songs into your games. Whether it's Lincoln Park, U2, Eminem, or some other group, having hit music in your games makes them a lot more enjoyable to play. Adding popular tunes to your games is fine if you are just creating them for yourself or your friends to play, but if you are trying to make a game that will be sold or available for download, you'll need to obtain permission to use the music from the artists and/or music publisher in order to avoid copyright infringement.

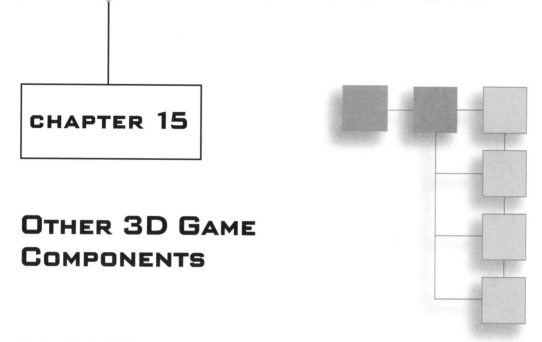

# CHAPTER 15

# OTHER 3D GAME COMPONENTS

So far this book has covered a lot of different components of a game, and we're almost ready to create our first fully functional game. Based on what you've learned so far, you could probably even create your first game on your own right now. There are a few key areas, however, that will help make your games look and play better, and I will cover them in this chapter. Think of this chapter as a potluck of different game elements that will improve your 3D game programming skills.

Here we will add on to some of the concepts you learned earlier by covering certain details and concepts that you weren't quite ready for until now.

## Gravity

The concept of gravity is important to many different types of games. Unless your game takes place in space or in some alternate gravity-less universe, you'll probably want your players or objects to either stay on the ground or float back to the ground when they jump in the air. There are several ways to create the illusion of gravity, and we'll explore one of the easiest in the following example.

Start by opening the program gravity.bb, which includes several features that have already been covered in the book. We have a sky, created by a sphere; a terrain with a collision set up between our character (a sphere with a pattern) so that he doesn't fall through the terrain; and controls set up to move around. Run the program and use the arrow keys and the A and Z keys to navigate around our little world.

**Figure 15.1**
To create the illusion of gravity, we'll move an object downward continually.

It's surprisingly easy to add code to create "gravity." Basically, what we'll do is move the object downward all of the time so that the character is always moving downward (see Figure 15.1).

We will apply just a light force of gravity so that our character will still be able to jump or move off the ground, but will then float gently to the ground. Add the following code in bold:

```
If KeyDown( 203 )=True Then x#=-0.1
If KeyDown( 205 )=True Then x#=0.1
If KeyDown( 208 )=True Then y#=-0.1
If KeyDown( 200 )=True Then y#=0.1
If KeyDown( 44 )=True Then z#=-0.1
If KeyDown( 30 )=True Then z#=0.1
MoveEntity sphere,x#,y#,z#
TranslateEntity sphere, 0,-.02,0
UpdateWorld

RenderWorld
Flip

Wend

End
```

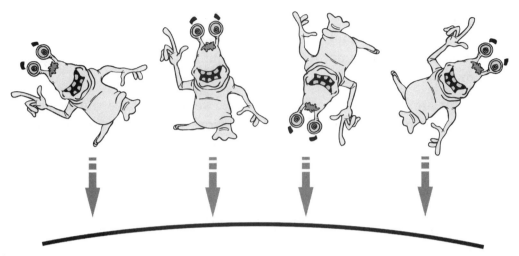

**Figure 15.2**
Use the `TranslateEntity` command rather than the `MoveEntity` command for the gravity so that no matter what direction the object is facing it will always float downward.

Take a look at the code that created the gravity:

```
TranslateEntity sphere, 0,-.02,0
```

We used the `TranslateEntity` command because we want the gravity to move downward on the y axis no matter what position our character is in (see Figure 15.2). The rest of the code is pretty straightforward: `sphere` is the name of the object we are applying gravity to, and `-0.02` is the force of the gravity. We use a negative value because we want the direction of the gravity to be downward along the y axis.

**N o t e**

**Not Too Much**

Don't make your force of gravity too high. Gravity levels that are too high will prevent your object from moving in any direction, as the downward force is too strong.

## Simple Jumping

Jumping is an integral part of many different types of games and can be achieved quite easily in Blitz3D. Whether it's your character jumping over obstacles, hurdles, or bad guys, the process of creating a bounce is fairly easy. I called this section "Simple Jumping" because it creates a code that will have an object jump only when a key is pressed on the keyboard. We haven't added any extra parameters. For example, the shape in this example doesn't have to be on the ground in order to jump; it can actually jump again midway through the first jump.

In order for jumping to work in this example, we need to have gravity already created on our object. Refer back to the previous section for information on creating gravity. Open the file called jumping.bb, which is the same file we used in the last section, with just a higher level of gravity (set at –0.1). The higher the level of gravity, the faster our object will fall back to the ground after it has jumped.

The actual process of jumping is just a matter of changing the object's position on the y axis. Add the following code in bold to the existing code:

```
While Not KeyDown( 1 )
x#=0
y#=0
z#=0

If KeyDown( 203 )=True Then x#=-0.1
If KeyDown( 205 )=True Then x#=0.1
If KeyDown( 208 )=True Then y#=-0.1
If KeyDown( 200 )=True Then y#=0.1
If KeyDown( 44 )=True Then z#=-0.1
If KeyDown( 30 )=True Then z#=0.1
If KeyDown (57)=True Then y#=0.5
MoveEntity sphere,x#,y#,z#
TranslateEntity sphere, 0,-0.1,0
UpdateWorld

RenderWorld
Flip

Wend

End
```

Run the program now and hit the space bar once. You should notice that your ball jumps in the air and then floats back down. Now press the left and right arrow keys or the A or Z keys to move the sphere, and then press the space bar to see the object jump as it moves (see Figure 15.3).

**Figure 15.3**
Pressing the space bar will make the sphere appear to "jump."

You can change how fast the object floats down by changing the gravity level. Let's take a look at the code we used to create the jump:

```
If KeyDown (57)=True Then y#=0.5
```

What this says is that when the space bar is pressed (key 57), the character's position should go up by 0.5 units along the y axis. We had already set up the code for movement (`MoveEntity sphere,x#,y#,z#`), so we only needed to add this one line of code to create the jump.

## Velocity

Creating the illusion of velocity can make your game feel more realistic. In real life, most objects don't just start and stop. Think of racers who sprint in the Olympics. When the gun sounds they aren't going their top speed instantly; it takes several seconds for them to reach their maximum stride. The same holds true when they cross the finish line. They don't stop instantly; it takes them a quite a few steps to apply the brakes and slow down. By controlling an object's velocity in your game, you can make its movement seem more realistic. In an earlier chapter, you learned how to have objects move on their own. Here you will learn to increase and decrease their speed or stop on a dime. These types of controls are great for games that contain any type of moving vehicle that the player controls.

Start by opening the program called velocity.bb. This program contains a textured sphere that is just sitting there. We are going to add controls that will act like a gas pedal, a brake, and an emergency brake to move and stop the sphere. To keep things simple, we will only add controls for the z axis. Add the following code in bold to create the controls, and then I'll discuss everything that we've added.

```
; The following code makes the program run
While Not KeyDown( 1 )

If KeyDown( 208 )=True Then velocity#=velocity#-0.001
If KeyDown( 200 )=True Then velocity#=velocity#+0.001
If KeyDown (31 ) Then velocity#=0
MoveEntity sphere,0,0,velocity#
TranslateEntity sphere, 0,-0.03,0
Collisions type_player,type_ground,2,2
Collisions type_ground,type_player,2,2
UpdateWorld

RenderWorld
Flip

Wend

End
```

With these four lines of code, we've created a gas pedal, a brake (or reverse), and an emergency brake. Let's look at the breakdown of the code we added:

**If KeyDown( 208 )=True Then velocity#=velocity#-0.001** – This code says that when the up arrow is pressed (key 208), then increase the current velocity by 0.001 units. In other words, every time you press the up arrow, the velocity will become greater and greater. By adjusting the velocity number (0.001), you can increase or decrease the speed of the acceleration. By the way, we created a variable here called velocity, but we could have called it anything we wanted— it's just a name we are assigning to this variable.

**If KeyDown( 200 )=True Then velocity#=velocity#+0.001** – This code is the opposite of the code above. It says that when the down arrow is pressed, decrease the current velocity by 0.001 units.

**If KeyDown (31 ) Then velocity#=0** – This is our emergency brake. The code says that if you press the S key on your keyboard (key 31), then the velocity will become 0.

**MoveEntity sphere,0,0,velocity#** – This is the code that sets everything in motion. It says that while the program is running, don't move the sphere at all along the x or y axes, but move it along the z axis by the velocity number. The velocity number will change depending on whether the up arrow, down arrow, or S key is being pressed.

Now go ahead and run the program. Pressing the up arrow will increase your velocity, while pressing the down arrow will slow you down (see Figure 15.4). If you keep pressing the down arrow, you will eventually start accelerating in reverse. You can press the S key at any time to stop the acceleration.

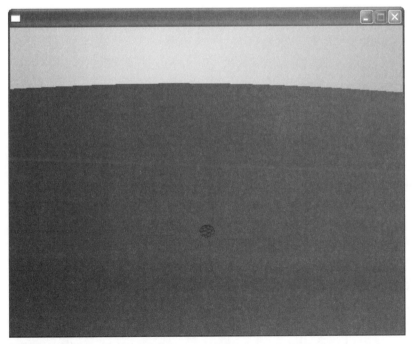

**Figure 15.4**
You can use the arrow keys to zoom the ball around the playing field.

```
; The following code makes the program run
While Not KeyDown( 1 )

If KeyDown( 208 )=True Then velocity#=velocity#-0.001
If KeyDown( 200 )=True Then velocity#=velocity#+0.001
If KeyDown (31 ) Then velocity#=0
If KeyDown (31 ) Then xvelocity#=0
If KeyDown( 203 )=True Then xvelocity#=xvelocity#-0.001
If KeyDown( 205 )=True Then xvelocity#=xvelocity#+0.001
MoveEntity sphere,xvelocity#,0,velocity#
TranslateEntity sphere, 0,-0.03,0
Collisions type_player,type_ground,2,2
Collisions type_ground,type_player,2,2
UpdateWorld

RenderWorld
Flip

Wend

End
```

# Chase Camera

A good percentage of 3D games use a feature called a chase camera. If you've ever played a modern-day "Mario Bros." type of game, then you've already seen a chase camera in use. A chase camera follows the action of the player of the game. Usually the player is always just a few feet in front of the camera, and wherever the player goes, he remains in sight because the camera follows him around. There's a good likelihood that you'll want to incorporate a chase camera into your games, and the good news is that it isn't all that difficult. Don't get me wrong, though—it can be made very complicated, as there are all sorts of features and enhancements you can add to the simple chase camera that we are about to create. For now, at least, I'm going to show you a simple way to create a chase camera.

Begin by opening the file called chase_camera.bb. This file contains a cone whose acceleration can be changed by pressing the up and down arrows and can be stopped by pressing the S key. The only problem is that if you press either arrow key for more than a second or two, the cone will zoom off the screen as the camera just stays put. We can create a chase camera with just a few lines of code.

Start off by rotating the camera by 45 degrees along the x axis. Right now, this wouldn't make much sense to do, but in a moment we are going to raise the camera, so having it rotated 45 degrees will help you see the cone since it will be looking downward toward the cone. Add the following code in bold:

```
; Create camera
camera=CreateCamera()
RotateEntity camera, 45,0,0
```

The next thing we are going to do is add the code that will tell Blitz3D to put the camera wherever the cone is and then position it a few units back. Add the following code in bold:

```
; The following code makes the program run
While Not KeyDown( 1 )

If KeyDown( 208 )=True Then velocity#=velocity#-0.001
If KeyDown( 200 )=True Then velocity#=velocity#+0.001
If KeyDown (31 ) Then velocity#=0
If KeyDown (31 ) Then xvelocity#=0
If KeyDown( 203 )=True Then xvelocity#=xvelocity#-0.001
If KeyDown( 205 )=True Then xvelocity#=xvelocity#+0.001
MoveEntity cone,xvelocity#,0,velocity#
TranslateEntity cone, 0,-0.03,0
PositionEntity camera,EntityX(cone),0,EntityZ(cone)
MoveEntity camera,0,0,-5
Collisions type_player,type_ground,2,2
Collisions type_ground,type_player,2,2
UpdateWorld

RenderWorld
Flip

Wend

End
```

**Figure 15.5**
Chase cameras are very popular in many 3D games. The camera follows the object around the screen.

Run the program now, and you should have a chase camera, as shown in Figure 15.5.

You've done it! You've created a chase camera. Let's take a close look at the code we used to create this wonderful effect:

`PositionEntity camera,EntityX(cone),0,EntityZ(cone)` — Here we are positioning the camera at the exact same spot of the location of the cone on the x axis and the z axis. The code `EntityX(cone)` enters the current location of the cone on the x axis, while `EntityZ(cone)` does the same for the z axis. This means that no matter where the cone is, the camera will be positioned in the exact same location on the x axis and z axis. Since we don't actually want the camera to be right on top of cone (we want it to be a few steps back), we enter the next line of code. Note that we left the position of the camera on the y axis at 0. This is because our player doesn't really jump or move up and down, so there is no need to enter a value for the y axis position. If it did we would have replaced the *0* with *EntityY(cone)*.

`MoveEntity camera,0,0,-5` — Because we don't want the camera over our cone (we want it to be a few steps back), we enter this line of code. Basically, we are saying take the current position of the camera (which at this point should be right on top of the cone) and move it back 5 units.

Go ahead and run the program now and watch as the camera follows the action.

## Mirror

In Chapter 12, "Setting the Stage," you learned how to create planes and terrains for your game. A great effect you can add to your terrains is the illusion that there is a reflection from the ground. This can be accomplished by using the mirror command. When you create a mirror, it reflects everything that is either above it or below it. The mirror command is very simple to add:

```
; This code creates a mirror
mirror=CreateMirror()
```

Here we've created a mirror called mirror, but you can call it anything you'd like. You can also reposition the mirror so that it is above or below your objects (see Figure 15.6).

**Figure 15.6**
Notice how the cone reflects in the mirror.

## Timing

Remember that your game is like a movie, going by frame by frame as seconds go by. You can use this to your advantage, not only in creating collisions and explosions, but for all types of effects in your game. Basically, you can create a countdown timer and have events take place before, during, or after a specific time. To do this, we will use the `Millisecs()` command. Before I start describing this command, it's important to know that 1000 milliseconds is equal to 1 second. Blitz3D is always counting the time, and the `Millisecs()` command will tell you what the current time is. You can use this command to create a timer and have events happen based on that time. Let's use this command to create a ticking time bomb!

Start by opening the program called bomb.bb and save it with a new name. This file is simply five spheres. One is very big, which will be the bomb, and the other four are smaller circles hiding behind the sphere that will act as the shrapnel. What we are going to do is create a countdown timer, and after 5 seconds we'll make the bomb disappear and send the shrapnel flying.

We need to start by creating the timer variable, and we will do this by adding the following code in bold. Enter this code outside of the game loop, right below the section where you created the shrapnel.

```
; This code creates a variable for the timer.
timer=MilliSecs()
```

It is very important that this code remain outside of the game loop—in other words, before the line that reads `While Not KeyDown (1)`; otherwise, the timer will continually reset as the game is running. So now we have a timer that has started counting every millisecond that goes by, which we have called `timer`. We could have given this timer any name since it is just a name we associated with the command. Now that we have a timer, we need to create some action to happen based on the timer. Add the following code in bold:

```
; This code makes the program run
While Not KeyDown( 1 )

; This code creates the explosion
If MilliSecs() < timer + 3000 ShowEntity bomb Else HideEntity bomb
If MilliSecs() > timer + 3000 MoveEntity shrapnel, -.3,+.8,.15
If MilliSecs() > timer + 3000 MoveEntity shrapnel1, .3,-.5,.05
If MilliSecs() > timer + 3000 MoveEntity shrapnel2, -.1,+.5,-.35
If MilliSecs() > timer + 3000 MoveEntity shrapnel3, .3,0,.0
```

```
RenderWorld
Flip

Wend

End
```

Run the program now. After 3 seconds, the bomb will explode. Now let's look at the code that we created:

**If MilliSecs() < timer + 3000 ShowEntity bomb Else HideEntity bomb** — This line basically says that after 3 seconds have passed, hide the sphere. Here's how it's done: If the current time (MilliSecs()) is less than the timer plus 3 seconds (< timer + 3000), then show the bomb (ShowEntity bomb). Otherwise, hide the bomb (HideEntity bomb).

The rest of the code deals with the particles flying. It's basically the same as the code above:

```
If MilliSecs() > timer + 3000 MoveEntity shrapnel, -.3,+.8,.15
If MilliSecs() > timer + 3000 MoveEntity shrapnel1, .3,-.5,.05
If MilliSecs() > timer + 3000 MoveEntity shrapnel2, -.1,+.5,-.35
If MilliSecs() > timer + 3000 MoveEntity shrapnel3, .3,0,.0
```

This code just says that after 3 seconds have passed, send the four spheres flying. The things you can do with timings are endless. As you've seen here, you can hide and move objects, but beyond that you can do just about anything.

## Text

You may be thinking to yourself, *This is 3D game programming; why do I need text?* Text can actually play a very important role in your 3D games since it allows the game to communicate with the players. If you think about it, text is a part of almost every game that you play. Some examples of how text is used in your games include: your score, the amount of ammunition you have left, your health, your current level, the time you have left, your position, and many others.

Adding text to your game is quite easy in Blitz3D. You simply have to indicate where on the screen you want the text to appear and what you want the text to say. You can also add variables to your text so that changing information can also be displayed.

## Adding and Positioning Text

Adding and positioning text in your games can all be done with one line of code, simply called the Text command. When you enter the Text command, you specify what text is to be included, where it is to be positioned, and how it should be justified. Here is an example of a line of code that will create a line of text that says "Your Score Is:":

```
Text 100,20, "Your Score Is: ",True,False
```

If you positioned this text in the right location and then ran the program, you should get the same result as seen in Figure 15.7.

Now let's dissect the code we created to see how we created this text:

**Text 100,20,** – The word Text starts the command and is followed by two numbers separated by commas. The first number represents the x coordinate for the position of the text, and the second number represents the y coordinate. In this example, the 100 represents how far in from the left the text should appear, and the 20 represents how far down from the top the text should appear. Figuring

**Figure 15.7**
Entering the code to create the text above is simply a matter of using the Text command.

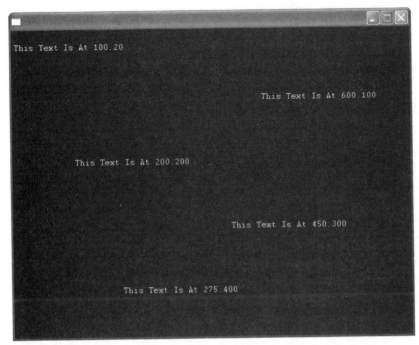

**Figure 15.8**
Figuring out the positioning of text on the screen will take some trial and error.

out the exact positioning of your text will take some trial and error, so experiment with different values. Figure 15.8 shows text positioned at different coordinates throughout the screen.

**"Your Score Is:"** – The actual text that you want to have appear on the screen should be entered between quotation marks. In this case, the text that is within the quotation marks, Your Score Is:, will appear onscreen.

**,True,False** – These next parts of the code are optional, but they allow you to justify the text within a line. Either one can be made True or False. The first word, in this case True, either turns off or on horizontal centering. When horizontal centering is turned on, the text is centered around the x position you have set; otherwise, it is left justified starting at the x coordinate. The best way to understand this is to look at an example. Following are four lines of code, each positioned at the 280 mark for the x coordinate (the 280 mark is actually marked with an x in the last line of text). Notice how the two lines of code that were set to True for horizontal centering are centered around the 280 point, while the ones that were set to False are left justified at the 280 mark. See the results of the following in Figure 15.9.

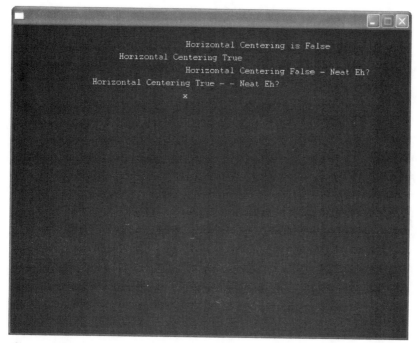

**Figure 15.9**
You can adjust the horizontal settings for your text. The x in this image represents the center point.

```
Text 280 ,20, "Horizontal Centering is False ",False,False
Text 280,40, "Horizontal Centering True ",True,False
Text 280,60, "Horizontal Centering False - Neat Eh?",False,False
Text 280,80, "Horizontal Centering True - - Neat Eh?",True,False
Text 280,100 ,"x", True,False
```

The code with the horizontal centering set to True is centered around the x-coordinate.

The second word of the code, in this case set to False, deals with the vertical centering around the y coordinate that you specify. True centers the text vertically, while False does not.

Now that you've seen the code, it's time to put it into action. The only hard part about adding the Text line of code is entering it in the right location. The Text code needs to be placed within the game loop, between the RenderWorld line and the Flip line. Open the file called text.bb, which is a program that contains a sphere and a cone and that has some collisions set up.

Add the following line of code (in bold) between the RenderWorld and Flip commands:

```
; This following code makes our program run
While Not KeyDown( 1 )
x#=0
y#=0
z#=0

If KeyDown( 203 )=True Then x#=-0.1
If KeyDown( 205 )=True Then x#=0.1
If KeyDown( 208 )=True Then y#=-0.1
If KeyDown( 200 )=True Then y#=0.1
MoveEntity sphere,x#,y#,z#
UpdateWorld

RenderWorld
Text 10 ,20, "Score: ",False,False
Flip

Wend

End
```

Take a look at Figure 15.10 to see the results.

**Note**

**Positioning**

The location where you enter code is very important when it comes to the Text command. It needs to be inserted between the RenderWorld and Flip commands. Don't believe me? Try placing the Text code anywhere else. Either the program won't run, or you won't be able to see the text on the screen.

## Adding Text Variables

As you can see by the example in the last section, having text without some sort of variable just isn't that effective. In that example, we have the word "Score," but more importantly, what we don't have is the actual score. This can be added by expanding our Text command. Think of the Text command as an equation; if you want to add something, just use the + sign.

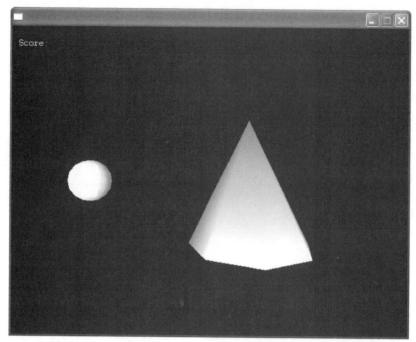

**Figure 15.10**
If you ran the program now, you would see the word "Score" in the top left corner.

Now we'll continue on with the example we used in the last section, so if for some reason you thought it would be a good idea to skip that section and jump to here, think again. Go back and add the "Score" line to the text.bb program.

Before we add the code necessary to display the score on the screen, we have to determine how we are going to keep score in this game. For this example, we'll say that every time the sphere touches the cone, a point will be earned. You learned in Chapter 13, "Collisions," that the CountCollisions command will count the number of times an object collides with another within each frame. We'll use this to act as our score. To actually add the score variable to the text onscreen, we simply use a + sign. Let's add the following code in bold to our program:

```
; The following code makes the program run
While Not KeyDown( 1 )
x#=0
y#=0
z#=0
```

```
If KeyDown( 203 )=True Then x#=-0.1
If KeyDown( 205 )=True Then x#=0.1
If KeyDown( 208 )=True Then y#=-0.1
If KeyDown( 200 )=True Then y#=0.1
If CountCollisions (sphere) Then score#=score#+1
MoveEntity sphere,x#,y#,z#
UpdateWorld

RenderWorld
Text 10 ,20, "Score: " + score# , False,False
Flip

Wend

End
```

Run the program now, and using the arrow keys, move the sphere into the cone. As soon as the sphere touches the cone, the score will start registering, as in Figure 15.11.

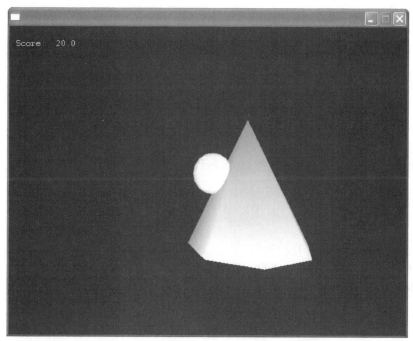

**Figure 15.11**
When the sphere touches the cone, the score will appear on the screen.

We added only two little snippets of code to create the score. Let's see how we did it:

**If CountCollisions (sphere) Then score#=score#+1** – Here we are saying that if a collision occurs between the sphere and the cone, then the variable we created called score# will become score# + 1. In other words, the score starts out at 0. If a collision occurs, then the score becomes 0 + 1, which would make the score 1. If another collision occurs, the score (which is now at 1) becomes 1+1, in other words, 2. This continues on, and we see the score getting higher and higher as long as the two objects are colliding.

**Text 10 ,20, "Score: " + score# , False,False** – Here we added the score variable to the existing text by using a + sign before adding the variable. You can add a variety of variables to your text strings simply by adding a + sign.

Let's now add some other variables to our text string. The only other variables we have in the program we are using are the x and y locations of the sphere, so let's add a line of text that displays the position of the sphere at all times. Add the following code in bold to the program:

```
; The following code makes the program run
While Not KeyDown( 1 )
x#=0
y#=0
z#=0

If KeyDown ( 203 )=True Then x#=-0.1
If KeyDown ( 205 )=True Then x#=0.1
If KeyDown ( 208 )=True Then y#=-0.1
If KeyDown ( 200 )=True Then y#=0.1
If CountCollisions (sphere) Then score#=score#+1
MoveEntity sphere,x#,y#,z#
UpdateWorld

RenderWorld
Text 10 ,20, "Score: "+ score#,False,False
Text 10 ,60, "Sphere x-coordinate: " + EntityX(sphere) + " Sphere y-coordinate:
  " + EntityY(sphere) , False,False
Flip

Wend

End
```

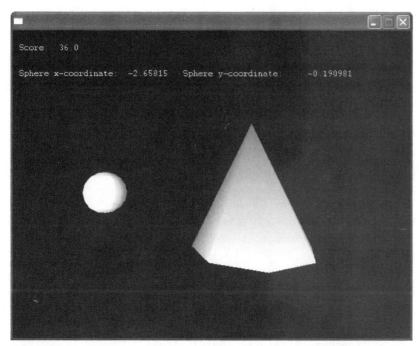

**Figure 15.12**
The code you added will display the x and y coordinates of the sphere.

Run the program now, and move the sphere around using the arrow keys. Your screen should look similar to Figure 15.12.

Let's take a closer look at the code we entered to see how we accomplished this:

**Text 10 ,60,** – This specified that the text needs to be placed 10 units from the left of the screen and 60 units down.

**"Sphere x-coordinate: "** – As you learned earlier, we need to add text in between quotation marks.

**+ EntityX(sphere)** – By adding a + sign, we are able to add additional variables or text. In this case, we used the variable EntityX(sphere), which displays the x-coordinate of the sphere.

**+ " Sphere y-coordinate: "** – Notice the spaces that were left between the ends of the text and the quotation marks, allowing space for the numbers.

**+ EntityY(sphere)** – This produces the y coordinate of the sphere.

**, False,False** – We turned off horizontal and vertical centering. We actually didn't need this part of the code at all, since these are the defaults.

## Setting Font Size and Appearance

As you can see by the previous examples, the appearance of the text didn't look too spectacular. It was plain white, relatively small, and used a standard font. You can change all that by loading fonts, specifying their attributes, and then applying those fonts and attributes to your string of text.

In Blitz3D, you use the LoadFont command to bring fonts into the program and specify their attributes. You can create different font variables so that applying different styles to your text becomes quite easy. Once your fonts are loaded, you can use the SetFont command to apply your font to a specific line of text.

Let's look at a typical line of code used to load a font:

```
FntArial14U=LoadFont("Arial",14,False,False,True)
```

This code may look a little long and involved, but it's actually pretty straight-forward. There are seven parts to the load font command:

```
Indentifier = LoadFont (fontname$[,height][,bold][,italic][,underlined])
```

Let's break down the code used as an example to see how it works:

**FntArial14U =** – This is the identifier, or name, that we've given to the font we're loading. It's a good idea to give it a descriptive name that you'll understand. Typically, the identifier for a font should start with Fnt so that you can quickly recognize what it is. In this case I called the font FntArial14U, which to me indicates that the font is Arial, it's size is 14, and it is underlined. Keep in mind that the identifier can be any name you choose.

**LoadFont** – This is the command that will initiate the font loading. Everything after this command will be within parentheses.

**("Arial",** – This is the font you are loading. You have to put the font name in quotation marks.

**14,** – This is the size of the font you are creating. The default size for fonts is 12.

**False,** – The first of three True or False parameters. This parameter controls whether or not the font is bold. True indicates that the font will be bold, while False will not be bold.

**False,** – This parameter controls whether or not the font is italicized. True indicates that the font will be in italics, while False will not be italicized.

**True)** – This parameter controls whether or not the font is underlined. True indicates that the font will be underlined, while False will not be underlined.

**Note**

**Now You Try**

Test your understanding of loading fonts. Take a look at the following code and try to determine how the font will appear:

```
F=LoadFont("Times",28,True,True,False)
```

If you guessed that it would be Times, size 28, bold, italic, and not underlined, then you'd be right!

It's a good idea to use only one or two different fonts in your games to avoid distracting players from your game. It's also a good idea to load all of your fonts in various configurations all at once so that accessing them is easy. For example, if you are going to be creating some text in the font Times, you probably should load a few different sizes, and some different configurations of attributes all at once so that you don't have to create them as you go along while programming your game. Here's a typical example of how you would create several different "flavors" of the same font so that you would have a library to choose from while programming:

```
fntTunga14=LoadFont(''Tunga'',14,False,False,False)
fntTunga 14B=LoadFont(''Tunga'',14,True,False,False)
fntTunga14I=LoadFont(''Tunga'',14,False,True,False)
fntTunga14U=LoadFont(''Tunga'',14,False,False,True)
```

Above I've created four different versions of the font Tunga. The first is simply size 14, the second is size 14 and bold, the third is size 14 and italicized, and the last one is size 14 and underlined. You can create any combination of fonts that you want; just keep in mind that every font you load takes up space in memory.

**Note**

**Font Defaults**

By default, fonts are set to size 12 with bold, italics, and underline set to False. This means that you do not need to include them as part of your code if you are accepting the defaults. For example, if we wanted to load the font Tunga at size 12, with no bold, italics, or underline, then rather than having to enter `fntTunga12=LoadFont(''Tunga'',12,False,False,False)`, we would only have to enter `fntTunga12=LoadFont(''Tunga'')` because all the other defaults are accepted.

Now that you know how to load a font, it's time to learn how to actually apply the font. You do this by using the SetFont command right before the line of text you are applying. For example, let's say you've loaded a font as follows:

```
FntArial14BI=LoadFont("Arial",14,True,True,False)
```

You would then apply this font using the following code right before your line of text.

```
SetFont Fntarial14BI
```

All the text that is created after the font is set will take on those attributes (in this case, Arial, size 14, bold, and italicized) until either a new font is set or the font is turned off.

Let's practice applying a font. Create a new program with the following code:

```
; Changing Fonts
;_____

Graphics3D 640,480
SetBuffer BackBuffer()

; Create camera
camera=CreateCamera()

;Create light
light=CreateLight()

;The following code makes the program run
While Not KeyDown( 1 )
RenderWorld
Text 300,20, "This is Arial 24", True
Text 300,120, "This is Arial 24 Bold", True
Text 300,220, "This is Arial 24 Italics",True
Text 300,320, "This is Arial 24 Underlined", True
Text 300,420, "This is Arial 24 Bold, Italics and Underlined", True
Flip

Wend

End
```

Now enter the following code in bold to load the fonts and then apply them.

```
; Changing Fonts
;_____

Graphics3D 640,480
SetBuffer BackBuffer()

; Create camera
camera=CreateCamera()

;Create light
light=CreateLight()

; Loading the fonts
fntArial=LoadFont("Arial",24)
fntArialB=LoadFont("Arial",24,True)
fntArialI=LoadFont("Arial",24,False,True,False)
fntArialU=LoadFont("Arial",24,False,False,True)
fntArialBIU=LoadFont("Arial",24,True,True,True)

;The following code makes the program run
While Not KeyDown( 1 )
RenderWorld
SetFont fntArial
Text 300,20, "This is Arial 24", True
SetFont fntArialB
Text 300,120, "This is Arial 24 Bold", True
SetFont fntArialI
Text 300,220, "This is Arial 24 Italics",True
SetFont fntArialU
Text 300,320, "This is Arial 24 Underlined", True
SetFont fntArialBIU
Text 300,420, "This is Arial 24 Bold, Italics and Underlined", True
Flip

Wend

End
```

Take a look at Figure 15.13, which shows how the program should look when you run it now.

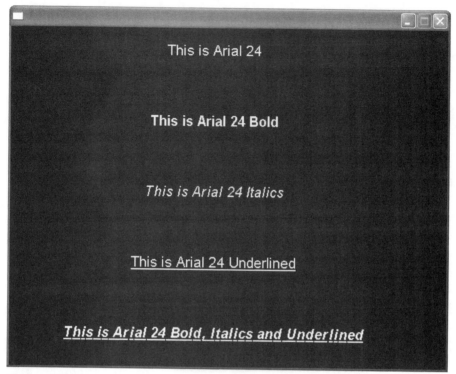

**Figure 15.13**
When you run the program now, you should see the different fonts applied.

**Note**

**Font Color**

You can change the color of your font by using the Color command before entering the Text line. To apply the color command, you simply type Color followed by the red, green, and blue values of the color you want to apply. For example, if you wanted to create some red text, you'd enter the code as follows:

Color 255,0,0

Text 200,300, "This text will be red because it is preceded by the Color command"

## Freeing Fonts

Fonts take up room in memory while they are loaded and therefore could potentially slow down your game. For this reason you should remove your fonts from memory using the FreeFont command after they have been applied. FreeFont works the same way that SetFont does in that you simply name the font that you want to free. You can free the fonts outside of the main loop of the program. Using the example from the previous section, free the fonts by adding the following code in bold:

```
While Not KeyDown( 1 )
RenderWorld
SetFont fntArial
Text 300,20, "This is Arial 24", True
SetFont fntArialB
Text 300,120, "This is Arial 24 Bold", True
SetFont fntArialI
Text 300,220, "This is Arial 24 Italics",True
SetFont fntArialU
Text 300,320, "This is Arial 24 Underlined", True
SetFont fntArialBIU
Text 300,420, "This is Arial 24 Bold, Italics and Underlined", True
Flip

Wend

FreeFont fntArial
FreeFont fntArialB
FreeFont fntArialI
FreeFont fntArialU
FreeFont fntArialBIU

End
```

## Math

Don't skip this section just because of the title! I know that math can be fairly intimidating for many people, but I promise that this will be easy. Math actually plays a huge role in all types of video games, but luckily for us, most of the calculations are done behind the scenes by the computer. That being said, there will be various instances where you will have to do some calculations in your programs. The truth is that throughout the examples in the book so far, we've actually done a bit a math, and you probably didn't even notice.

Let's start with a simple example of how you would use math. Earlier in this chapter, we used math when we were determining the score when a sphere bumped into a sphere. Do you remember the code we entered? It was score#=score#+1. See? Just simple addition. The beauty of doing math in Blitz3D is that you can not only work with numbers, but you can also include variables in your equations. The following chart shows you the commands you can use in Blitz3D to write equations:

+        Addition

-        Subtraction

*        Multiplication

/        Division

=        Equals

Let's put our math skills to use by writing a small program that does some math (by the way, all programs you create use math.) We are going to write a program that does a simple conversion for us. I happen to live in Canada where we use the metric system, which makes things difficult when driving through the States because our speed limits are in kilometers per hour and the U.S. speed limits are in miles per hour. So, as an example, let's start by creating a program that converts kilometers to miles. Start by creating a blank program that contains the following code:

```
; Km conversion
;_____

Graphics3D 640,480
SetBuffer BackBuffer()

; Create camera
camera=CreateCamera()

;Create light
light=CreateLight()

;The following code makes our program run
While Not KeyDown( 1 )

RenderWorld
Flip

Wend

End
```

In order for this program to work, players will first need to enter the number of kilometers they want converted. To do this, we will add something called a *string variable*. You'll learn more about string variables in Chapter 16, "Programming Fundamentals," so for now just enter the code in bold in the location specified:

```
;Create light
light=CreateLight()

;Inputting the text
Km = Input (''Please enter the number of km you want to convert to miles '')
;The following code makes our program run
While Not KeyDown( 1 )
```

Now it's time for the math. At this point, the player has entered in a number for the amount of kilometers he wants converted. This number becomes the variable called Km#. Since there are about 0.62137 miles for every kilometer, we need to do some multiplication to figure out the number of miles. To do this, we are going to have Blitz3D calculate the answer to Km# * 0.62137 and then display it on screen. Remember that * is multiplication in Blitz3D. Enter the following code in bold:

```
;Create light
light=CreateLight()

;Inputting the text
Km = Input (''Please enter the number of km you want to convert to miles '')

;The following code makes the program run
While Not KeyDown( 1 )

RenderWorld
Text 100,50, ''There are '' +km*0.62137 + '' miles in '' + km + '' kilometers''
Flip

Wend

End
```

Run the program now, and you'll see your math skills in action. You enter a number in kilometers, and you get your answer in miles (see Figure 15.14). Pretty cool, eh? (That's Canadian talk for "Pretty cool, isn't it?")

While this is just one simple example of how math can be used, you can see that we didn't create any special variables for our equation; we just multiplied our variable (km#) by an amount to get our answer.

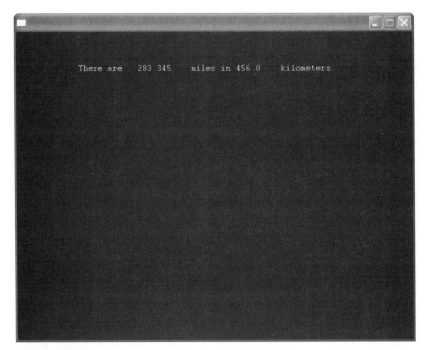

There are   283.345   miles in 456.0   kilometers

**Figure 15.14**
Your math skills have created a conversion calculator.

# Random

Random is your best friend. Well, maybe not your best friend, but a really, really, really good friend. You can do a lot of cool stuff with the Random command in Blitz3D. Okay, enough already, what is Random? The Random command . . . well . . . makes thing random. So far in this book, whenever we've wanted to specify an attribute for an object—for example, the color or size or position of a shape—we would actually tell Blitz3D what that attribute should be. Using the Random command, you can have Blitz3D randomly set the attributes for your object.

Why would you want to use random? Let me count the ways. There are literally thousands of different applications for the Random command, but I'll give you just a few. Typically, the Random command is used when you are dealing with more than one object. Here are a few examples of scenarios where you would use the random command:

- Image you had a game with 100 different aliens. Rather than having to provide a color to each alien, you could have Blitz3D randomly give them each a color.

- Let's say you are creating a series of objects like an asteroid field. You'd probably want each asteroid to be a little different in shape. Rather than having to shape each asteroid individually, you could use the Random command to randomly create different shapes for your asteroid.

- In a game with different enemies, you want the enemies to be in a different location each time the game is played. Using the Random command, you could have the enemies positioned randomly around the playing field.

So far we've been calling it the Random command but the actual command you use when coding looks something like this:

```
Rand (-10,50)
```

The two numbers that you put in parentheses after the Rand command are very important because they allow you to control the range. The number on the left is the lowermost limit for the number, and the number on the right is the uppermost number. In other words, if we were to run this code right now, Blitz3D would randomly choose a number between –10 and 50.

Let's create some code using the Random command so that you can get a better understanding as to what it does. In the following example, we will create a sphere and then randomly give it a color. Start by entering the code for the following program that just creates the sphere:

```
; Random color
;_____

Graphics3D 640,480
SetBuffer BackBuffer()

; Create camera
camera=CreateCamera()

;Create light
light=CreateLight()

;Create a sphere
sphere=CreateSphere()
PositionEntity sphere, 0,0,6

;The following code makes our program run
While Not KeyDown( 1 )
```

```
RenderWorld
Flip

Wend

End
```

Now let's add the code to color the sphere. As you should recall, when we color an object we provide a number for the Red, Green, and Blue values. This number is anywhere between 0 and 255 for each color. In this case, we will have Blitz3D randomly select the number for each color by entering the following code in bold:

```
;Create a sphere
sphere=CreateSphere()
PositionEntity sphere, 0,0,6
EntityColor sphere, Rand(0,255),Rand(0,255),Rand(0,255)
```

If you run the program now, you'll see that the sphere has been given a random color. We set the lowest possible number for each color value to be 0 and the highest to be 255 with the code Rand(0,255).

Now let's try something really interesting. I want you to cut the line you just added and paste it into the game loop. The code for the program should now look like this:

```
; Random color
;_____

Graphics3D 640,480
SetBuffer BackBuffer()

; Create camera
camera=CreateCamera()

;Create light
light=CreateLight()

;Create a sphere
sphere=CreateSphere()
PositionEntity sphere, 0,0,6

;The following code makes our program run
While Not KeyDown( 1 )
EntityColor sphere, Rand(0,255),Rand(0,255),Rand(0,255)
```

```
RenderWorld
Flip

Wend

End
```

Go ahead and run the program now. Because we added the command to randomly assign a color to the sphere inside the game loop, the color of the sphere changes with each loop of the game. By the way, you are seeing 30 different color changes per second! Here we have randomly changed the color of an object, but you could have just as easily randomly changed its shape or location or any other attribute.

## Note

### Rand, Rnd and SeedRnd

There are actually three different commands you can use for generating a random value. The Rand command will result in an integer value, while the Rnd command will produce a floating-point value. You'll learn more about floating-point values and integers in the next chapter, but in a nutshell, an integer cannot have decimal places while a floating-point value can. The Rand and Rnd numbers don't *really* create random numbers; they choose a random number based on a starting point called a *seed value*. The seed value is always the same, so if you ran a Rnd or Rand command, you'd get the same number every time you ran the program. The SeedRnd command changes the seed value so that the numbers it generates are truly random.

As I mentioned earlier, using the Rand command comes in very handy when working with multiple objects. In the next example, we will code a program that creates multiple spheres. We are then going to use the Random command to change the shape of the sphere.

The code used to create the multiple spheres is a For...Next statement. I'll discuss this type of statement further in the next chapter. For now we are just concerned with the Random command that will be used to change the shape of the spheres.

Enter the following code to create the program:

```
; Random Sphere Shapes
;_____

Graphics3D 640,480
SetBuffer BackBuffer()

; Create camera
camera=CreateCamera()
PositionEntity camera, 25,28,-40
```

```
;Create light
light=CreateLight()
;Creating Many Spheres
For x = 1 To 10
For y = 1 To 10
sphere=CreateSphere()
PositionEntity sphere, x*5,y*5,6
Next
Next

;The following code makes the program run
While Not KeyDown( 1 )

RenderWorld
Flip

Wend

End
```

Run the program now, and you should see 100 spheres as in Figure 15.15.

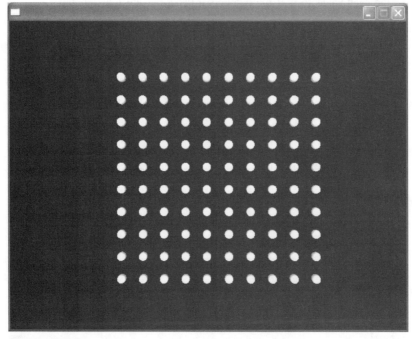

**Figure 15.15**
We've created 100 spheres using a For...Next statement.

Now we will use a Random command to randomly change the shape of each sphere. We are going to add a `ScaleEntity` command to change the size and shape of the spheres, and we will set the range to be any integer between −3 and 3. Do this by adding the following code in bold:

```
;Creating Many Spheres
For x = 1 To 10
For y = 1 To 10
sphere=CreateSphere()
PositionEntity sphere, x*5,y*5,6
ScaleEntity sphere, Rand(-3,3), Rand(-3,3), Rand(-3,3)
Next
Next
```

When you run the program now, you should have randomly shaped spheres as in Figure 15.16.

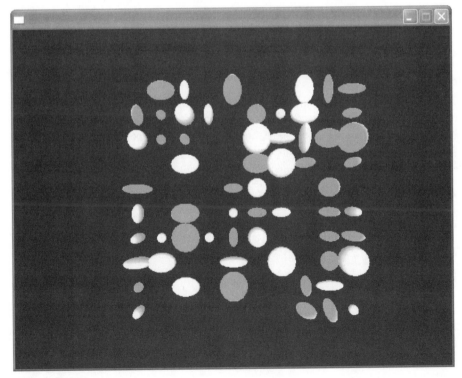

**Figure 15.16**
Using the Rand command, we created randomly shaped spheres.

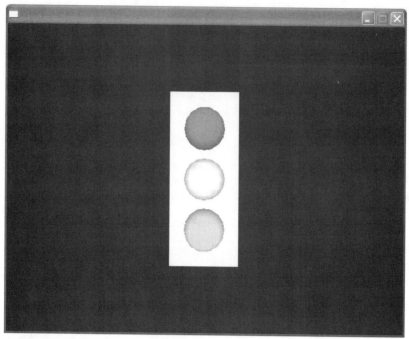

**Figure 15.17**
Your traffic light should look something like this.

## Note

**Now You Try**

I want you to try to create a traffic light that is out of order. It should be a cube stretched to look like a rectangular shape. Within the rectangle, there should be three spheres that will act as lights: one red on the top, one yellow in the middle, and one green on the bottom. Make each of the three lights flicker between different shades of their color. Take a look at Figure 15.17 to get a reference for what the shape should look like. When you are finished, compare your code with the following code. You can also open the file called traffic.bb to preview the program.

```
; Out of Order Traffic Light
;_____

Graphics3D 640,480
SetBuffer BackBuffer()

; Create camera
camera=CreateCamera()

;Create light
light=CreateLight()
```

```
;Create a cube
cube=CreateCube()
ScaleEntity cube, 0.7,1.7,1
PositionEntity cube, 0,0,5
EntityColor cube, 234,234,23

;Create red light
red=CreateSphere()
PositionEntity red, 0,1.2,4.9
ScaleEntity red, 0.5,0.5,0.5
EntityOrder red,-1

;Create yellow light
yellow=CreateSphere()
PositionEntity yellow, 0,0,4.9
ScaleEntity yellow, 0.5,0.5,0.5
EntityOrder yellow,-1

;Create green light
green=CreateSphere()
PositionEntity green, 0,-1.2,4.9
ScaleEntity green, 0.5,0.5,0.5
EntityOrder green,-1

;The following code makes our program run
While Not KeyDown( 1 )
EntityColor red, Rand(177,255),Rand(0,110),Rand(0,87)
EntityColor yellow, Rand(236,255),Rand(193,255),Rand(0,85)
EntityColor green, Rand(0,113),Rand(193,255),Rand(0,120)

RenderWorld
Flip

Wend

End
```

## Guns and Bullets

A major component to almost every game are guns and bullets. You have several options when it comes to creating your weapons. You can design and create them from scratch using a 3D modeling program, you can download existing weapons that other people have created and are willing to share, or you can create them from basic shapes from directly within Blitz3D. Whichever method you choose, there are a few little tricks that you should be aware of when inserting these weapons into your game. This section will cover some of these hints that will make it easier for you to position and use the weapons in your game.

## Positioning a First-Person Shooter Gun

In most first-person shooter games, the player's weapon stays in the middle of the screen throughout the entire game. The easiest way to accomplish this is to move the weapon along with the camera. Let's create a simple game that has a small cylinder as our weapon. Our goal is to have the cylinder positioned at the bottom of the screen that moves along with the movement of the player. Start by opening the program called "weapon.bb." Save the file with a new name and make sure that the files sky.jpg and grass1.jpg are copied to the same folder as the program.

The first thing we'll do is create a weapon for our game. In this case, our weapon will be a simple cylinder that is slightly stretched to give it the look of a cannon. Add the following code in bold:

```
sky_tex = LoadTexture ( "sky.jpg" )
EntityTexture sky,sky_tex

;Creating the Weapon
gun=CreateCylinder(12)
EntityColor gun, 100,100,100
ScaleEntity gun ,0.1,0.6,0.1
PositionEntity gun ,48,1,52

; This following code makes our program run
While Not KeyDown( 1 )
```

Run the program now to see what you've created. We've created a cylinder, given it a gray color, and slightly stretched it. Your screen should look the same as Figure 15.18.

We've created a cylinder that will act as our gun, but it still need to be rotated and positioned properly.

Our next step is to rotate and position the "gun" so that it is sticking out from the bottom of our screen. To do this, we will change the PositionEnity gun

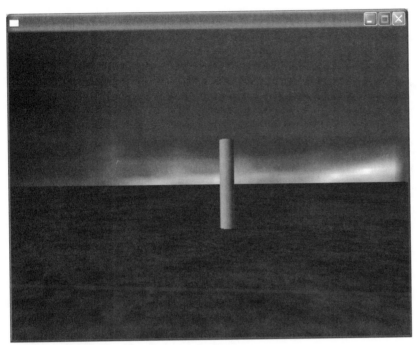

**Figure 15.18**
At this point your gun should look like this cylinder.

coordinates and add a RotateEntity gun command. Let's start rotating our gun by adding the following line in bold:

```
;Creating the Weapon
gun=CreateCylinder(12)
EntityColor gun, 100,100,100
ScaleEntity gun ,0.1,0.6,0.1
PositionEntity gun ,48,1,52
RotateEntity gun, 55,0,45
```

When you run the program now, your gun should be rotated as in Figure 15.19.

Now that we have our gun rotated, we need to reposition it so that it appears at the bottom of our screen. To do this, simply change the coordinates of the PositionEntity gun line as seen in bold:

```
;Creating the Weapon

gun=CreateCylinder(12)
EntityColor gun, 100,100,100
ScaleEntity gun ,0.1,0.8,0.1
```

**Figure 15.19**
We've rotated the gun along the x and z axes to make it appear like it's pointing outward and upward.

```
PositionEntity gun ,49.2,0.02,50.3
RotateEntity gun, 55,0,45
```

Run the program now. The gun should be positioned as you see in Figure 15.20.

As the program is running, use the left and right arrow keys to move. See the problem? While the camera moves, the gun stays still, and therefore quickly moves off the screen. To resolve this problem, we will associate the gun with the camera by making the camera the parent entity of the gun. I touched on parent entties earlier in the book, but to recap: by making an entity a parent of another object, you are in essence "gluing" them together. Whenever you move the parent item, the child item will move along with it. In this instance, the gun will be the child, and the camera will be the parent. The following code in bold is how we create a parent for the gun.

```
;Creating the Weapon

gun=CreateCylinder(12)
EntityColor gun, 100,100,100
ScaleEntity gun ,0.1,0.8,0.1
```

**Figure 15.20**
We've positioned the gun at the bottom of the screen. It's almost ready to start blowing away enemies!

```
PositionEntity gun ,49.2,0.02,50.3
RotateEntity gun, 55,0,45
EntityParent gun,camera
```

Run the program now, and you'll see that wherever you move the gun follows along because we have attached the camera and the gun using the `EntityParent` command. When using the `EntityParent` command, the first element after `EntityParent` is the object you want to be the child (in this case, `gun`), which is followed by a comma and the next element, the parent itself (in this case, `camera`).

## Bullets

Typically, I don't suggest jumping back and forth in this book because most chapters build on one another. Here is the one exception. Before proceeding with this section on bullets, you may want to jump to the next chapter and review the section on Arrays, Functions, and Looping Conditionals. Creating a bullet itself is really quite simple. You can use an image from a 3D modeling program, but in most cases, spheres or cylinders work just fine. You can fancy up your bullet by applying a bright texture or giving it a color. One idea would be to have the bullet flash by randomly changing its color as it flies. Regardless of how you create your bullet, the trickly part is to make it fly, create multiple bullets, and have them go in the right direction. That's what I'll be covering in this section. The method I describe here is not the only way to create and fire bullets, but it's one of the easiest. We'll explore different options for bullets, including setting a maximum number of bullets, reloading, and changing the direction of the bullets.

For this example, we'll use a program similar to the one we created in the previous section, with just a few positioning differences. Start by opening the file called bullet.bb. Once you have the file open, save it with a new name. If you ran the program now, you'd see a gun made from a cylinder with controls that move the camera (which the gun is attached to), as seen in Figure 15.21.

The goal of our program is to create a bullet that flies out of our gun when the mouse button is pressed. We want the bullet to fly for a few seconds and then disappear. It sounds fairly simple, but there are a few steps involved. We are

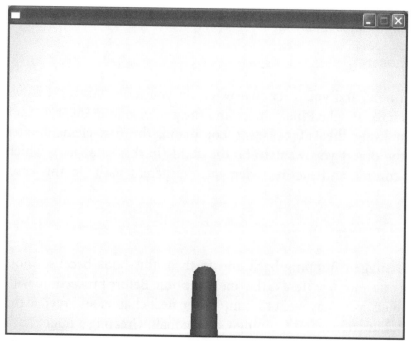

**Figure 15.21**
You can move this gun around by pressing the left and right arrow keys.

going to put the code for the bullet firing in the main game loop. Whenever the space bar is pressed, a bullet will fire. Let's start by adding the following code in bold to execute this command:

```
MoveEntity camera, 0,cy#,cz#
RotateEntity camera, 0,rx#,0

;Firing bullets

If KeyDown(57) Then

EndIf
```

What we have done here is said that whenever the space bar is pressed, then run the following code, until the EndIf is reached. We haven't added the code to actually fire any bullets yet; we'll do that shortly and place the code in between those two lines. To do this, we will create an *array*. Arrays will be discussed in detail in the next chapter, but for now, just know that arrays are used to create multiple variables with just a few lines of code. The bullets themselves are simply spheres that are slightly stretched out. Enter the following code in bold to create the bullets, and then I'll explain:

```
EntityOrder gun, -1
EntityParent gun,camera
EntityColor gun, 100,100,100

;Creating the bullets

fullcart=100
Dim bullet(fullcart)
For i=0 To fullcart
bullet(i)=CreateSphere()
EntityColor bullet(i), 100,100,100
ScaleEntity bullet(i),0.2,0.4,0.2
HideEntity bullet(i)
Next
```

Let's take a look at the code we just entered.

**fullcart=100** – Here we are creating a variable called fullcart, to represent a full cartridge of bullets. In this case, we are saying that the cartridge has 100 bullets available.

**Dim bullet(fullcart)** – This is how we create an array. This array, which is started with the code Dim, will help create and control the 100 available bullets.

**For i=0 To fullcart** – This is the start of a For...Next statement. These statements will also be discussed in full detail in the next chapter. Here we are telling Blitz3D to loop the next statements 100 times.

```
bullet(i)=CreateSphere()
EntityColor bullet(i), 100,100,100
ScaleEntity bullet(i),0.2,0.4,0.2
```

These three lines of code create the bullets. Notice the letter i in parentheses beside each bullet name. This i corresponds with the i in the statement For i=0 To fullcart, which allows us to create 100 individual bullets.

**HideEntity bullet(i)** – This will hide the bullets until we are ready to fire them.

**Next** – This ends the For...Next loop.

So now that we've got 100 bullets loaded, we need to create the code to fire them. We will add this code in between the code we created earlier that starts an action whenever the space bar is pressed. So let's add the following code in bold that will fire our bullets:

```
MoveEntity camera, 0,cy#,cz#
RotateEntity camera, 0,rx#,0

;Firing bullets
If KeyDown(57) Then
ShowEntity bullet(t)
PositionEntity bullet(t) ,EntityX(gun,1),EntityY(gun,1),EntityZ(gun,1)
EntityColor bullet(t),Rand(0,255),Rand(0,255),Rand(0,255)
t=t+1

EndIf
```

Let's take a look at the four lines of code to see what we've done:

**ShowEntity bullet(t)** – When the bullets were first created we hid them. This command will show the bullets. Notice the letter t in parentheses after the word bullet. This is a variable that we made up for each individual bullet, and we'll need to use this variable in a moment. We used the letter t, but you can use any variable name.

`PositionEntity bullet(t) ,EntityX(gun,1),EntityY(gun,1),EntityZ(gun,1)` — This places the bullet right at the position of the gun.

`EntityColor bullet(t),Rand(0,255),Rand(0,255),Rand(0,255)` — For a neat little effect, we'll have each bullet be a different color as it comes out of the gun.

`t=t+1` — This bumps up the variable t by one so that a new bullet is created whenever the space bar is pressed. If this code wasn't there, each time you pressed the space bar, the same bullet would be fired, replacing the existing one. We'll experiment with this code in a moment.

So far, when the space bar is pressed, a bullet will appear at the location of the gun. The bullet will be behind the gun, so you won't be able to see it. In order to make the bullet move, we are going to add another For...Next statement. This time, we'll create a new variable, the letter q, that will move each of our 100 bullets as they are fired. Add the following code in bold:

```
;Firing bullets
If KeyDown(57) Then
ShowEntity bullet(t)
PositionEntity bullet(t) ,EntityX(gun,1),EntityY(gun,1),EntityZ(gun,1)
EntityColor bullet(t),Rand(0,255),Rand(0,255),Rand(0,255)
t=t+1
EndIf

For q = 0 To fullcart
MoveEntity bullet(q), 0,1,3
Next
```

So the code we created here will move the bullets whenever they are fired. It's time to run our program. When you press the space bar, you should see bullets fly, as in Figure 15.22.

Our code isn't quite done for a couple of reasons. If you move the left or right arrow keys as you fire, you'll notice a problem. The bullets won't follow the direction of the gun. The gun has moved, but the bullets continue to fly in their original direction, as seen in Figure 15.23.

We need to alter the direction of the bullet to follow the gun by rotating the bullet based on the rotation angle of the gun. Here's how:

```
If KeyDown(57) Then
ShowEntity bullet(t)
```

**Figure 15.22**
When you press the space bar, different color bullets will fly out of the gun.

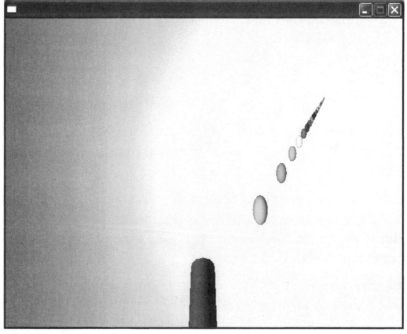

**Figure 15.23**
When you move the gun, the bullets still fly in their original direction.

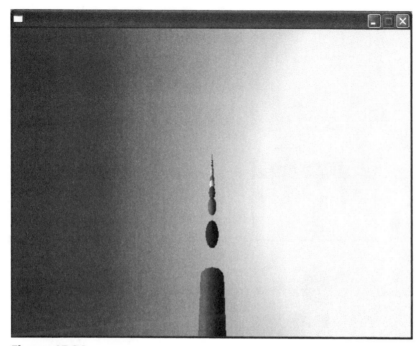

**Figure 15.24**
After adding the `RotateEntity bullet(t)` code, the bullets now follow the direction of the gun.

```
PositionEntity bullet(t) ,EntityX(gun,1),EntityY(gun,1),EntityZ(gun,1)
RotateEntity bullet(t),EntityPitch#(gun,1)-
  35,EntityYaw#(gun,1),EntityRoll#(gun,1)
EntityColor bullet(t),Rand(0,255),Rand(0,255),Rand(0,255)
t=t+1
EndIf
```

Run the program now, and you'll see that the bullets follow the direction of the gun, as seen in Figure 15.24.

If you continue to fire, you will notice that after 100 bullets have been fired, an error message appears as seen in Figure 15.25.

The reason for this is that the cartridge we created has only 100 bullets (fullcart=100). We can either increase this number to be incredibly high so that the player will never run out of bullets, or we can have our cartridge reload. I'll cover reloading in a moment, but for now, let's experiment a little with the code we've already created. Remember earlier that we added the code t=t+1. I want you to temporarily delete this code and then run the program. Notice now that you can fire only one bullet at a time (as seen in Figure 15.26) because the same bullet is being reused. Go ahead and put that code back into the program.

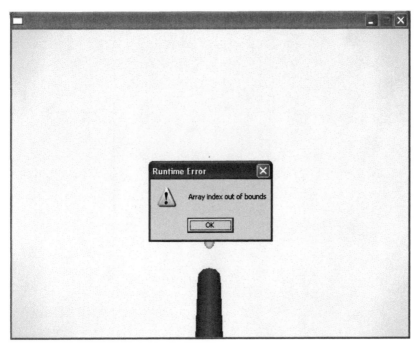

**Figure 15.25**
When you run out of bullets, a Runtime Error dialog box appears.

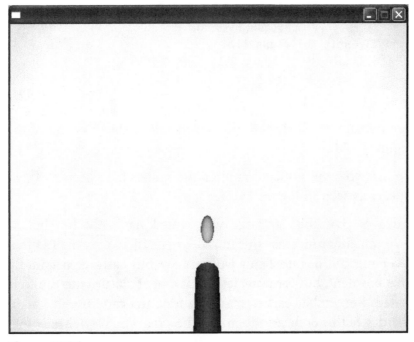

**Figure 15.26**
You'll only be able to fire one bullet when you remove the t=t+1 code.

You can also experiment with the direction of the bullets. You can have them fly higher or lower by changing the y variable in the code `MoveEntity bullet(q),` `0,1,3`. You can also make the bullets fly faster or slower by changing the z variable—in this case, changing the number 3.

### Reloading

As just discussed, once you hit 100 bullets, an error will occur because you go beyond the cartridge total. Let's start by getting a better idea of how many bullets we have fired, which we'll do by adding the following code in bold:

```
bulletcount=100-t
RenderWorld
Color 0,0,0
Text 0,15,"Bullets Remaining: "+bulletcount
```

Here we create a variable called `bulletcount`, which is created by subtracting the value of t (the variable we associated with each bullet) from the total number of bullets in our cartridge, `100`. We then added a line of text that will display the value of the `bulletcount`. When you run the program now, you'll see the bullets that you have remaining listed at the top left of the screen, as seen in Figure 15.27. Although this is nice, it doesn't solve our problem of the error that appears when we run out of bullets.

The variable t that we created represents each individual bullet. By adding an `If` statement, we can say that whenever t reaches 100 bullets fired, it should revert back to 1, this way we won't run out of bullets and the error won't appear. Enter the following code in bold:

```
bulletcount=100-t
If t=100 Then
t=1
Endif
RenderWorld
```

Run the program now, and you'll see that whenever the bullet count gets down to 1, it will revert back to 100. We purposely put this `If . . . Then` statement on three different lines so that we can add to it in the next section. So we've now gotten rid of the error, but it's not really an authentic reload. Usually a player will have to press a button in order to have his weapon reload. In this case, we'll make it so that when the player presses the letter R on the keyboard, his cartridge

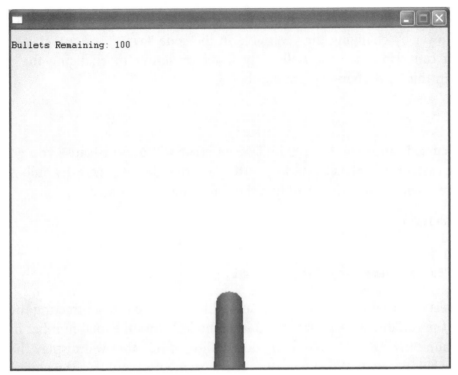

**Figure 15.27**
The text you entered (Bullets Remaining:) will appear on the screen.

will be reloaded. We can accomplish this by adding a condition to the firing process and creating a new variable. The new variable we are going to create is called reload. We'll change the code so that in order to be able to fire a bullet, reload has to be equal to 0; otherwise, we can't fire. Start by adding this line in bold to the "Firing bullets" area of the code:

```
If KeyDown(57) And reload=0 Then
```

By adding the code And reload=0 Then we've made it so that two conditions have to be true in order for a bullet to be fired. First, the space bar needs to be pressed, and secondly, the variable we just created called reload needs to equal 0. By default, all variables equal zero unless something changes them, so the program will run just the same at this point.

Now we need to change the value of the reload variable once we run out of bullets. Remember that we run out of bullets when the variable t equals 100.

Since we already have an If statement with the variable t=100, we'll just add to it by entering the following code in bold:

```
If t=100 Then
t=1
reload=1
Endif
```

What we've said here is that once 100 bullets have been fired, the reload variable will equal 1. Since the reload variable needs to equal 0 in order to fire, you will no longer be able to fire. Go ahead and run the program now and press the space bar until you run out of bullets. You'll notice that once the counter reaches 0, you'll no longer be able to fire.

Let's now incorporate a message to the player, letting him know that he has run out of bullets and that he needs to press the letter R in order to reload. We do this by adding the following Text code in bold:

```
UpdateWorld
RenderWorld
Color 0,0,0
Text 10,15,"Bullets Remaining: "+bulletcount
If reload=1 Then Text GraphicsWidth()/2, GraphicsHeight()/2,"Press R to
   Reload",1,1
Flip

Wend

End
```

This code tells Blitz3D to display the text "Press R to Reload" when the reload variable is equal to 1. Rather than putting in coordinates for where to place the text, we entered the code GraphicsWidth()/2, GraphicsHeight()/2, which places the text halfway on the screen both vertically and horizontally, or, in other words, we put the text in the center of the screen. When you run the program now, a message will appear on the screen as seen in Figure 15.28 when you run out of bullets.

Now we need to add the code that will reload our cartridge back to 100 bullets and let us fire again. We can accomplish this with a simple If statement:

```
If KeyDown (19) = True then
t=1
```

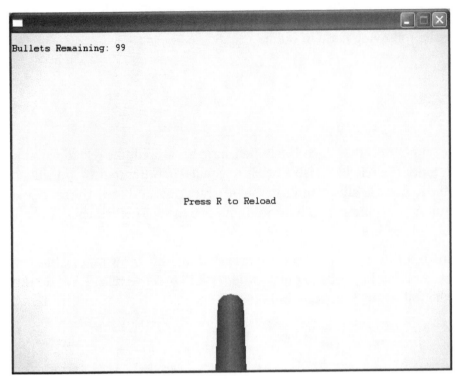

**Figure 15.28**
The player will see this message when he runs out of bullets.

```
reload=0
EndIf

RenderWorld
```

Here we are telling Blitz3D that when the letter R is pressed, the variable t should equal 1, or in other words, load 100 bullets. We also change the variable called reload so that it will equal 0 and we can fire again.

### Note

**Bullet Timing**

The bullets that we've created so far in this program come out at rapid fire. As the space bar is pressed, bullets seem to flow out of the gun at Mach speed, and after a moment you are out of bullets. The easiest way around this is to change the code for firing bullets from If KeyDown(57) to If KeyHit(57). This will require the player to actually press and let go of the space bar in order to fire another bullet. In other words, holding down the space bar will fire only one bullet.

**Figure 15.29**
Try to create these two guns that fire different color bullets.

## Note

**Now You Try**

Take a look at Figure 15.29. Try to create two different guns that appear out of the bottom corners of the screen. Make it so that the gun on the left fires red bullets when the left mouse button is pressed, and the gun on the right fires blue bullets when the right mouse button is pressed. Once you are done, compare your program to the following code:

```
;Double Gun Fire
;_____

Graphics3D 640,480
SetBuffer BackBuffer()

; Create camera
camera=CreateCamera()

;Create light
light=CreateLight()
```

```
; Creating the background
background=CreateSphere(32)
ScaleEntity background, 200,200,200
FlipMesh background
EntityColor background, 255,214,100

;Creating the gun
gun=CreateCylinder(12)
ScaleEntity gun,0.2,0.6,0.4
RotateEntity gun,45,0,0
PositionEntity gun, EntityX(camera)+2.5,EntityY(camera)-2, EntityZ(camera)+3
EntityOrder gun, -1
EntityParent gun,camera
EntityColor gun, 100,100,100
maxbull=100

;Creating the gun

gun1=CreateCylinder(12)
ScaleEntity gun1,0.2,0.6,0.4
RotateEntity gun1,45,0,0
PositionEntity gun1, EntityX(camera)-2.5,EntityY(camera)-2, EntityZ
  (camera)+3
EntityOrder gun1, -1
EntityParent gun1,camera
EntityColor gun1, 100,100,100

;Creating the bullets

Dim bullet(maxbull)
For i=0 To maxbull
bullet(i)=CreateSphere()
EntityColor bullet(i), 100,100,100
ScaleEntity bullet(i),0.2,0.2,0.2
HideEntity bullet(i)
Next
Function Fire()
End Function
While Not KeyDown( 1 )

;Camera Controls
If KeyDown(200)= True Then cz#=cz#+.01
If KeyDown (208)= True Then cz#=cz#-.01
```

```
If KeyDown(205)= True Then rx#=rx#-1
If KeyDown (203)= True Then rx#=rx#+1
If KeyDown(30)= True Then cy#=cy#+.01
If KeyDown (44)= True Then cy#=cy#-.01
If KeyDown (48) Then cy#=0 cz#=0

;Control camera turning radius
If rx# > 180 Then rx#=-180
If rx# < -180 Then rx# = 180
MoveEntity camera, 0,cy#,cz#
RotateEntity camera, 0,rx#,0

;Firing bullets
If MouseDown(1)
ShowEntity bullet(t)
PositionEntity bullet(t) ,EntityX(gun,1),EntityY(gun,1),EntityZ(gun,1)
RotateEntity bullet(t),EntityPitch#(gun,1)-
  35,EntityYaw#(gun,1),EntityRoll#(gun,1)
EntityColor bullet(t),0,0,255
t=t+1
EndIf

If MouseDown(2)
ShowEntity bullet(t)
PositionEntity bullet(t) ,EntityX(gun1,1),EntityY(gun1,1),EntityZ(gun1,1)
RotateEntity bullet(t),EntityPitch#(gun1,1)-
  35,EntityYaw#(gun1,1),EntityRoll#(gun1,1)
EntityColor bullet(t),255,0,0
t=t+1
EndIf

For q = 0 To maxbull
MoveEntity bullet(q), 0,1,3
Next

If t=100 Then
t=1
EndIf

RenderWorld
Flip

Wend

End
```

# Pausing

Imagine that you are in the middle of playing the game of your life. Everything is coming together, all cylinders are firing, and the high score is in sight. Just then the telephone rings, the dog starts barking, the doorbell goes off, your mother starts yelling, and nature calls. You don't want to ruin your chances at getting that high score, but what do you do? Easy: You pause the game. Thankfully, programming a pause into your game is easy because Blitz3D has a command that will pause all the action in your game until you press a key. The command for pausing is WaitKey(), which will pause the game until any key is pressed. Let's incorporate it into a game. Open the file called atom1.bb, which contains several spheres flying around a nucleus. Save this file to a new location on your computer and make sure the files sunskin.jpg, and orgit.jpg are saved in the same location. We'll add a command that initiates the pause whenever the letter P is pressed. Add the following code in bold to the program:

```
While Not KeyDown(1)
If KeyDown(25) Then WaitKey()

; Turn pivots, making atom orbit around the nucleus.
TurnEntity pivot,0,3,0
TurnEntity pivot2, 3,0,0
TurnEntity pivot3, 0,0,3
```

Now run the program and press the letter P. The action on the screen will stop. Press any other key on the keyboard and the action will resume.

### Note

**WaitJoy() and WaitMouse()**

In addition to using the WaitKey() command, you can also use WaitJoy(), which will pause the program until a joystick button is pressed, or WaitMouse(), which will pause the program until a mouse button is pressed.

Typically, when you pause a program, you'll want something on the screen to indicate that the game has been paused—for example, the words "Game Paused." Earlier in this chapter you added text using the Text command, which is how we'll indicate that the game is paused.

Replace the code If KeyDown(25) Then WaitKey() with this:

```
If KeyDown(25) Then
Text 100,150, ''Game Paused - Press any key (except P) to continue''
```

**Figure 15.30**
When the game is paused, this text should appear. It will disappear as soon as the game is resumed.

```
Flip
WaitKey()
EndIf
```

Run the program now, and press the letter P. The game should pause, and you should see the same text that appears in Figure 15.30. Notice in the code that we added the command called Flip. We need this command because the text is drawn on the back buffer, and we wouldn't be able to see it otherwise. To bring it to the front buffer (directly on screen), we need to use the Flip command.

**Note**

**Pause Function**

Rather than putting the pause code in the main game loop, you should create a function for it. It's always the best practice to put as little code in the main game loop as possible. You'll learn more about functions in the next chapter.

One other option you might want to use when creating a pause in your program is to clear the screen of action while the game is paused. To do this, you can use the Cls command. This command will clear the front buffer (everything on the

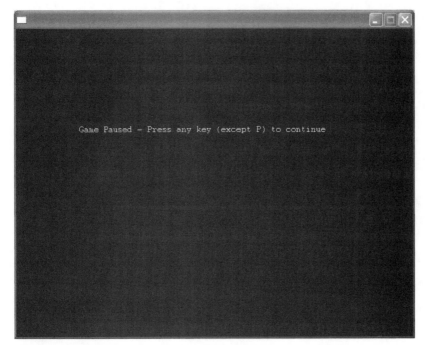

**Figure 15.31**
Using the `Cls` command clears the front buffer so that all you will see is the text we created until the game is resumed.

screen) until the game is resumed. Simply add the `Cls` command as seen here in bold. After you've added the code, run the program and then press the P key. The screen should be clear, except for the text as seen in Figure 15.31.

```
If KeyDown(25) Then
Cls
Text 100,150, "Game Paused - Press any key (except P) to continue''
Flip
WaitKey()
EndIf
```

Earlier in the book we created a fancy looking Pause screen that we can incorporate when the game is paused rather than just having boring text. Make sure that the image pause.bmp is saved to the same location as the program. Replace the existing pause code with the following to load your pause image whenever the letter P is pressed:

```
If KeyDown(25) Then
Cls
```

```
pause=LoadImage ("pause.bmp")
DrawImage pause,0,0
Flip
WaitKey()
EndIf
```

You can see that all of the code created here is almost identical to the pause code that just contained text. The difference is that we used the command `pause=LoadImage ("pause.bmp")` to load the image into the program. We then drew it, starting at point 0,0 (the top left corner of the screen) by using the code `DrawImage pause,0,0`. Once again, notice how we used the `Flip` command to bring the image to the front buffer. Since our image is exactly the same size as the screen of our program, when we placed it starting at point 0,0, it took up the entire screen. When you run the program now and press P, you should see the Pause screen image appear.

### Note

**Exit Screen**

You can use the same technique covered here to create an Exit screen, asking users if they are sure they want to quit before exiting.

## Welcome Screens

Almost every game should have a Welcome screen that provides the player with information on how to start the game, how to control the game, and how to end it. Earlier in the book, we designed a Welcome screen that we will now incorporate into our program. The code we are going to use to load our Welcome screen will be a function (I'll cover functions in greater detail in the next chapter) that we'll include at the very beginning of our program. Start by opening atom2.bb, which is a program with several spheres pivoting around each other. Save the file with a new name in another location on your computer, and make sure the files sunskin.jpg, and orgit.jpg are saved in the same location. Make sure that the image welcome.bmp is also located in the same location.

The key to the Welcome screen code is to put the function right at the beginning of our program, before all other code. After the function is executed, the main program will start at the point where the function ended. Enter the following code in bold right at the beginning of the program:

```
; Atom2
; -------------------
```

```
welcome()
Function welcome()
Graphics 640,480
screen=LoadImage ("welcome.bmp")
DrawImage screen,0,0
While Not KeyDown(1)
If KeyDown(31) Then Return
Wend
End Function

Graphics3D 640,480
SetBuffer BackBuffer()
```

Let's take a look at the code line by line to see what we've just done:

`welcome()` – This launches the function called welcome().

`Function welcome()` – This is the start of the definition of the function we have called welcome.

`Graphics 640,480` – This line sets the screen resolution.

`screen=LoadImage ("welcome.bmp")` – This will load the image called "welcome.bmp" into the program, but will not display it.

`DrawImage screen,0,0` – This will display the image we have loaded, starting at the 0,0 point on the screen.

`While Not KeyDown(1)` – This starts a loop within the function.

`If KeyDown(31) Then Return` – If the letter S is pressed, the function will end, and we will be returned to the main program.

`Wend` – This ends the loop.

`End Function` – This ends the function.

Run the program now, and you should see the Welcome screen appear. When you press the letter S, the Welcome screen should disappear and the game should begin.

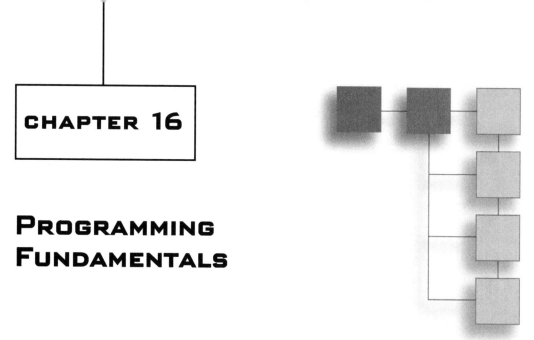

# CHAPTER 16

# PROGRAMMING FUNDAMENTALS

Wow, you've covered a lot of material so far, and you're one step away from creating your first fully functional 3D game. Before you continue, though, I need to cover some important fundamentals of programming. I've actually touched on many of these fundamentals throughout the programming we've done so far, but now it's time to identify them and look at some specific examples. Understanding these elements is really important, not only for programming in Blitz3D, but for just about every other compiler. The topics covered here—including variables, functions, arrays, conditionals, and others—can be applied to almost every computer language.

## Variables

Variables play a very important role in the world of programming. A variable is something that has the ability to change. Take, for example, a program that has a sphere that you can move across a playing surface. The coordinates of the sphere (the, x, y, and z coordinates) change as the sphere moves, so they are variables. Another example of a variable would be the score of your game. As the player accumulates points, the score changes, so it is a variable. All variables need to be declared, which means you have to tell Blitz3D what the variables are. There are four types of variables that you can create in Blitz3D, and in the following sections I'll discuss how to declare them and what their differences are.

## Integer Variables

An integer variable is one whose value must be an integer. In other words, the value of a variable that is an integer variable can't have a decimal. A good example of an integer variable would be a score for your video game. Most games have integers as their score—you'd rarely see a score of 10.732, but you would see a score of 10 or 11. Integer variables are declared using a percent sign: %. Here are a couple of examples of integer variables being declared:

```
Number_of_lives%=9
Highscore%=50000
```

### Note

**The % (Percent) Sign**

You only have to use the % sign when you are declaring the variables. Later in your code, if you use the variable, you can just use its name; you don't have to include the %. And the nice part is that you don't really need to use the % sign because, by default, variables are integers.

## Floating-Point Variables

Floating-point variables are used when the variable needs to have decimal places. An example of this type of variable might be the speed of a player or his location onscreen. Floating-point variables are declared using a pound sign: #. Here's an example of how floating-point variables would be declared:

```
x# = 0.235
roll#=124
```

### Note

**Identifiers**

The names that you give to your variables are called identifiers. For example, if I said temp#=7, the temp# would be called the identifier. There are several words that are built into Blitz3D that cannot be used as identifiers, including: After, And, Before, Case, Const, Data, Default, Delete, Dim, Each, Else, Elself, End, Endlf, Exit, False, Field, First, Float, For, Forever, Function, Global, Gosub, Goto, If, Insert, Int, Last, Local, Mod, New, Next, Not, Null, Or, Pi, Read, Repeat, Restore, Return, Sar, Select, Shl, Shr, Step, Str, Then, To, True, Type, Until, Wend, While, Xor, and Include.

## String Variables

String variables are used when you want to enter text as or make text into a variable. These are particularly useful when using player names and are always entered using a $ (dollar) sign at the end of the variable name. Here's how you would declare a string variable:

```
Player1$="Kara"
TopPlayer$="Eric"
```

Let's create a very simple program that references these string variables. Enter the following code. The code in bold specifically references the string variables.

```
Graphics3D 640,480
SetBuffer BackBuffer()
camera=CreateCamera()
light=CreateLight()
Player1$="Kara"
TopPlayer$="Eric"
While Not KeyDown( 1 )
Text 100,0, "Player One is "+Player1+""
Text 100,100, "The top player is "+TopPlayer+""
RenderWorld
Wend
```

When you run the program you'll see two lines of text appear with the string variables you have entered, as seen in Figure 16.1. Let's quickly break down the lines of code that made this happen:

```
Player1$="Kara"
TopPlayer$="Eric"
```

These two lines of code created the variables, one called Player 1 and the other called Top Player. You can give string variables just about any name as long as you follow them with the $ sign.

```
Text 100,0, "Player One is "+Player1+""
Text 100,100, "The top player is "+TopPlayer+""
```

Earlier in the book, you learned how to enter text. You can see here that adding a variable to a block of text isn't really that difficult. You just need to surround the variable with quotation marks and + signs.

### Inputting String Variables

Not only can you create and call upon string variables, you can actually create them on the go and have players input the variable. I'll give you a great example

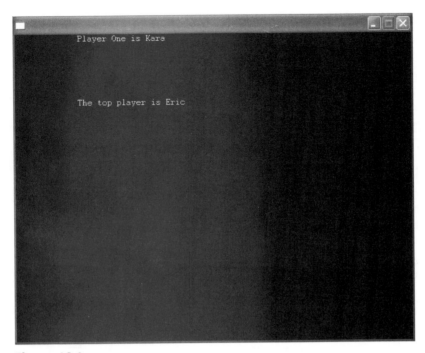

**Figure 16.1**
The string variables will appear in the text when you run the program.

of when you would use this. Let's say you wanted players to enter their names so that their names appear onscreen as they play. You could have them enter their names using a string variable.

Here's an example of how you would have a player input her name using the Input$ string:

```
Playername$ = Input$ ("Please Enter Your Name")
```

Now let's put this to use in some actual code. Enter the following program code and then run the program. Your end result should look like Figure 16.2. The sections in bold deal with the string variable.

```
Graphics3D 640,480
SetBuffer BackBuffer()
camera=CreateCamera()
light=CreateLight()
Playername$ = Input$ ("Please Enter Your Name ")
While Not KeyDown( 1 )
Text 100,0, "Hi "+Playername$+" are you ready to play?"
RenderWorld
Wend
```

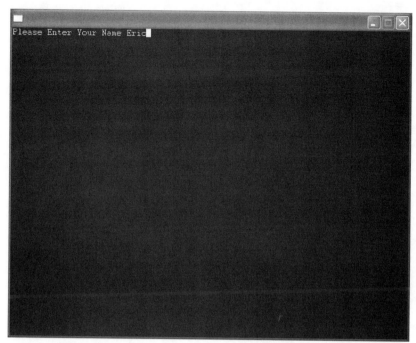

**Figure 16.2**
You can use string variables to have players input information into your games.

---

**Note**

**Spaces**

Be sure to leave a space between your question and the closing question mark when creating your Input$ code; otherwise, the input won't look right onscreen. For example, in the code Playername$ = Input$ ("Please Enter Your Name ") notice that there is a space between Name and the ". Take a look at Figure 16.3 to see the difference from a player's perspective between leaving a space before the quotation and not leaving a space.

In this example, we started by creating a variable called Playername. We then added the Input$ command before the text that asked the question. Anything that the user types after being posed the question will become the value of the Playername variable.

---

## Inputting with Other Variables

Asking the players to enter information can be used with all types of variables, not just string variables. Here are some examples of how you could use a player's input to create variables:

```
no_of_players%=Input$ ('Please Enter the Number of Players ")
levels%=Input$ ("How Many Levels Do You Want")
y#=Input$ ("How High Do You Want To Be Able To Jump")
```

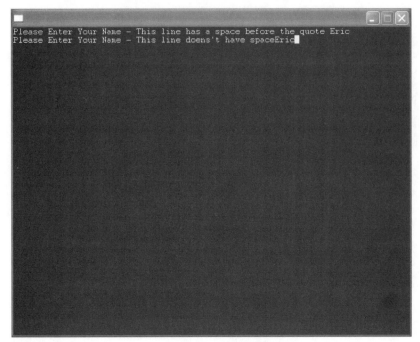

**Figure 16.3**
Leave a space before the quotation marks for your input strings or the text
won't look right, as seen in the second line above.

---

**Note**

**Wrong Answers**

Blitz3D won't prevent you from entering a "wrong" answer to a question, but it will change your
answer. Here's what I mean. Let's say that you entered the code `levels%=Input$ ("How Many
Levels Do You Want")`. By using the % sign, you have indicated that you need this variable to
be an integer. Thinking that he was pretty clever, one of your players entered his name rather than
a number. If Blitz3D doesn't get the answer that it is looking for, in this case an Integer number, it
will revert to 0 or the closest number. What I mean by closest number is, let's say that same clever
player had entered 10.2 in response to the same question. Blitz3D would make the levels variable
equal to 10.

---

## Global versus Local Variables

In order to understand local versus global variables, you should have an
understanding of functions. I will cover functions a little later in this chapter, but,
in a nutshell, a user-created function is a section of code that is grouped together,
usually to perform a specific task. A global variable is a variable that can be
used in any location in your program, while a local variable can be used only in

the function where it was declared. In other words, if you want to create a variable that can be used anywhere in your program, it has to be made a global variable.

Typically, you would declare all of your global variables at the beginning of your program. To define a variable as global, you simply have to put the word Global in front of it. Here's an example of how you would declare global variables:

```
Global strength#=50
Global point# = 1
Global bang = LoadSound (bang.mp3)
```

## Functions

As I touched on briefly in the last section, a function is a group of code instructions that you can call upon at any time in your program to perform a specific task or tasks. Functions are huge timesavers, since they allow you to create mini-programs within your program. In fact, you should be in the habit of creating most of the events in your games as functions rather than directly in the game loop. This will free up resources and allow your games to run faster.

Take, for example, an explosion in a game. Every time an explosion occurs, you want several spheres to be created and then have them fly off in different directions. Rather than having to create the code that makes the explosion over and over, you can create a function. The function will contain the code for the explosion and can be called upon whenever you need to blow something up. In the following example, we will create a program in which an explosion will occur every time the mouse button is clicked. Start by entering this code for an empty program:

```
; Function
;_____

Graphics3D 640,480
SetBuffer BackBuffer()

; Create camera
camera=CreateCamera()

;Create light
light=CreateLight()
```

```
;The following code makes our program run
While Not KeyDown( 1 )

RenderWorld
Flip

Wend

End
```

Now that we have an empty shell of a program created, we will create a function that can be called upon at any time. Remember to keep the function outside of the game loop. We'll start by adding a function that simply creates three spheres:

```
;Create a function
Function Explosion()
bomb1=CreateSphere(15)
ScaleEntity bomb1, 0.2,0.2,0.2
bomb2=CreateSphere(15)
ScaleEntity bomb2, 0.2,0.2,0.2
bomb3=CreateSphere(15)
ScaleEntity bomb3, 0.2,0.2,0.2
End Function
```

Before we add more to this function, let's take a look at what we've done so far. The code Function Explosion() creates a function that we have called "Explosion." The rest of the code is simply three spheres with different names followed by the code End Function that signifies the end of the function. If we ran the program now, we still wouldn't see anything because we haven't called upon the function at any point. Let's add a statement into our game loop that runs the function whenever the left mouse button is pressed. Do this by adding the following code in bold to the game loop.

```
;The following code makes our program run
While Not KeyDown( 1 )
If MouseDown(1) Then explosion

RenderWorld
Flip

Wend
```

This statement says that if the left mouse button is pressed, then run the explosion function. Running the program now still won't produce anything because the spheres are out of view. Now add the following code in bold that will position the bombs into view:

```
;Create a function
Function Explosion()
bomb1=CreateSphere(15)
ScaleEntity bomb1, 0.2,0.2,0.2
PositionEntity bomb1, 0,0,5
bomb2=CreateSphere(15)
ScaleEntity bomb2, 0.2,0.2,0.2
PositionEntity bomb2, 0,0,5
bomb3=CreateSphere(15)
ScaleEntity bomb3, 0.2,0.2,0.2
PositionEntity bomb3, 0,0,5
End Function
```

Run the program now and press the left mouse button. You should see a sphere appear on the screen when you click the mouse button (see Figure 16.4).

**Figure 16.4**
When you run the program and press the left mouse button, this is what you should see onscreen.

The reason that only one sphere seems to appear on the screen is that we've positioned all three in the exact same position. So we have a good start to our explosion, but nothing has really exploded yet. We want to send these three spheres flying in different directions. We also want the spheres to disappear after a few seconds. The reason for this is that we don't want these particles that we've created for our explosion continuing on and on forever since they would bog down system resources. Every time we press the mouse button, three spheres are created. Imagine if we pressed the mouse button 100 times: we'd have hundreds of spheres flying around our program, bogging down system memory.

To create the motion of the spheres, we will create a While statement that runs for 3 seconds. (I'll discuss While statements further on in this chapter.) To have it run for 3 seconds, we'll add a Millisecs command to the function. Add the following code in bold to finish the function.

```
;Create a function
Function Explosion()
bomb1=CreateSphere(15)
ScaleEntity bomb1, 0.2,0.2,0.2
PositionEntity bomb1, 0,0,5
bomb2=CreateSphere(15)
ScaleEntity bomb2, 0.2,0.2,0.2
PositionEntity bomb2, 0,0,5
bomb3=CreateSphere(15)
ScaleEntity bomb3, 0.2,0.2,0.2
PositionEntity bomb3, 0,0,5
timer=MilliSecs()
While MilliSecs() < timer+3000
MoveEntity bomb1,.3, .05, .07
MoveEntity bomb2,-.1, .18, .16
MoveEntity bomb3,.6, -.25, .07
UpdateWorld
RenderWorld
Flip
Wend
FreeEntity bomb1
FreeEntity bomb2
FreeEntity bomb3
End Function
```

Run the program now and press the mouse button. What you should see onscreen are your three spheres flying off in different directions (see Figure 16.5).

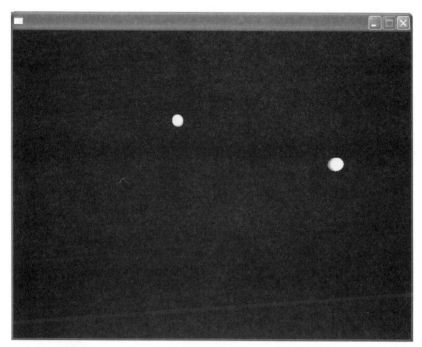

**Figure 16.5**
Your "explosion" should occur when you press the mouse button.

While it may not look like much of an explosion now, you can certainly spice up the sphere by adding textures and colors, or perhaps even make it flicker as you learned to do in the previous chapter. Let's take a look at the code we used to create this moving explosion within our function.

`timer=MilliSecs()` – This defined a variable called `timer` that is equal to the time when the function is run.

`While MilliSecs() < timer+3000` – This begins a loop that will last for 3 seconds. I'll discuss this type of `While` statement later in this chapter.

**MoveEntity bomb1,.3, .05, .07**
**MoveEntity bomb2,-.1, .18, .16**
`MoveEntity bomb3,.6, -.25, .07`

These three lines of code move each sphere in a different direction while the function is looping.

```
UpdateWorld
RenderWorld
Flip
```

These three lines of code ensure that our spheres are drawn on the screen.

**Wend** – This command ends the `While` statement loop.

```
FreeEntity bomb1
FreeEntity bomb2
FreeEntity bomb3
```

After the function is complete, the three bombs are removed from the program using the `FreeEntity` command.

### Note

**FreeEntity**

The `FreeEntity` command will remove an object from the screen and free up any resources that it was using.

## Arrays

*Arrays* are a terrific way to create many different variables at once. (In the next section, I'll cover *types,* which are actually a better way to control many different objects, but for now let's take a look at what we can do with arrays.)

With arrays you can create many different variables at once, each one being a numbered clone of the original. What does that mean? Let's say you invented a cloning machine that would make an exact copy of anything that you put inside it. To experiment, you decided to put a puppy in the machine and clone it 100 times. After you have finished cloning it, you have 100 puppies that look exactly the same. The problem is that it is hard to tell one puppy from the next, so you decide to give the puppies names. You can't possibly think of 100 different names, so you decide that you'll number the puppies, and put little puppy t-shirts on them with their numbers. That's how arrays work in Blitz3D: each copy of a variable is assigned a number. For example, if you created 100 spheres, the first would be sphere(1), the second would be sphere(2) and so on, up to 100.

To create a variable, you start with the command Dim followed by, in parentheses, the number of copies you want to make. Here is a sample of our code to declare our array with 100 puppies:

```
Dim puppies (100)
```

Here puppies is the name of our array and the number of puppies that can fit in this array is 100. We now actually have 100 different variables: puppies(1), puppies(2), puppies(3) .... puppies(100). But just having the variable created doesn't do much. We now need to define what the puppies are and actually create them. For the sake of simplicity, let's say that each of our puppies was a cylinder. We could define each variable separately, for example:

```
puppies(1) = CreateCylinder()
puppies(2) = CreateCylinder()
puppies(3) = CreateCylinder()
puppies(4) = CreateCylinder()
```

And so on, until we reached 100, but that would really defeat the point of having an array as a timesaver. Later in this chapter you'll learn about For...Next statements in detail, but for now we'll use one to create all 100 puppies at once:

```
Dim puppies (100)
For p = 0 to 100
puppies(p)=CreateCylinder()
Next
```

This statement just creates a cylinder for each one of our 100 puppies. All 100 puppies at this point would be at the exact same location. Here we have created 100 cylinders, but as you saw in the last chapter, arrays are great for creating bullets or other types of objects that you need in mass quantities. Let's create the illusion of a winter storm by creating an array of snowballs (spheres) and have them fall from the sky.

Start by creating a blank program by entering the following code:

```
; Snowballs
;_____

Graphics3D 640,480
SetBuffer BackBuffer()

; Create camera
camera=CreateCamera()

; Creating a light
light=CreateLight()

; The following code makes the program run
While Not KeyDown( 1 )
```

```
RenderWorld
Flip

Wend

End
```

Now we are going to create an array called snowballs by adding the following code in bold:

```
; Creating a light
light=CreateLight()

;Creating the building array
Dim snowball (100)
```

Now that we have created the array, we'll use a For . . . Next statement to create 100 snowballs, change their size, and position them:

```
;Creating the building array
Dim snowball (100)
For b = 0 To 100
snowball(b)=CreateSphere()
PositionEntity snowball(b),Rnd(-30,30),Rand(20,70),30
ScaleEntity snowball(b),0.5,0.5,0.5
Next
```

Let's take a look at the code we've entered to see what we've done:

**For b = 0 To 100** – This will start a For . . . Next statement that will loop 100 times.

**snowball(b)=CreateSphere()** – This code will create the snowballs in the shape of a sphere.

**PositionEntity snowball(b),Rnd(-30,30),Rand(20,70),30** – This will position the snowballs randomly from left to right. We'll also position them in random locations above the screen to begin with.

**ScaleEntity snowball(b),0.5,0.5,0.5** – This code will size the snowball.

**Next**– Next ends the For . . . Next statement.

If you ran the program now, you wouldn't see anything on the screen because all of the snowballs are above the screen. They'll stay there until we make them move with the following code in bold:

```
; This following code makes our program run
While Not KeyDown( 1 )
For i = 0 To 100
MoveEntity snowball(i),0,Rnd(-.002,-1),0
Next

RenderWorld
Flip

Wend

End
```

Here we created a For . . . Next statement that loops 100 times. Notice that we created a new variable called i, which is one we simply made up. We then assigned it to the variable snowball by adding the code snowball(i). To make the snowballs fall from the sky, we use the MoveEntity command and randomize the speed of the snowballs falling. When you run the program, you should see snowballs falling, as in Figure 16.6.

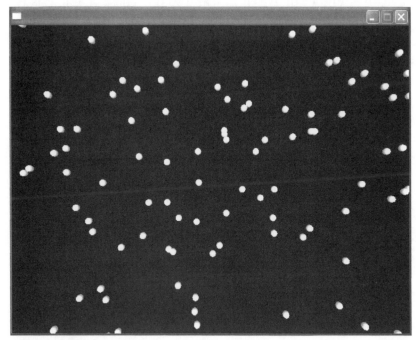

**Figure 16.6**
With an array, you can create hundreds of variables with just a few lines of code.

## Types

Types are an important part of programming in Blitz3D and can save you hundreds of lines of codes. Think of a type as a "team." You can assign different objects and characteristics to that team and then define different qualities for the team and its members. Working with and understanding types can be a little confusing, so take things slow, step-by-step, until you have a good understanding of what a type does and how it can be applied to your game. Let's use the example of creating a maze for your game that is made up of different spheres. Rather than creating each sphere individually and defining the characteristics of each sphere, we can create a team of spheres (our type) and then define what characteristics (size, color, shape, health) that the team members should have. The first step is to give your team a name by defining the type. This is done as follows:

```
; Defining our type
Type Maze
```

In this case we called our type Maze, but you can give your types any name you choose. The next thing that we need to do is tell Blitz3D what type of characteristics our type will have. These characteristics can include things like its position, its shape, the number of lives it has, and so on. These characteristics are called *fields*. To keep things simple, let's give our maze only two characteristics and call those characteristics *Health* and *Shape* by adding the following code in bold. But before entering the code, let me discuss why we would want to create a characteristic like Health. Let's say that whenever a player bumped into a piece of the maze, the maze piece would change colors. After being hit three times, the maze piece would disappear. Using types, you can verify the status of different fields by checking each piece of the maze simultaneously. You can assign a variable that says that the Health of a maze piece is equal to 3 to begin with. Each time it is hit by the player, its Health is reduced by 1. When the health is equal to 0, the maze piece will disappear. Using types, we don't have to create code that will check each piece of the maze separately; we can just check all pieces that are a certain type. Still a little confused? It should become clear as we go through this example:

```
; Defining our type
Type Maze
Field Health
Field Shape
```

Our type is now created, so we have to end it by adding the following code in bold:

```
; Defining our type
Type Maze
Field Health
Field Shape
End Type
```

So now that we have our type, called Maze, and our characteristics, called Health and Shape, we now have to create our full team. To do this we need to create a variable for the type we created. Variables for your types are created by putting a "." (period) between the variable and the type. In this case, we will create a variable called player by adding this code:

```
player.maze = New Maze
```

The code we just added basically says that we should add a player to our maze. The "players" are actually going to be the spheres that make up the maze. Now we have to define the shape of our players and their health status. To define the fields within a type you have to use the "\" (backslash) character. Here's how we would define the shape of our players:

```
player\shape = CreateSphere()
player\health = 3
```

So let's recap what we've done so far. We've created a type called Maze that has one characteristic called Health. We've also assigned a variable called player to the maze and defined it as the creation of a sphere. Are you thoroughly confused yet? If so, you're not alone. Understanding types takes time and practice. We'll now put the components together into a program to see how it all works and what we can do. Start by opening the file called empty.bb and save it with a new name. Alternatively, you can just enter the following code. If you've opened empty.bb, make sure to add the UpdateWorld command as seen below.

```
; Empty Program
;_____
```

```
Graphics3D 640,480
SetBuffer BackBuffer()

; Create camera
camera=CreateCamera()

;Create light
light=CreateLight()

;The following code makes our program run
While Not KeyDown( 1 )
UpdateWorld

RenderWorld
Flip

Wend

End
```

Now let's enter the code we created earlier in this section to our program outside of the main loop (the new code is in bold):

```
; Empty Program
;_____

Graphics3D 640,480
SetBuffer BackBuffer()

; Create camera
camera=CreateCamera()

;Create light
light=CreateLight()

; Defining our type
Type Maze
Field Shape
Field Health
End Type
player.maze = New Maze
player\shape = CreateSphere()
player\health = 3
```

```
;The following code makes our program run
While Not KeyDown( 1 )
Updateworld

RenderWorld
Flip

Wend

End
```

Running the program now will produce absolutely nothing because we haven't positioned our player\shape anywhere. Add the following code in bold to position our entity player\shape:

```
; Defining our type
Type Maze
Field Shape
Field Health
End Type
player.maze = New Maze
player\shape = CreateSphere()
player\health = 3
PositionEntity player\shape ,0,0,6
```

Now run the program. Ooooh! Ahhhhh! You see a sphere (Figure 16.7). Big whoop! Actually, it is a big deal as you'll see in the next step. This sphere is part of a type called "Maze" so we can create many players and check and alter their characteristics all at once.

Now we are going to surround part of the code with a For...Next statement (I'll discuss For...Next statements later in the chapter, but for now just know that it creates a loop.) The reason we are going to do this is because we are going to create 1000 spheres with just a few lines of code.

Start off by deleting the code you just entered: PositionEntity Team\shape ,0,0,6. Now that this is gone, we can start creating our 1000 spheres. Let's make a grid of spheres that are 10 × 10 × 10, which will yield 1000 spheres. Rather than creating each sphere individually, we will use a For...Next statement to replicate the sphere we created called player\shape that is part of the type Maze.

Enter the following code in bold, and then I'll discuss each line we've added:

```
; Empty Program
;_____
```

**Figure 16.7**
Although it doesn't seem like much, this sphere that you created is part of the
type called `Maze`. That means you can quickly check its characteristics.

```
Graphics3D 640,480
SetBuffer BackBuffer()

; Create camera
camera=CreateCamera()
PositionEntity camera ,30,15,-20
RotateEntity camera, 0,30,0

;Create light
light=CreateLight()

; Defining our type
Type Maze
Field Health
Field Shape
End Type
For x= 1 To 10
For y = 1 To 10
For z = 1 To 10
```

```
player.maze = New Maze
player\shape = CreateSphere(32)
player\health = 3
PositionEntity player\shape, x*2,y*2,z*2
Next
Next
Next

;The following code makes our program run
While Not KeyDown( 1 )
Updateworld

RenderWorld
Flip

Wend

End
```

Run the program now and you should see a grid of 1000 spheres (see Figure 16.8).

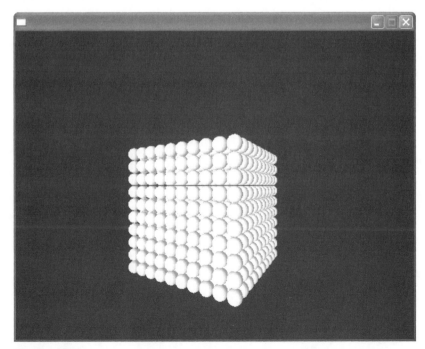

**Figure 16.8**
You have just created 1000 spheres all of the type Player.

Let's now take a close look at the few lines of code we added:

```
PositionEntity camera ,30,15,-20
RotateEntity camera, 0,30,0
```

We moved and rotated the camera so that we could get a better view of the grid we created.

```
For x= 1 To 10
For y = 1 To 10
For z = 1 To 10
```

This is the beginning of three different For statements. Basically, this will loop the creation of our sphere ten times so that we end up with 10 spheres along the x axis, 10 along the y axis and 10 along the z axis, leaving us with a $10 \times 10 \times 10$ grid.

PositionEntity player\shape, x*2,y*2,z*2 – This statement positioned each sphere in a different location, two units apart from one another. If we wanted the spheres to be spaced out further, we would have entered a larger number.

To be honest, creating a grid of 1000 spheres can be done easily without creating a type. The beauty of having each sphere as a member of the type called Maze is that we can check the characteristics of each sphere and then control each sphere individually or the entire group. Let's now put this to the test. We defined the Health of each sphere as 3 to begin with. In the game loop, we'll create a statement saying that if the Health of a sphere is 3 (which it should be), then move that sphere in a random direction. Let's add the following code in bold to our game loop:

```
;The following code makes our program run
While Not KeyDown( 1 )
For player.maze = Each Maze
If player\health = 3 Then MoveEntity player\shape, Rand(-3,3), Rand(-3,3),
Rand(-3,3)
Next
Updateworld

RenderWorld
Flip

Wend

End
```

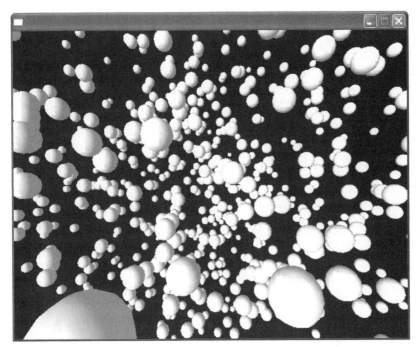

**Figure 16.9**
All of the spheres are moving in random order.

Run the program now and you should see all 1000 spheres moving in random order. The reason they are all moving is because the Health of each is equal to 3 (see Figure 16.9).

To check each one of the spheres in the maze, we entered the code For player.maze = Each Maze. This line of code is very powerful because in one quick sweep it examines each member of our maze, which happens to be comprised of 1000 spheres. It checks each to see if its Health is equal to 3. If the Health of a sphere is equal to 3, then it moves the sphere around in random order.

While the effect that this code produces may look neat, it isn't very practical. Let's change this code so that if the Health of the sphere is equal to 3, its color will be red, and otherwise it will become blue. Let's do this by replacing this code:

```
If player\health = 3 Then MoveEntity player\shape, Rand(-3,3), Rand(-3,3),
Rand(-3,3)
```

with the following:

```
If player\health=3
EntityColor player\shape, 255,0,0
```

```
Else
EntityColor player\shape, 0,0,255
EndIf
```

When you run the program now, all of the spheres should be red, because all of their Healths are equal to 3. Let's now get really fancy. We are going to create a cube that will be our ship. If the cube crashes into the maze, then the health of the maze piece will be reduced by one and the sphere will change its color. To do this, we'll need to set up some collisions and some controls for the cube. Since we've covered how to accomplish this in the book already, I want you to try to create the cube and set up the collisions on your own. We're also going to reduce the number of spheres and spread them out. When you are done, compare your code to the code in bold below.

```
; Types
;_____

Graphics3D 640,480
SetBuffer BackBuffer()

; Create camera
camera=CreateCamera()
PositionEntity camera ,30,15,-20
RotateEntity camera, 0,30,0

;Create light
light=CreateLight()

; Creating the collision types
type_player=1
type_obstacle=2

;Creating the game player
cube=CreateCube()
ScaleEntity cube, 1.5,1.5,1.5
PositionEntity cube, 30,15,5
EntityType cube, type_player

; Defining the collisions
Collisions type_player,type_obstacle,1,2

; Defining our type
Type Maze
Field Health
```

```
Field Shape
End Type
For x= 1 To 4
For y = 1 To 4
For z = 1 To 4
player.maze = New Maze
player\shape = CreateSphere(32)
player\health = 3
PositionEntity player\shape, x*5,y*5,z*5
EntityType player\shape, type_obstacle
NameEntity player\shape, Handle (player)
Next
Next
Next

;The following code makes our program run
While Not KeyDown( 1 )
a#=0
b#=0
c#=0

If KeyDown( 203 )=True Then a#=-0.1
If KeyDown( 205 )=True Then a#=0.1
If KeyDown( 208 )=True Then b#=-0.1
If KeyDown( 200 )=True Then b#=0.1
If KeyDown( 30)=True Then c#=-0.1
If KeyDown( 44 )=True Then c#=0.1
MoveEntity cube,a#,b#,c#

For player.maze = Each maze
If player\health=3
EntityColor player\shape, 255,0,0
Else
EntityColor player\shape, 0,0,255
EndIf
Next
Updateworld

RenderWorld
Flip

Wend

End
```

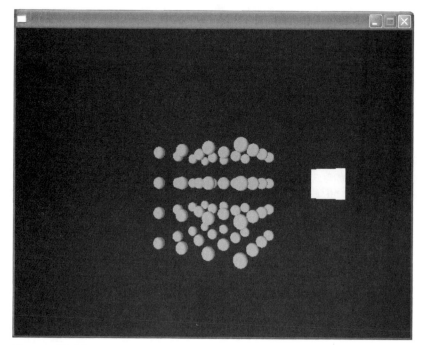

**Figure 16.10**
This cube will act as our ship that we can use to smash into the maze.

If you run the program now, you should notice a cube that will act as our "player," as seen in Figure 16.10.

Now that you have the collisions set up, it's time to create the code that will reduce the Health of the maze, which in turn will change the color of the spheres whenever a collision occurs. We will use a For...Next statement that will inspect every sphere in the maze and check to see whether a collision has occurred. If so, the Health of the sphere will be reduced and its color will change. Enter the following code in bold:

```
For player.maze = Each maze
If player\health=3
EntityColor player\shape, 255,0,0
Else
EntityColor player\shape, 0,0,255
EndIf
Next

If CountCollisions (cube) > 0
entity = EntityCollided (cube, Type_obstacle)
```

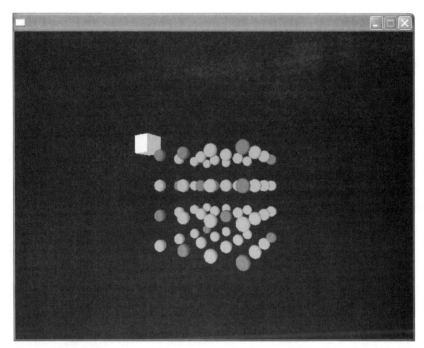

**Figure 16.11**
As the cube hits a sphere, the sphere will change color.

```
player.maze =Object.maze (EntityName (entity))
player\health = player\health-1
EndIf
UpdateWorld

RenderWorld
Flip

Wend

End
```

Run the program now, and as your player, the cube, bumps into the spheres, the spheres will turn blue as in Figure 16.11.

## Conditionals

Whether you've known it or not, you've actually used conditionals throughout this book. Here we are going to look at the different types of conditionals and how they can be used. The truth is, we've actually used a conditional in every program we've created so far by using the code `While Not KeyDown( 1 )` to make our programs run. As you learned earlier, that code says that as long as the Esc key isn't pressed, run the program. This is just one of many different types of conditionals we can create.

A conditional basically takes a look at a situation in your game, and based on that situation, it will make a decision. Think of a common decision you have to make on a daily basis. You look out the window and see that it is raining outside. Based on the fact that it is raining (the situation) you put on your raincoat (the decision). If it was snowing, you'd put on your ski jacket, and if it was sunny and hot, you wouldn't wear a coat at all. That's how a conditional works; it looks to see if a certain circumstance is true or false, and then makes a decision based on the result of that circumstance.

## Operators

You can't have a conditional without an operator. An operator is the test you use to see if a condition is true or false. That may sound a little confusing, so let's look at an example. Recall the example of the weather and appropriate clothing. If we converted that into a programming code, it might look something like this:

```
If Weather = Rainy then wear Raincoat
```

The equals sign in the middle of the equation is the operator. Let's look at the same type of scenario using a slightly different operator. This time, let's make our decision based on the temperature outside. If it's less than 20 degrees out, we'll wear our ski jacket:

```
If Temperature < 20 degrees then wear ski jacket
```

Notice the < (less than) sign in this equation. This is the operator. There are several other operators that you can use in Blitz3D as seen in the following chart:

| | |
|---|---|
| = | Equals |
| > | Greater than |
| < | Less than |
| <> | Not equal to |
| >= | Greater than or equal to |
| <= | Less than or equal to |

All of the preceding are known as *relational operators*. There are several other types of operators called *logical operators* that allow you to combine or work with two or more equations. These include:

```
And, Or, Xor, Not
```

I'll cover these in specific examples in the following sections.

## If...Then Statements

If...Then statements are probably the most common form of conditionals. You test to see if a condition is true or false, and you tell Blitz3D what action to take. Remember our raincoat example from the previous section? It is a good example of an If...Then statement:

**If** Weather = Rainy **then** wear Raincoat

Let's use an actual example in a program. Enter the code below to create a program that contains a cone. We'll then add an If...Then statement to our code that will color the cone when the space bar is pressed.

```
; Cone
;_____

Graphics3D 640,480
SetBuffer BackBuffer()

; Create camera
camera=CreateCamera()

;Create light
light=CreateLight()

;Create a cone
cone=CreateCone()
PositionEntity sphere, 0,0,6

;The following code makes our program run
While Not KeyDown( 1 )

RenderWorld
Flip

Wend

End
```

Now add the following If...Then statement in bold to the game loop in order to color the cone when the space bar is pressed:

```
;The following code makes our program run
While Not KeyDown( 1 )
If KeyDown (57) = True Then EntityColor cone, 0,255,0

RenderWorld
Flip

Wend

End
```

The If statement we created is one that you've seen many times throughout the book. It says that If the space bar is pressed, Then change the color of the cone to the color we've specified.

**Note**

**A Sloppy Shortcut**

> It's always a good idea to properly format your code so it's easy for other people to understand and follow. Also, when properly formatted, you can find mistakes and bugs easily. That being said, certain code isn't essential. Take a look at the code you just entered: If KeyDown (57) = True Then EntityColor cone, 0,255,0. Certain parts of that code are unnecessary, since they are accepted by default. In this code we could take out the = True Then because by default an If statement is true and anything following the If will be carried out whether or not the Then is included. Test this yourself: Enter If KeyDown (57) EntityColor cone, 0,255,0 in the last example, and then run the program. You'll notice that it works just the same.

How you format the If...Then statement is important if you want to add more than one condition. Notice how our entire statement in the previous section was all on one line. We can actually split this onto multiple lines to add more than one function to the statement. For example, let's say not only did we want the cone to turn green when the space bar was pressed, but we also wanted it to stretch upward (see Figure 16.12). To do this, you start by entering the If conditions and you put the Then options on separate lines. You will, however, have to add an EndIf command so that Blitz3D knows you are ending the If statement. Delete the If statement you created earlier and replace it with the following code in bold:

```
;The following code makes our program run
While Not KeyDown( 1 )
If KeyDown (57) = True Then
EntityColor cone, 0,255,0
```

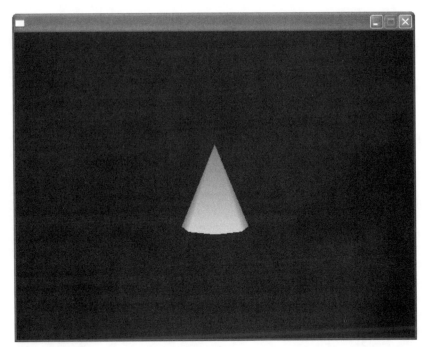

**Figure 16.12**
We colored and stretched our cone using one If...Then statement.

```
ScaleEntity cone, 1,1.2,1
Endif
```

```
RenderWorld
Flip
```

```
Wend
```

With our If...Then statements, you can add multiple conditions on separate lines as long as you end the statement with the EndIf command.

## If...Then...Else

The If...Then...Else statement takes things one step further. It basically says that if something is true or false do one thing; otherwise, do something else. Let's start by creating a program that tells us the weather conditions based on a temperature we enter. We'll use an If...Then...Else statement to accomplish this. Start by entering the following code to create an empty program:

```
; If, Then, Else
;_____
```

```
Graphics3D 640,480
SetBuffer BackBuffer()

; Create camera
camera=CreateCamera()
End
```

We first need the player to input some information. We'll do this by adding the following input string in bold:

```
; Create camera
camera=CreateCamera()
```

**;Asking for temperature**
**temp# = Input ("What is the current temperature? ")**

```
; The following code makes our program run
```

We now have a variable called `temp#` that contains the current temperature. Based on that information we will create an `If...Then...Else` statement that will create a text string based on the temperature. Add the following code in bold:

```
; If, Then, Else
;_____
```

```
Graphics3D 640,480
SetBuffer BackBuffer()

; Create camera
camera=CreateCamera()

;Asking for temperature
temp# = Input ("What is the current temperature? ")
```

**; The If, Then, Else Statement**
**If temp# > 20 Then**
**Print ("Not too bad out, wonder if I even need a coat?")**
**Else**
**Print ("Brrr...Getting cold, must be winter!!")**
**EndIf**

**;Wait 3 Seconds**
**Delay 3000**

```
End
```

**Figure 16.13**
Using an If . . . Then . . . Else statement, you can have two possible outcomes to a condition.

Run this program now and you should see results similar to Figure 16.13.

Notice that we had to end the statement with an EndIf to signify the end of the If statement.

**Note**

**Delay**

In the code that we entered above, we used a command that we have not used before, called Delay. The Delay command will pause the program for an amount of time that you specify. The time is in milliseconds, and every 1000 milliseconds is equal to one second. In the example we used, we entered the code Delay 3000 which paused the program for 3 seconds.

The example we just created used an If . . . Then . . . Else statement in a 2D environment. Let's now create a program that uses this type of statement with 3D objects. We'll create a program that has a ball that can be moved around the screen. Using an If . . . Then . . . Else statement, we'll change the color of the ball when it moves in different directions. Start by opening the file entitled colorball.bb, and then enter the code in bold below:

```
;The following code makes our program run
While Not KeyDown( 1 )
If KeyDown( 205 )=True Then x#=x#+0.005
If KeyDown( 203 )=True Then x#=x#-0.005
If KeyDown( 208 )=True Then y#=y#-0.005
If KeyDown( 200 )=True Then y#=y#+0.005
If x#> 0 Then
EntityColor ball, 255,0,0
Else
EntityColor ball, 0,255,0
EndIf
MoveEntity ball, x#,y#,z#

RenderWorld
Flip

Wend

End
```

Run the program now and use the left and right arrow keys to move around the ball. In this code, we have basically said that when the ball is moving to the right, its color should be red; otherwise, it should be green. Notice again that each statement is on a separate line, and we've added the EndIf code at the end to signify the end of the statement.

Using an If...Then...Else statement, you can create multiple Else options by adding the ElseIf command. Let's look at this option by first creating a two-dimensional guessing game. In this game, the computer will randomly pick a number between 1 and 10, and you will try to guess the number. Based on your guess, the computer will provide you with some feedback. Enter the following code to create the guessing game:

```
; Guessing Game
;_____

Graphics3D 640,480

;Generate a random number between 1 and 10
number#=Rand (1,10)
```

```
;Asking for number
guess# = Input ("What is your guess? ")
If guess# = number# Then
Print ("Wow, great guess, you should become a mind reader.")
ElseIf guess#-number# < 2
Print ("Oh so close, the actual number was " + number# )
ElseIf guess#-number# < 4
Print ("Pretty close, the actual number was " + number# )
Else
Print ("Not even close, the actual number was " + number# )
End If
Delay 5000
End
```

Run the program and enter a number. Based on the difference between your guess and the number that the computer generated, a different comment will appear. When using the ElseIf command, Blitz3D will go through each line until it finds one that is true. Let's go through this example line by line to see how the ElseIf statement worked. Let's say the computer chose the number 10 (this would be the number# variable), and we guessed 2 (which would be the guess# variable). Here's the first If statement:

STEP 1
```
If guess# = number# Then
Print ("Wow, great guess, you should become a mind reader.")
```

In our case, 2 does not equal 10, so Blitz3D continues to the next ElseIf statement:

STEP 2
```
ElseIf guess#-number# < 2
Print ("Oh so close, the actual number was " + number# )
```

Since $10 - 2$ equals 8, which is not less than 2, Blitz3D continues to the next ElseIf statement:

STEP 3
```
ElseIf guess#-number# < 4
Print ("Pretty close, the actual number was " + number# )
```

Since $10 - 2$ equals 8, which is not less than 4, Blitz3D has not found any true statements, so it defaults to the final Else statement:

STEP 4
```
Print ("Not even close, the actual number was " + number# )
```

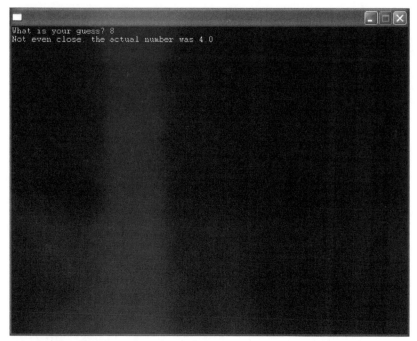

**Figure 16.14**
A quick guessing game using If...Then...Else.

If we had entered a different number — let's say we had guessed 9 as our number—Blitz would have stopped at Step 2 above because it would have been true. Figure 16.14 illustrates one iteration of the game.

## Goto

I'm sure that it's safe to assume that at some point or another you've surfed the Web. While surfing, you may have bookmarked a site or sites that you'd want to revisit again sometime in the future. Once you have a site bookmarked, you can easily jump to that page by clicking on the saved bookmark. That's pretty much how the Goto command works in Blitz3D. You can specify certain areas of your program with a mark and then jump to that mark when a certain action takes place. The Goto command is convenient in that it can save you from having to create a lot of code. Applying the Goto command is a two-step procedure. The first step is to create your bookmark at a specific location in your code, which is done by placing a period before the bookmark name. You can give your bookmark any name, just make sure it begins with a period. After you've created your bookmarks, you can access them by using the Goto command followed by the bookmark name. Truth be told, it's much smarter to use functions in Blitz3D rather than the Goto command, but just so you know how it works, I'll give you an example that you can follow although we will not actually be using it in any code.

You start by labeling a series of code with a bookmark. In this instance, we'll create a bookmark called name. Remember that bookmarks, or labels, are created by adding a period before the bookmark name:

```
.name
Print (''What is your name'')
```

Now to jump to that code at any point in your program, enter the command:

```
Goto name
```

Notice that when using the Goto command, we don't put the period in front of the name of the bookmark. In other words, we didn't enter Goto .name, we entered Goto name. Now that you know what the Goto command is, remember to only use it when absolutely necessary.

## Select...Case

The Select...Case option is very similar to If...Then...Else or ElseIf statements in that it allows you to test a variable and then run one of a variety of consequences if the expression is true. To be quite honest, you can accomplish the same thing with an If...Then...Else statement, but the formatting is just a little different. Which statement you end up using is simply a matter of preference. You use the Select command to choose your variable and then offer different cases based on the value of that variable. It'll make much more sense when you see it in a program. In the following example, we will have the player choose the level of difficulty for the game. If he chooses Easy, then 10 "aliens" will be created; if he chooses Medium, then 25 "aliens" will be created; and if he chooses Hard, then 50 "aliens" will be created. In this section, we are not really concerned with how the aliens will be created; we are just looking at how we can use a Select...Case command. Let's create a new program where we enter the level of difficulty and then prove that our Select...Case command worked by printing out our selection.

```
; Select Case
;_____
```

```
Graphics3D 640,480
SetBuffer BackBuffer()

;Getting the level of difficulty
Difficulty = Input$ ("Enter 1 for Easy, 2 for Medium or 3 for Hard? ")

; Choosing the case
Select Difficulty
Case 1
aliens#=10
Case 2
aliens#=25
Case 3
aliens#=50
Default
aliens#=10
End Select

;To prove it worked
Print ( +aliens#+ " aliens will be created." )

Delay 5000

End
```

Now run the program four different times. The first three times, enter 1 then 2 then 3 for the difficulty level. For the last time, enter any other number or don't enter a number at all. You'll notice that whatever number you enter or if you just press the Return or Enter key, the number of aliens will default to 10 because we set a default value in the code. Speaking of the code, let's take a closer look to see how we did it:

```
Difficulty = Input$ ("Enter 1 for Easy, 2 for Medium or 3 for Hard? ")
```

The code above created a variable with the identifier Difficulty. Because we used an Input$ string, the player was able to enter a number for the difficulty level.

```
; Choosing the case
Select Difficulty
```

This is how you start a Select statement. You begin with the word Select followed by the identifier for the variable. In this case the identifier was Difficulty.

```
Case 1
aliens#=10
```

This is like an `If` statement. It says that if `Difficulty` is equal to 1, then there should be 10 aliens.

```
Case 2
aliens#=25
```

This says that if the player entered 2, then there should be 25 aliens.

```
Case 3
aliens#=50
```

This says that if the player entered 3, then there should be 50 aliens.

```
Default
aliens#=10
```

The default option is very important, especially when you are asking the players of your game to enter values. If they enter anything except for the specific options set out in the cases, then the variable will revert to the default value. In this example, if the player enters anything other than 1, 2, or 3, the number of aliens that will be created will be 10, the value set as the default.

```
End Select
```

This is the code that you use to end any `Select` statement.

## Looping Conditionals

If you remember back to the beginning of the book, I mentioned that your game works a lot like a movie or cartoon. It proceeds frame by frame in a loop until the game is over. The part of the code that contains the main information for the running of your game is called the *game loop*. Think of a loop like the tire on your bicycle. Imagine you painted a white mark on the side of your tire. As your tire spins, the white mark would start at the top and then come back around to the top after one complete spin. Think of a loop as one complete spin of your tire. As your program runs, the game loop repeats over and over until something happens to stop the game. The game loop is just one type of loop that can be created. You can use loops in functions and in other areas to help you in the creation of your game elements. There are several different types of statements that create loops, the most relevant of which I will discuss in this section.

### For...Next

The For...Next loop works particularly well with types but doesn't have to be used with them solely. Think of a For...Next loop as a counter with which you can specify how many times you want a loop to go around. This type of loop is particularly useful when creating or working with a large number of objects. Here's an example of how a For...Next loop would be formatted:

```
For x#= 1 to 20
Spheres=CreateSphere()
Next
```

The loop we just created would create 20 spheres. Notice that right after the word For, you place the name of the variable—in this case we called the variable x#. This is followed by the range of the loop—the 1 is the beginning number, and the 20 is the end number, meaning that this loop will repeat itself 20 times. At the end of the loop, we add the code Next to signify the end of the loop. If you ran this loop now, you wouldn't see much on your screen because all 20 spheres would be created in the exact same spot. So let's modify the code so that the position of each sphere also changes with each loop. We'll also make this loop part of a function that is called upon when the space bar is pressed. Create a new program with the following code:

```
; For...Next
; ———————————

Graphics3D 640,480
SetBuffer BackBuffer()
camera=CreateCamera()
PositionEntity camera, 6,0,-15
light=CreateLight()
Function Make20Spheres()
For x= 1 To 20
Spheres=CreateSphere()
ScaleEntity Spheres, 0.2,0.2,0.2
PositionEntity spheres, x,y,3
Next
End Function
While Not KeyDown (1)
If KeyDown (57) Then Make20Spheres

RenderWorld
Flip
```

```
Wend

End
```

Run the program now and press the space bar. You should see 20 spheres appear. Let's dissect the code and look at the important parts that made this program possible:

`PositionEntity camera, 6,0,-15` – We moved the camera back 15 units so that we could see the spheres once they were created.

```
Function Make20Spheres()
For x= 1 To 20
Spheres=CreateSphere()
ScaleEntity Spheres, 0.2,0.2,0.2
PositionEntity spheres, x,0,3
Next
```

This is the For...Next statement that will actually create the spheres. The variable x will change 20 times, going from 1 to 20 as the loop goes round. We then position the spheres, based on the x value.

`If KeyDown (57) Then Make20Spheres` – This code runs the function when the space bar is pressed.

### Note

**Now You Try**

In the code above, you created 20 spheres with your For...Next statement. Now try to create 1000 spheres by modifying the code above to create 10 spheres along the x, y, and z axes. Hint: You'll have to create three For...Next statements—one for the x, one for the y, and one for the z values. Also, if you're really stuck you can refer back to the code we used in the section called "Type" where we did something similar. Once you're done, compare your code to the following code and the results you see in Figure 16.15

```
; For...Next
; ----------------

Graphics3D 640,480
SetBuffer BackBuffer()
camera=CreateCamera()
PositionEntity camera, 6,0,-15
light=CreateLight()
Function Make20Spheres()
```

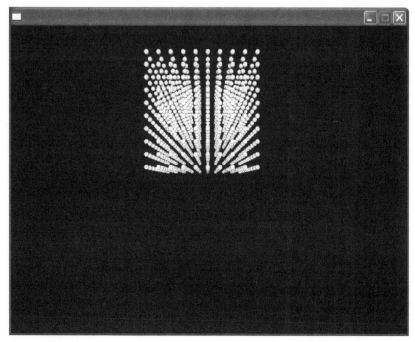

**Figure 16.15**
Create 1000 spheres with just a few lines of code using a For...Next statement.

```
For x= 1 To 10
For y = 1 To 10
For z = 1 To 10
Spheres=CreateSphere()
ScaleEntity Spheres, 0.2,0.2,0.2
PositionEntity spheres, x,y,z
Next
Next
Next
End Function

While Not KeyDown (1)
If KeyDown (57) Then Make20Spheres

RenderWorld
Flip

Wend

End
```

As I mentioned in the opening paragraph of this section, For...Next statements are particularly useful in types, since you can go through the type with the statement, examining each to make sure that it meets certain criteria. Start by opening the file called fornext.bb. This file contains a series of spheres that we created using a type. Using a For...Next statement, we'll have the program check each sphere to see if it meets a certain requirement. In this case, we'll have the colors of the spheres change after 5 seconds have passed. The For...Next statement will check each sphere and check to see how many seconds have passed. If less than 5 seconds have passed, the spheres will remain red; otherwise, they will turn blue. We'll use an If...Then...Else statement to actually change the colors.

Add the following For...Next statement in bold to the existing code:

```
While Not KeyDown( 1 )
For player.maze = Each Maze
Next

RenderWorld
Flip

Wend

End
```

The For...Next statement that you just added will check each sphere that you have created to see if it meets a certain set of criteria. We haven't added any criteria yet—that's what we'll do next with the following If statement in bold:

```
timer=MilliSecs()
;The following code makes our program run
While Not KeyDown( 1 )
For player.maze = Each Maze
If MilliSecs() < timer + 5000
EntityColor player\shape, 255,0,0
Else
EntityColor player\shape, 0,0,255
EndIf
Next
```

As this program runs, Blitz 3d will check each sphere and see how much time has passed. After 5 seconds have passed, the spheres will turn blue. This is just one example of how you can use a For...Next statement to evaluate each member of a type. Earlier in the chapter, when we first explored types, we used a `For...Next` statement to check the health status of each item in our type. How you end up using `For...Next` statements will depend on the type of game you are creating and the number of variables you would like to create.

### While...Wend

In almost every chapter in this book you've used `While...Wend` statements as part of the game loop, by using the following code:

```
While Not KeyDown (1)
Wend
```

This basically says that while the Esc key isn't pressed, run the following code. The `Wend` statement signifies the end of the `While` loop. A `While` statement will continue to loop until the statement is no longer true. In the example above, when the Esc key is pressed, the statement is no longer true, so the loop will end and the program will close. Typically, we use this type of statement only for our game loop, but that being said, there are instances where you might want to use it within the game loop or within other functions.

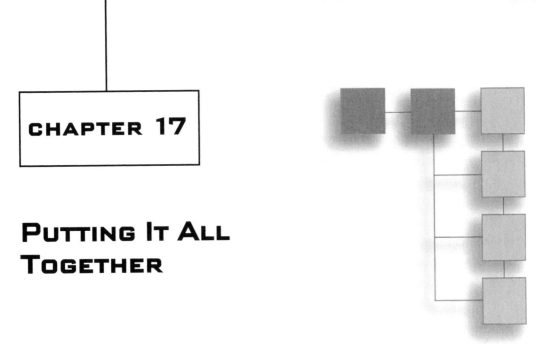

# CHAPTER 17

# PUTTING IT ALL TOGETHER

Think of everything that you've learned so far in this book as a semester of learning leading up to your final exam. This chapter is the final exam, in which you'll put together many of the concepts that you've learned so far and apply them while creating an actual video game. The game won't be like Doom, Halo, Half-Life, or any of the other commercial games that you see on the market. It will actually be quite simple. That being said, it will apply many of the concepts you've learned, and you should be proud of the work that you've done to bring you to this point.

Rather than just copying the code you see in this chapter, try to actually think of it as an exam. Before each block of code, I'll create a section describing what we are trying to accomplish. Read these sections and try to create the game on your own. If you get stuck, refer to the code and see where you went wrong.

## Planning the Game—"3D Gallery"

If you think back to Chapter 3, "Designing a Game," you'll recall that I discussed the importance of taking the time to plan your game—defining the characters, the action, and the environment, and the process of playing the game. Here is the breakdown of the game that we will now create called "3D Gallery." The game will be a 3D version of a shooting gallery at a local fair. The player will shoot at different objects moving around the game environment. The goal of the game is to find and shoot all of the moving objects. Here are the key points of the game:

- The game will be a third-person shooter, meaning that the player won't actually be seen.

- The player will have a gun that will be seen at the bottom of the screen wherever the player is moved.

- When the player fires the gun (by pressing the space bar) a missile will fly out of the gun, moving forward and slightly upward.

- There will be five different types of items in the gallery.

- The targets will be grouped in five and will be constantly moving.

- If the target hits the ground, it will randomly be placed at another position in the sky.

- The world will have gravity and all objects will float to the ground.

- The world of the game will contain water and hills.

- The player will earn one point for every target hit.

- The targets will disappear when a bullet hits them.

- The game ends when all the targets have been destroyed or when 3 minutes have elapsed.

- Using the up and down arrow keys, you can move the player forward and back.

- Using the left and right arrow keys, you can rotate the player horizontally.

- The player will have 100 missiles, but can reload by pressing the R key.

- The game can be paused by pressing the P key.

- When the game ends, the player will be presented with a screen instructing him how to restart or exit.

- When the game starts, the player will be presented with a Welcome screen showing instructions for controlling the player and the game.

- When the game is paused, a screen will appear indicating to the player that pressing the mouse button will restart the game.

- The score, time remaining, and bullets remaining will be displayed on the screen.

## Files for the Game

Most of the files that we will use in this game we have either created earlier in the book or will create specifically for this game. That being said, we are going to use some existing 3D models for the targets. Special thanks to Adam Kruvand at Studio2a for providing the models. Make sure that you create a new folder on your computer and copy the following files from the CD into the folder:

duck.3ds

seahorse.3ds

donkey.3ds

flamingo.3ds

dolphin.3ds

snake.3ds

bullet.3ds

welcome.bmp

pause.bmp

end.bmp

ground.jpg

explode.wav

phaser.wav

## Creating the Water Texture

The only file that we are going to create from scratch is that of the water. Using Corel Photo-Paint, we'll create a texture that looks like water. One problem with the textures that we've created so far is that they weren't seamless. We need to create textures that look identical where they start and end so that there are no "seams." I'll show you a technique you can use in Photo-Paint so that your textures are seamless.

1. Launch Photo-Paint and click the New button in the Welcome screen that appears. In the dialog box that appears (see Figure 17.1), change the units of measurement to pixels. Make the height and width of the document 256 pixels, and change the resolution to 72 dpi. Also change the Color mode to 24-bit RGB and click OK.

2. Click Edit > Fill to bring up the Fill dialog box (see Figure 17.2). Click the Texture Fill button (the last large colored button) and then click the Edit button. You can now select and modify the fill.

3. Click on the Texture Library drop-down menu and select Samples from the list (see Figure 17.3). Now scroll through the list of different textures and choose Swimming pool2. Click OK, and you will be returned to the main dialog box. Click OK to close the dialog box. The fill will now be applied to your document, and you should see an image of some clouds.

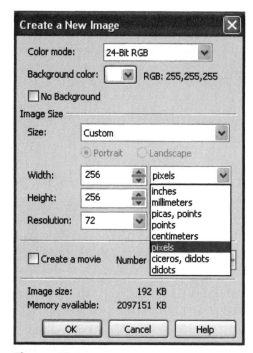

**Figure 17.1**
Enter the dimensions in this dialog box to create a texture document.

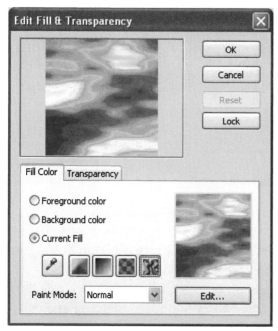

**Figure 17.2**
Click the Texture Fill button and then the Edit button.

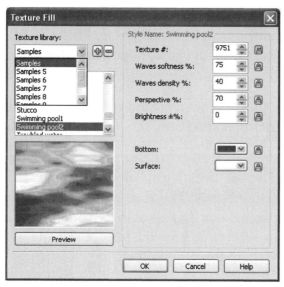

**Figure 17.3**
Choose the Swimming pool2 fill to create a water-like texture.

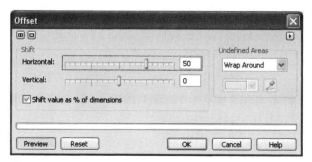

**Figure 17.4**
Shift the texture vertically and you'll see the seam.

4. We are now going to make the texture "seamless" by making sure that when copies of the texture are placed side by side, the player won't be able to tell where the texture begins or ends. Click Effects > Distort > Offset. This will bring up a dialog box (see Figure 17.4), from which we can shift texture horizontally or vertically. Enter 50 in the horizontal box and 0 in the vertical box and then click OK. This will shift the texture over by 50% so that you can see the "seam" that will be created when the textures are placed side by side. To remove this, we will use the Clone tool.

5. Click and hold the tool right under the letter A in the toolbox. A flyout of tools will appear. From that flyout (see Figure 17.5), click the Clone tool (which is the button with two little brushes.)

6. Click on the Shape drop-down button from the toolbar (see Figure 17.6). From the menu that appears, select the feathered option with a 60 on it.

7. Right-click on an area beside the stitch, but not including the stitch. This area will now be the source. Now click on the stitch and you'll see the stitch area disappear. Repeat this step for other areas until the stitch is completely removed as seen in Figure 17.7.

8. Click Effects > Distort > Offset. This will bring up a dialog box from which we can shift texture horizontally or vertically. This time we will change the vertical offset. Enter 0 in the horizontal box and 50 in the vertical box and then click OK. You will now see a preview of how the texture will appear when the segments are lined up one on top of the other.

9. Repeat Step 7 to remove the vertical stitch (see Figure 17.8). You will now have a seamless texture.

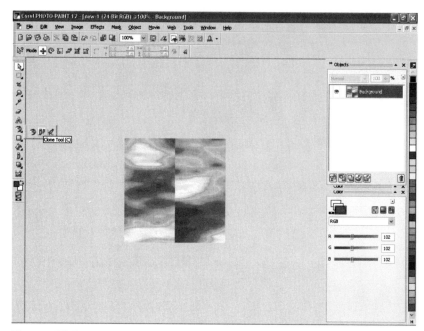

**Figure 17.5**
Choose the Clone tool from the flyout.

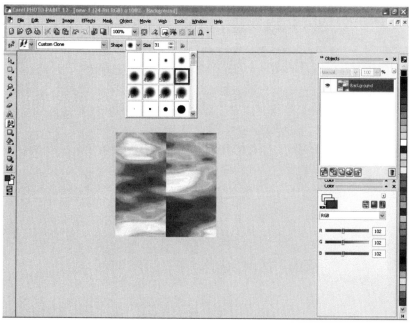

**Figure 17.6**
Choose the size 60 brush from the drop-down menu.

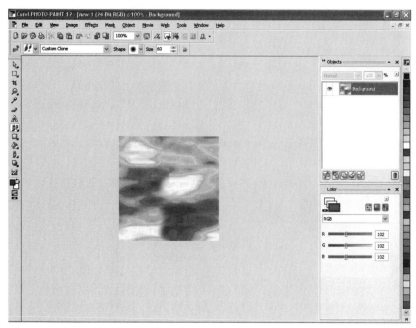

**Figure 17.7**
Clone the area beside the stitch onto the stitch so that it will disappear.

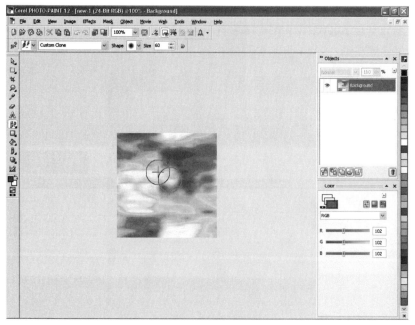

**Figure 17.8**
Remove the vertical stitch using the Clone tool.

10. Click Effects > Distort > Offset. Enter a 0 in both the horizontal and vertical boxes and then click OK. You'll be left with your final texture that is now seamless.

11. Click File > Save As to bring up the Save As dialog box. Click the drop-down menu, choose the file type called JPG, and give the file the name water.jpg. Save the file into the folder where you saved the other game files.

## Welcome Screen

In almost every game, you'll find a Welcome screen that gives the player instructions on the controls needed to play the game. Our game will be no different. We'll use the Welcome screen that we created in Chapter 8, "Getting Graphic." If you happened to have skipped that chapter, now would be a good time to go back and go over the process of creating your Welcome screen since you'll need it for this section of code. Start off by creating a new program in Blitz3D and save it with any name to the folder where you stored all of the files necessary for this game. The first thing that we are going to do is create a function that will initiate the Welcome screen. While creating our program, we'll use lots of comments so that keeping track of where things are will be a breeze. Let's start by adding the following code to create our function:

```
;Shooting Gallery
;_____

;This line launches the welcome function
    welcome()

;Creating the welcome function

    Function welcome()
        Graphics 1024,768
        screen=LoadImage ("welcome.bmp")
        DrawImage screen,0,0
        While Not KeyDown(1)

            If KeyDown(28) Then Return

        Wend

    End Function
```

### Note

**Tabs**

Notice how there are different tab indentations for different lines. Since our program is going to contain many lines of code, indenting groups of code will make it easier to identify.

Most of this function should already make sense to you. If it doesn't, refer back to Chapter 16, "Programming Fundamentals," to go over functions. That being said, the process of loading an image was only briefly covered, so let's look at the following two lines of that code in particular:

```
screen=LoadImage ("welcome.bmp")
DrawImage screen,0,0
```

These two lines of code start by creating an identifier called `screen`, and then the `LoadImage` command loads the image called welcome.bmp into the program. The code `DrawImage screen` will draw the image starting from the top left corner of the screen (position, 0,0). Go ahead and run the program now, and, with any luck, you should see the Welcome screen appear. When you press the Enter or Return key, the program should end. Notice that the display was set at 1024 × 768, which means the game should take up the entire screen on most monitors. If you run the program now, you should see the Welcome screen, as in Figure 17.9.

## Setting Up the Graphic Elements and Camera

As done for all our programs, we'll need to set the resolution and the buffer. Even though we set the resolution for earlier in the function, we need to set it for the rest of the program. To do this, we'll enter the following code in bold:

```
    EndIf
    Wend
    End Function

;Setting the graphics for the program
    Graphics3D 1024,768
    SetBuffer BackBuffer()

; Creating the camera
    camera=CreateCamera()

; Creating a light
    light=CreateLight()
```

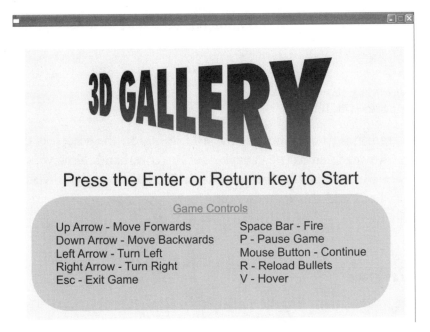

**Figure 17.9**
The Welcome screen is generated in the function run at the beginning of the program.

## Setting Up the Game Elements

Now we'll create the game loop for the program using the same code we've used throughout the book. Add the code in bold:

```
; Creating a light
    light=CreateLight()

; The following code makes our program run

While Not KeyDown( 1 )
    Renderworld
    Flip
Wend
End
```

## Creating the World

The world for our game is going to be made up of three different elements. The water in the lakes will be a plane on which we will apply the texture we created earlier. For the hills, we will use a heightmap on which we will apply another texture. The sky won't actually be an object–instead, we'll change the color of the camera, which will make everything that is black appear the color that we specify.

To do this, we'll use the `CameraClsColor` command. Let's start by applying that command in bold:

```
; Create camera
    camera=CreateCamera()
    CameraClsColor camera, 0,125,255
```

If you run the program now, you'll notice that everything on the screen is the light blue color that we specified in the `CameraClsColor` command. Now we are going to create the water, which, as mentioned earlier, is just a plane with a texture applied to it. Let's add this code in bold:

```
; Creating a light
    light=CreateLight()

;Creating a the water plane

    water=CreatePlane()
        PositionEntity water, 0,-15,0
        watertexture=LoadTexture ("water.jpg")
        EntityTexture water, watertexture
        ScaleTexture watertexture,15,15
```

At this point, every part of that code should make sense to you. It's simply a plane with the water texture that we created earlier applied to it. We scaled the texture to make it look more spread out, and we positioned the plane 15 units below the 0 level on the y plane.

Now we will create the terrain for the game. It will be a heightmap with a texture applied to it, scaled and positioned.

```
ScaleTexture watertexture,15,15
```

```
; Loading the heightmap
    terrain=LoadTerrain ( "ground.jpg" )
        ScaleEntity terrain,5,50,5
        PositionEntity terrain,-500,-20,-500
        tex=LoadTexture( "greenery.jpg" )
        ScaleTexture tex, 50,50
        EntityTexture terrain,tex
        EntityType terrain, type_scenery
```

Run the program now and you should see the sky, mountains, and water, as seen in Figure 17.10.

**Figure 17.10**
Create the sky, mountains, and water.

## Gallery Items

The gallery items that will serve as targets for our game will be made up of seven different animals. There will be five copies of each animal for a total of 35 animals. For each animal, we'll create an array of five of the animals and position them, scale them, and color them. Each of the animals will be a .3ds file that we will load. Let's start by creating the ducks, and then we'll create the other animals. Add the following code in bold:

```
EntityTexture terrain,tex
EntityType terrain, type_scenery

;Creating the gallery items
    Dim ducks(5)
        For x = 1 To 5
            ducks(x)= LoadMesh ("duck.3ds")
            PositionEntity ducks(x), x*15,0,90
            EntityColor ducks(x), 255,255,0
            ScaleEntity ducks(x), 0.2,0.2,0.2

    Next
```

**Figure 17.11**
The array you created should produce five yellow ducks.

Run the program now, and with any luck you should have five ducks across the screen, as in Figure 17.11.

Now we need to recreate this array for the other animals. The code will look almost exactly the same with the exception that we'll change the animal name and adjust their position and size.

```
;Creating the gallery items
   Dim ducks(5)
      For x = 1 To 5
         ducks(x)= LoadMesh ("duck.3ds")
         PositionEntity ducks(x), x*15,0,90
         EntityColor ducks(x), 255,255,0
         ScaleEntity ducks(x), 0.2,0.2,0.2
   Next

   Dim seahorse(5)
      For x = 1 To 5
         seahorse(x)= LoadMesh ("seahorse.3ds")
         PositionEntity seahorse(x), x*6,10,45
         EntityColor seahorse(x), 255,102,0
         ScaleEntity seahorse(x), 0.03,0.03,0.03
      Next
```

```
Dim donkey(5)
    For x = 1 To 5
        donkey(x)= LoadMesh ("donkey.3ds")
        PositionEntity donkey(x), x*5,35,85
        EntityColor donkey(x), 204,204,204
        ScaleEntity donkey(x), 0.3,0.3,0.3
    Next

Dim flamingo(5)
    For y = 1 To 5
        flamingo(y)= LoadMesh ("flamingo.3ds")
        PositionEntity flamingo(y), y*6,8,25
        EntityColor flamingo(y), 102,51,51
        ScaleEntity flamingo(y), 0.003,0.003,0.003
    Next

Dim dolphin(5)
    For x = 1 To 5
        dolphin(x)= LoadMesh ("dolphin.3ds")
        PositionEntity dolphin(x), x*6,45,0
        EntityColor dolphin(x), 102,153,255
        ScaleEntity dolphin(x), 0.3,0.3,0.3
    Next

Dim snake(5)
    For x = 1 To 5
        snake(x)= LoadMesh ("snake.3ds")
        PositionEntity snake(x), x*16,10,10
        EntityColor snake(x), 153,255,153
        ScaleEntity snake(x), 0.06,0.06,0.06
    Next
```

Run the program now, and you should see many of the animals, as in Figure 17.12.

## Note

### Changing the Animals

Feel free to import the animal models into 3ds Max and alter them using some of the techniques you learned earlier in the book.

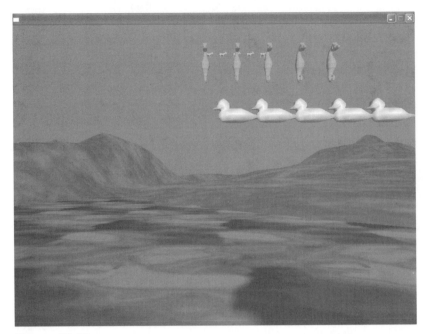

**Figure 17.12**
You'll see some of the animals at this point, but not all because they are
spread out in different locations around the playing field.

## Creating the Guns and Bullets

The gun for our game will simply be a cylinder that we will "attach" to the
camera so that wherever we move the camera, the gun will follow. The bullets will
be copies of the missile that we created in 3ds Max earlier in the book. If you
happened to skip Chapter 9, "3D Modeling" or that exercise, you have two
options: you can either go back and create the missile or grab the file from the CD
or download it from our Web site. Let's start by creating the code in bold below
for the gun:

```
EntityType snake(x), type_gallery
     EntityRadius snake(x), 5
  Next

;Creating the gun
     gun=CreateCylinder(12)
        ScaleEntity gun,0.2,0.6,0.4
        RotateEntity gun,45,0,0
        PositionEntity gun, EntityX(camera),EntityY(camera)-2,
     EntityZ(camera)+3
```

```
        EntityOrder gun, -1
        EntityParent gun,camera
    EntityColor gun, 100,100,100
```

The code that we've used to create the gun simply creates a cylinder, colors it, positions it at the bottom of our screen, and then assigns the camera as its parent so that wherever the camera goes, it goes. The code we'll use for the bullets is very similar to that which we used in Chapter 15, "Other 3D Game Components." It will be an array that contains 100 bullets and loads the missile we created earlier. We'll also create a variable called maxbull that will limit the number of bullets in our cartridge to 100 before having to reload. We'll deal with reloading later; for now, let's create the bullets by adding the following code in bold:

```
    EntityParent gun,camera
    EntityColor gun, 100,100,100

;Creating the bullets
   maxbull = 100
      Dim bullet(maxbull)
         For i=0 To maxbull
             bullet(i)=LoadMesh ("bullet.3ds")
             EntityColor bullet(i), 100,100,100

      Next
```

Run the program now, and you should see the gun at the bottom of the screen. You won't see any bullets because we haven't positioned them; we'll do that during the firing process a little later on in the program.

## Game Control and Gravity

The controls for the game are actually quite simple. The arrow keys will move the player back and forth or rotate the view from side to side. In this section, we'll also create the illusion of gravity by constantly moving the player downward, and we'll allow the player to jump by moving the camera upward every time the letter V is pressed. I chose the letter V because it is close to the space bar (which is what will be used for firing bullets later) so that the player can jump and fire using the same hand. Add the following code in bold to add controls and gravity for the game:

```
; The following code makes our program run
   While Not KeyDown( 1 )
```

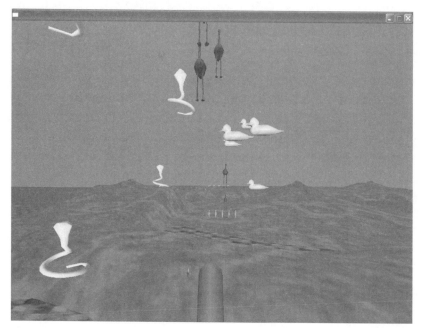

**Figure 17.13**
If you hold down the letter V and press the arrow keys, you can get a good view of your playing field.

```
If KeyDown( 205 )=True Then TurnEntity camera,0,-1,0
If KeyDown( 203 )=True Then TurnEntity camera,0,1,0
If KeyDown( 208 )=True Then MoveEntity camera,0,0,-1
If KeyDown( 200 )=True Then MoveEntity camera,0,0,1
If KeyDown( 47 )=True Then TranslateEntity camera,0,3,0

MoveEntity camera, 0,-0.8,0
```

If you run the program now, you may be in for a little shock. Because we created gravity, the camera will move downward and fall right through the ground because we have yet to set up collisions. If you hold down the letter V you can hover above the plane to get a good look of your playing field, as in Figure 17.13.

## Moving Targets

Right now, the targets in the game would be really easy to hit because they aren't moving. We'll change that right now by adding the code to move the different objects at different speeds. We'll create different speeds and different directions for each of the types of targets so that it will be difficult to hit them with the bullets. We'll use a For. . . Next statement to move each of the five copies of each animal. Add the follow code in bold:

```
If KeyDown( 47 )=True Then TranslateEntity camera,0,3,0
MoveEntity camera, 0,-0.8,0
```

```
; Moving the targets
    For a = 1 To 5
        MoveEntity ducks(a), 0.1,-.02,0
        MoveEntity seahorse(a), 0,-.02,0
        MoveEntity donkey(a), 0,-.02,0
        MoveEntity flamingo(a), 0.1,-0.2,0
        MoveEntity snake(a), -0.2,-0.2,0
        MoveEntity dolphin(a), 0,-0.2,-0.3
    Next
```

## Firing Bullets

The ability to fire bullets is one of the most important aspects of our game and will involve quite a bit of code. As stated earlier, we have a cartridge of 100 bullets, and we want the player to have to reload when he runs out of bullets. We'll also need to create collisions so that when a bullet strikes a target the target disappears and the score goes up by one. We'll take care of that in a bit; for now, we'll just create the code that fires the bullets.

```
        MoveEntity dolphin(a), 0,-0.2,-0.3
    Next

;Firing bullets
    If KeyHit (57)
        PositionEntity bullet(t)
,EntityX(gun,1),EntityY(gun,1),EntityZ(gun,1)
        RotateEntity bullet(t),EntityPitch#(gun,1)-
35,EntityYaw#(gun,1),EntityRoll#(gun,1)
        EntityColor bullet(t),0,0,255
    EndIf

    For q = 0 To maxbull
        MoveEntity bullet(q), 0,0.8,3
    Next
```

If you ran the program now, you could fire by pressing the space bar—the only problem being that you are still falling through the ground because the gravity isn't offset by a collision. In a moment, we'll create our collisions, but before that, let's cover pausing the game.

## Pausing the Game

If the player needs to take a break, he can always pause the game by pressing the letter P. When the letter P is pressed, a new image will appear on the screen, informing the player that he can press the mouse button to resume the game. Add the following code in bold to create the pause code:

```
For q = 0 To maxbull
        MoveEntity bullet(q), 0,0.8,3
    Next

;Pausing the game
    If KeyDown(25) Then
        Cls
        pause=LoadImage ("pause.bmp")
        DrawImage pause,0,0
        Flip
        WaitMouse()
    EndIf
```

## Creating Collisions

Collisions are of utmost importance to our game for several reasons. Using collisions, we'll have the bullets destroy the targets, we'll prevent the player from falling through the ground, and we'll randomly reposition the targets when they hit the ground. We need to identify our collisions, assign a collision type to each object, and then define the collisions. We'll start with the easy part, identifying the collision types. There are four different groups of collision objects that we will create for this game, including the scenery, the bullets, the player, and the gallery items. To define these groups, add the following code in bold:

```
    Graphics3D 1024,768
    SetBuffer BackBuffer()

;Setting the type values
    type_player=1
    type_scenery=2
    type_gallery=3
    type_bullet=4
```

Now that we have the types identified, we need to assign each object in our game to one of these types by using the EntityType command. Since many of the objects, such as the targets and the bullets, are part of an array, we need to enter this code within the actual array scattered throughout the program. There are actually eleven different lines of code you need to add in different locations. Here is a list of the eleven lines of code that you can use as a checklist as you go through your program:

```
EntityType camera, type_player
EntityType water, type_scenery
EntityType terrain, type_scenery
EntityType ducks(x), type_gallery
EntityType seahorse(x), type_gallery
EntityType donkey(x), type_gallery
EntityType flamingo(y), type_gallery
EntityType dolphin(x), type_gallery
EntityType snake(x), type_gallery
EntityType bullet(i), type_bullet
```

While we're at it, were also going to set the radius size for each of the objects using the EntityRadius command. Here are the eleven lines of EntityType commands code in bold, within the actual text of the program along with the corresponding EntityRadius commands.

```
;Shooting Gallery
;_____
    welcome()
    Function welcome()
        Graphics 1024,768
        screen=LoadImage ("welcome.bmp")
        DrawImage screen,0,0
        While Not KeyDown(1)
            If KeyDown(28) Then
                Return
            EndIf
        Wend
    End Function

;Setting the graphics for the program
    Graphics3D 1024,768
    SetBuffer BackBuffer()

;Setting the type values
    type_player=1
    type_scenery=2
```

```
    type_gallery=3
    type_bullet=4; Creating the camera
    camera=CreateCamera()
    CameraClsColor camera ,0,125,255
    EntityType camera, type_player
    EntityRadius camera, 5

; Creating a light
    light=CreateLight()

; Creating a the water plane
    water=CreatePlane()
    PositionEntity water, 0,-15,0
    watertexture=LoadTexture ("water.jpg")
    EntityTexture water, watertexture
    ScaleTexture watertexture,15,15
    EntityType water, type_scenery

; Loading the heightmap
    terrain=LoadTerrain ( "ground.jpg" )
    ScaleEntity terrain,5,50,5
    PositionEntity terrain,-500,-20,-500
    tex=LoadTexture( "greenery.jpg" )
    ScaleTexture tex, 50,50
    EntityTexture terrain,tex
    EntityType terrain, type_scenery

;Creating the gallery items
    Dim ducks(5)
        For x = 1 To 5
            ducks(x)= LoadMesh ("duck.3ds")
            PositionEntity ducks(x), x*15,0,90
            EntityColor ducks(x), 255,255,0
            ScaleEntity ducks(x), 0.2,0.2,0.2
            EntityType ducks(x), type_gallery
            EntityRadius ducks(x), 3
        Next

    Dim seahorse(5)
        For x = 1 To 5
            seahorse(x)= LoadMesh ("seahorse.3ds")
            PositionEntity seahorse(x), x*6,10,45
            EntityColor seahorse(x), 255,102,0
            ScaleEntity seahorse(x), 0.03,0.03,0.03
```

```
            EntityType seahorse(x), type_gallery
            EntityRadius seahorse(x), 3
        Next

    Dim donkey(5)
        For x = 1 To 5
            donkey(x)= LoadMesh ("donkey.3ds")
            PositionEntity donkey(x), x*5,35,85
            EntityColor donkey(x), 204,204,204
            ScaleEntity donkey(x), 0.3,0.3,0.3
            EntityType donkey(x), type_gallery
            EntityRadius donkey(x), 3
        Next

    Dim flamingo(5)
        For y = 1 To 5
            flamingo(y)= LoadMesh ("flamingo.3ds")
            PositionEntity flamingo(y), y*6,8,25
            EntityColor flamingo(y), 102,51,51
            ScaleEntity flamingo(y), 0.003,0.003,0.003
            EntityType flamingo(y), type_gallery
            EntityRadius flamingo(y), 3
        Next

    Dim dolphin(5)
        For x = 1 To 5
            dolphin(x)= LoadMesh ("dolphin.3ds")
            PositionEntity dolphin(x), x*6,45,0
            EntityColor dolphin(x), 102,153,255
            ScaleEntity dolphin(x), 0.3,0.3,0.3
            EntityType dolphin(x), type_gallery
            EntityRadius dolphin(x), 3
        Next

    Dim snake(5)
        For x = 1 To 5
            snake(x)= LoadMesh ("snake.3ds")
            PositionEntity snake(x), x*16,10,10
            EntityColor snake(x), 153,255,153
            ScaleEntity snake(x), 0.06,0.06,0.06
            EntityType snake(x), type_gallery
            EntityRadius snake(x), 5
        Next
```

```
;Creating the gun
    gun=CreateCylinder(12)
    ScaleEntity gun,0.2,0.6,0.4
    RotateEntity gun,45,0,0
    PositionEntity gun, EntityX(camera),EntityY(camera)-2, EntityZ(camera)+3
    EntityOrder gun, -1
    EntityParent gun,camera
    EntityColor gun, 100,100,100

;Creating the bullets
    maxbull = 100
    Dim bullet(maxbull)
        For i=0 To maxbull
            bullet(i)=LoadMesh ("bullet.3ds")
            EntityColor bullet(i), 100,100,100
            EntityType bullet(i), type_bullet
        Next
```

Wow, that was a lot of fishing through our code, but we got it done! Now that we have our objects assigned to different collision types, we must create the collisions themselves. We want to set the collisions for the gallery items and the scenery, the bullets and the gallery items, the player and the scenery, and the scenery and the gallery items. All will be set to slide (a collision value of 2) except for the collision between the player and the scenery, in which case we want the collision to stop, so we assign it a collision value of 1. Enter the following code in bold:

```
bullet(i)=LoadMesh ("bullet.3ds")
    EntityColor bullet(i), 100,100,100
    EntityType bullet(i), type_bullet
Next

; Defining the Collisions
    Collisions type_gallery,type_scenery,2,2
    Collisions type_bullet,type_gallery,2,1
    Collisions type_player,type_scenery,2,2
    Collisions type_scenery, type_gallery, 2,2
```

Before we can run our program and test to see if our collisions work, there is one important line of code we need to enter: UpdateWorld. UpdateWorld checks for

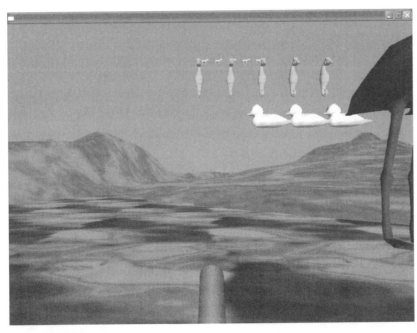

**Figure 17.14**
After creating collisions, the game should start to come together.

collisions and takes the appropriate actions, and we need to enter it before
RenderWorld near the end of the program:

```
Updateworld
RenderWorld
Flip
Wend
End
```

Now run the program, and, with any luck, what you see on your screen should
look similar to Figure 17.14. Notice how your player no longer falls through the
ground because of the collisions we've created.

## Changing the Gallery

Because we have our collisions set up, we can now control how different objects
in our game interact with one another. To add an additional element of difficulty
to our game, we'll have the gallery items change their location whenever they hit
the ground. We'll use a For. . . Next statement that will check every gallery

item to see if it has collided with the ground. If a collision has occurred, we'll reposition the item that has collided with the ground to a random location on the playing field. If you are unclear on the code used here, review Chapter 13, "Collisions." Enter the following code in bold:

```
        MoveEntity dolphin(a), 0,-0.2,-0.3
    Next


;Changing the position of gallery items
    For q = 0 To maxbull
        If CountCollisions (terrain)
            smash=CollisionEntity (terrain,1)
            PositionEntity smash, 0,Rand(10,100),Rand(-100,100)
        EndIf
    Next
```

## Destroying Gallery Items

The goal of the game is to destroy the gallery items by hitting them with the bullets that you fire from your gun. To accomplish this, we need to check to see whether a bullet has collided with a gallery item and, if so, hide the gallery item that has been hit.

```
    For q = 0 To maxbull
        MoveEntity bullet(q), 0,0.8,3
        If CountCollisions (bullet(q))
            crash=CollisionEntity (bullet(q),1)
            HideEntity crash
        EndIf

    Next
```

Run the program now and start firing away. You should notice that whenever a gallery item is hit, it disappears.

## Reloading Bullets

We only want our players to have 100 bullets before they reload. In order to accomplish this, we will need to add another condition to our If statement that controls the firing of the bullets. We'll then use the R key (19) to reload the bullets. We created code similar to this in Chapter 15 so if any of the following code in bold doesn't make sense, then go back and review that chapter.

```
;Firing bullets
    If KeyHit (57) And reload = 0
        PositionEntity bullet(t)
,EntityX(gun,1),EntityY(gun,1),EntityZ(gun,1)
        RotateEntity bullet(t),EntityPitch#(gun,1)-
35,EntityYaw#(gun,1),EntityRoll#(gun,1)
        EntityColor bullet(t),0,0,255
        t=t+1
    EndIf

    For q = 0 To maxbull
        MoveEntity bullet(q), 0,0.8,3

        If CountCollisions (bullet(q))
            crash=CollisionEntity (bullet(q),1)
            HideEntity crash
        EndIf
    Next

    bulletcount=100-t
    If t=100 Then
        reload=1
    EndIf

    If KeyDown (19) = True Then
        t=0
        reload=0

    EndIf
```

## Score

Every time a bullet collides with a gallery object, we want the score to go up by one. This is easy to accomplish. We'll create a variable called score# and have it go up by one whenever a bullet-to-gallery object collision occurs. Enter the following code in bold in the "Firing bullets" section:

```
    For q = 0 To maxbull
        MoveEntity bullet(q), 0,0.8,3
        If CountCollisions (bullet(q))
```

```
        crash=CollisionEntity (bullet(q),1)
        HideEntity crash
        score#=score#+1
    EndIf
Next
```

## Time Remaining

As discussed earlier in this chapter, the game will end when one of two things happen: either all the gallery items have been destroyed, or 3 minutes have elapsed. In order to time the game, we need to create two timers—one outside the game loop that will start the timer, and one inside the game loop that will indicate the current time in the game. When we subtract the current time from the start time, we'll end up with how much time has elapsed. Start by creating a variable called starttime just before the game loop:

```
;Defining the starting time of the game
    starttime=MilliSecs()

;The following code makes our program run
    While Not KeyDown( 1 )
```

Now we'll create two more variables within the game loop: one called currenttime that will indicate the current time in the game and will change with every loop of the game, and then another one called timeleft.

```
UpdateWorld
RenderWorld
currenttime = MilliSecs()
timeleft= 180000 - ((currenttime - starttime))
```

Let's take a closer look at the variable we created called "timeleft." Keep in mind that we want our game to be 3 minutes long, which is 180,000 milliseconds. So we subtract the starttime from the currenttime to see how many milliseconds have passed. We then subtract this from 180,000 to see how many milliseconds are left in the game.

## Ending the Game

For the game to end, all of the gallery items need to be destroyed (in other words, the score has to equal 35), or the time elapsed will need to equal zero. Whenever one of those two conditions is met, a graphic will appear allowing the user to exit the game or start over. If he elects to start over, we need to have the program jump back to the beginning. We'll accomplish this by using a Goto command. Remember that with Goto commands we need to create a bookmark so the computer knows where to jump to. In this case, we'll create a bookmark at the beginning of the program. Add the following bookmark in bold to the game code:

```
;Creating a bookmark
   .start

;Setting the graphics for the program
   Graphics3D 1024,768
   SetBuffer BackBuffer()
```

Now we need to create the code that will load the graphic and jump to the starting point if the space bar is pressed when the game is over or will end the program if the Esc key is pressed. Enter the following code in bold.

```
;Ending the game
   If score# = 35 Or timeleft < 0 Then
   Cls
   End=LoadImage ("end.bmp")
   DrawImage End,0,0
   Flip
   WaitKey()
   If KeyDown(1) Then End
   If KeyDown (57) Then Goto start
   EndIf

UpdateWorld
RenderWorld
```

Play the game now and wait three minutes. At the end, the end.bmp image should appear, as in Figure 17.15

## Text

We need to add three different text elements to the screen: the score, the time remaining, and the bullets remaining. Since we already have variables created for all three, we'll just have to add a line of code to display each of them. Notice how we divide the timeleft variable by 1000 so that the player will see the time

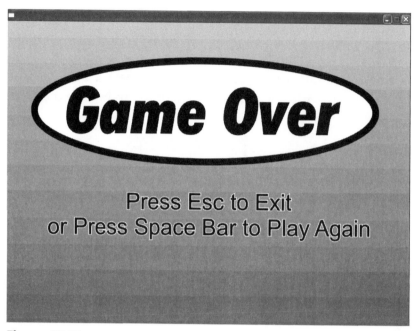

**Figure 17.15**
When all the gallery items are destroyed or 3 minutes have elapsed, the end.bmp image will appear.

remaining in seconds. We'll also add a line of text to appear when the player has run out of bullets. Add the following code in bold:

```
Text 100,10,"Score: " +score#,True,False
Text 400,10,"Bullets Remaining: "+bulletcount
Text 800,10,"Time Remaining: "+TimeLeft /1000
If reload=1 Then Text GraphicsWidth()/2, GraphicsHeight()/2,"Press R to
Reload",1,1

Flip

Wend

End
```

Run the game now, fire 100 bullets, and you should see text appear on your screen as in Figure 17.16.

## Sounds

Before we're ready to sit down and play our game for hours, let's add just a few sound effects. In particular, we'll create sounds when a bullet is fired and when a gallery target is hit. If you remember back to Chapter 14, "Sounds and Music,"

**Figure 17.16**
You should see the text indicating the time and bullets remaining, along with
the score. When you run out of bullets, the reload message will appear.

you'll know that we need to start by loading our sounds, which we'll do right after
the Welcome function at the beginning of the game:

```
Return
EndIf
Wend
End Function

; Loading the sounds
    phaser=LoadSound("phaser.wav")
    explosion=LoadSound("explode.wav")
```

Next we need to associate the sound whenever a bullet is fired:

```
;Firing bullets
    If KeyHit (57) And reload=0
        PlaySound phaser
        PositionEntity bullet(t)
,EntityX(gun,1),EntityY(gun,1),EntityZ(gun,1)
```

We also need to add a sound whenever a gallery item is destroyed, also in the "Firing bullets" section:

```
For q = 0 To maxbull
    MoveEntity bullet(q), 0,0.8,3
    If CountCollisions (bullet(q))
        crash=CollisionEntity (bullet(q),1)
        HideEntity crash
        score#=score#+1
        PlaySound explosion

    EndIf
```

That's it! Your game is complete. Congratulations. Now. . .enjoy!

## Note

**Not Working?**

If for any reason your game isn't working, open the file called shooting gallery.bb, which contains a working version of the final game. Compare your code to the code in the final version to see where things went wrong.

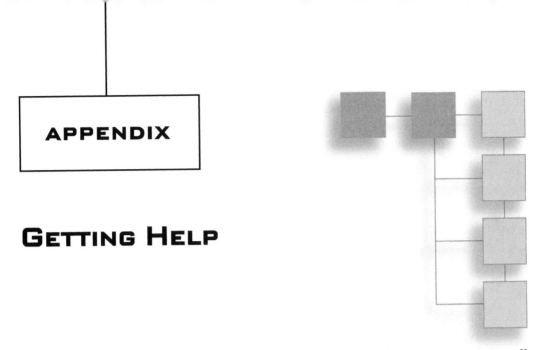

# APPENDIX

# GETTING HELP

While this book provides a good grounding in Blitz3D, it by no means covers all of the functionality and commands that you may need when creating your own games. The good news is that there is help out there, not only within Blitz3D itself, but also from the online community. This appendix shares some of the resources available to you.

## Scancodes Picker

As you know, every key on the keyboard is represented by a number in Blitz3D. Trying to figure out what number represents a particular key would be a bit of a guessing game without the help of the Scancodes Picker. This is a little program built into Blitz3D that will produce the code when you click on a specific key.

1. Click the Home icon on the toolbar and then click the Command Reference link in the window that appears.

2. Click on the Scancodes Picker option in the left portion of the window. A picture of a keyboard will appear in the right portion of the window.

3. Click on any key. The number representing that key will appear in the Scan Code box at the top of the page, as seen in Figure A.1.

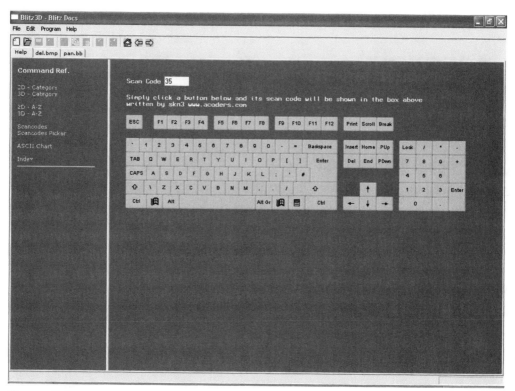

**Figure A.1**
Click on any key in the Scancodes Picker to see the corresponding code.

## Command Reference

Throughout the book, we've used dozens of lines of code to initiate different commands in our games. We certainly haven't touched on every single command available. If you're interested in finding out more about the different commands, you can explore the Command Reference library. Here you can look through an alphabetical list of different commands to see their syntax and examples of how they are used. The commands are grouped into two categories: 2D and 3D commands. 3D commands are specific to Blitz3D, while the 2D commands can be used in Blitz3D along with several other Blitz languages.

1. Click the Home icon on the toolbar and then click the Command Reference link in the window that appears.

2. Click on 3-D A-Z in the left part of the window. This will display a list of the alphabet. Click on the letter that contains the code you are looking for. For example, if you were looking for the definition of the LoadMesh command, you would click on the letter L.

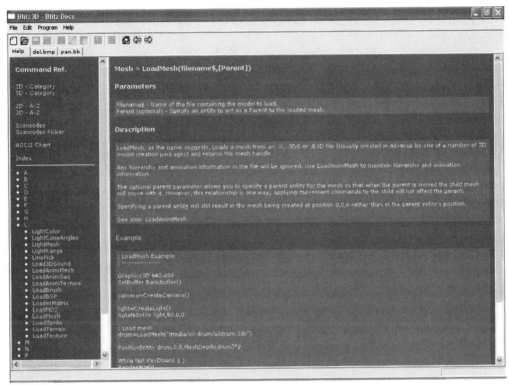

**Figure A.2**
Clicking on a code name will provide a description and an example of how to use it.

3. Click on the desired command. A definition of that command and an example of how it may be used will appear in the right side of the window, as in Figure A.2.

# Online Resources

There are several great online resources that can help you when you get stuck programming your game. It's a good idea to get the help of other programmers if you can't seem to get your code to work the way you want it to or need an idea on how to approach a specific problem. Sometimes another set of eyes is all it takes to get your problem fixed. You can be sure that if you are stuck with a particular issue, someone else has gone through it in the past. Check out these sites:

- **Coders Workshop Forum** (www.codersworkshop.com). This site has a specific Blitz3D section where you can post your code and ask questions of your fellow game programmers. It's free to join and is quite easy to use. You can search through existing postings to see if similar questions have been posted.

- **Blitz Basic Community** (www.blitzbasic.com/Community/_index_.php). This site has five forums specifically dedicated to helping users of Blitz3D. You'll find sample code, answers to common questions, tutorials, and samples from other users' programs. The only drawback of this site is that in order to post, you must be registered with Blitz3D, meaning you need to have purchased the full working version.

# INDEX

415

# License Agreement/Notice of Limited Warranty

By opening the sealed disc container in this book, you agree to the following terms and conditions. If, upon reading the following license agreement and notice of limited warranty, you cannot agree to the terms and conditions set forth, return the unused book with unopened disc to the place where you purchased it for a refund.

## License

The enclosed software is copyrighted by the copyright holder(s) indicated on the software disc. You are licensed to copy the software onto a single computer for use by a single user and to a backup disc. You may not reproduce, make copies, or distribute copies or rent or lease the software in whole or in part, except with written permission of the copyright holder(s). You may transfer the enclosed disc only together with this license, and only if you destroy all other copies of the software and the transferee agrees to the terms of the license. You may not decompile, reverse assemble, or reverse engineer the software.

## Notice of Limited Warranty

The enclosed disc is warranted by Thomson Course Technology PTR to be free of physical defects in materials and workmanship for a period of sixty (60) days from end user's purchase of the book/disc combination. During the sixty-day term of the limited warranty, Thomson Course Technology PTR will provide a replacement disc upon the return of a defective disc.

## Limited Liability

THE SOLE REMEDY FOR BREACH OF THIS LIMITED WARRANTY SHALL CONSIST ENTIRELY OF REPLACEMENT OF THE DEFECTIVE DISC. IN NO EVENT SHALL THOMSON COURSE TECHNOLOGY PTR OR THE AUTHOR BE LIABLE FOR ANY OTHER DAMAGES, INCLUDING LOSS OR CORRUPTION OF DATA, CHANGES IN THE FUNCTIONAL CHARACTERISTICS OF THE HARDWARE OR OPERATING SYSTEM, DELETERIOUS INTERACTION WITH OTHER SOFTWARE, OR ANY OTHER SPECIAL, INCIDENTAL, OR CONSEQUENTIAL DAMAGES THAT MAY ARISE, EVEN IF THOMSON COURSE TECHNOLOGY PTR AND/OR THE AUTHOR HAS PREVIOUSLY BEEN NOTIFIED THAT THE POSSIBILITY OF SUCH DAMAGES EXISTS.

## Disclaimer of Warranties

THOMSON COURSE TECHNOLOGY PTR AND THE AUTHOR SPECIFICALLY DISCLAIM ANY AND ALL OTHER WARRANTIES, EITHER EXPRESS OR IMPLIED, INCLUDING WARRANTIES OF MERCHANTABILITY, SUITABILITY TO A PARTICULAR TASK OR PURPOSE, OR FREEDOM FROM ERRORS. SOME STATES DO NOT ALLOW FOR EXCLUSION OF IMPLIED WARRANTIES OR LIMITATION OF INCIDENTAL OR CONSEQUENTIAL DAMAGES, SO THESE LIMITATIONS MIGHT NOT APPLY TO YOU.

## Other

This Agreement is governed by the laws of the State of Massachusetts without regard to choice of law principles. The United Convention of Contracts for the International Sale of Goods is specifically disclaimed. This Agreement constitutes the entire agreement between you and Thomson Course Technology PTR regarding use of the software.